IAN DURY & THE BLOCKHEADS
SONG BY SONG

Printed in the United Kingdom by MPG Books Ltd, Bodmin

Distributed in the US by Publishers Group West

Published by Sanctuary Publishing Limited, Sanctuary House
45–53 Sinclair Road
London W14 0NS
United Kingdom
www.sanctuarypublishing.com

Photographs courtesy of The Blockheads, unless otherwise stated

Cover image courtesy of Redferns Picture Library

ISBN: 1-86074-648-9

IAN DURY & THE BLOCKHEADS
SONG BY SONG

JIM DRURY

Sanctuary

Contents

In memory of Ian Dury and Charley Charles

Foreword

"Arseholes, bastards, fucking cunts and pricks..." How many people when first playing 'Plaistow Patricia' on *New Boots And Panties* must have sustained near whiplash at such a barrage of unrepentant Anglo-Saxon invective. The fact that it came so suddenly off the back of the long fade on 'Blockheads' somehow adds to the effect. So much so in fact, that whenever I play the latter on the radio, there's a slight flutter of nerves at the bottom of my stomach as the song finishes. That so sophisticated an album should have been released during the height of the punk explosion has always struck me as quite ironic. The 'death to hippies' ethos of punk seemed to grant a curious amnesty to The Blockheads, some of whom were members of a 'more hippy than hippy' outfit called Loving Awareness. Post 1976, this absurdly talented and sartorially disparate combo would provide a rock-solid groove over which one of England's finest lyricists could parade his pantomime brutality and gruff Essex whimsy. So much more than a backdrop to Dury, The Blockheads were intrinsically woven into his sound, and accordingly, he into theirs.

I loved this band like no other from the age of 16. In addition to the gigs and records I lived by, they were a gateway to a deeper exploration of funk, soul, reggae and jazz. Their live performances were always a satisfying melee of bar-room chaos and sub-military precision. Hammersmith Odeon, the Brixton Academy, even Ilford Odeon – Ian and The Blockheads stripped back the rock pretences of these grandiose halls and turned them, for one night only, into bawdy palaces of delight. Songs as much informed by Sly Stone as they were by Max Miller had audiences baying for more night after night. That fate threw together all these men to make such a beautiful racket is something that almost has one believing in a higher power. In the wake of Ian's death the Blockheads took one of their boldest decisions, and that was to carry on. The catharsis of those early gigs spent without the great man at the helm has seen them grow into something beautiful and new. Current shows have a generous complement of both old and new songs balancing out the celebration with a healthy dose of innovation. One night after one of these gigs in South Wales, I took the Blockheads into a quiet hotel bar, plied them with sandwiches and booze and just sat back and listened to stories tumble out of them like gold. The more they drank, the more they meandered down memory lane. Then came the moment when Norman revealed that they established a kind of rota for babysitting Ian when he was in his cups and demanding further forays into the local nightlife whilst on tour. They called it 'Dury duty.' As the shivers coursed up my spine, I sat there grinning like a child on Christmas Day. It was that or burst into tears of pure joy. It remains one of the best nights of my whole life...

Phill Jupitus
November, 2003

Introduction

The death of Ian Dury on 27 March 2000 deprived the world of one of the finest rock lyricists of all time. His courageous five-year battle with cancer had touched the hearts of the nation, but the extraordinary sense of loss felt by the British public came from something far deeper than sympathy. Ian's immense contribution to late 20th-century British culture meant that he was not merely respected by the people of his country. He was loved.

The public's affection for Ian was based largely on his ability to sing about the mundane nature of people's lives and somehow make it sound both interesting and amusing. Characters like Billericay Dickie, Clevor Trever and Geraldine the sandwich girl were far from standard rock fare, but Ian succeeded in bringing them to life in the listeners' imagination.

Ian's songwriting touched the hearts of people across the social spectrum, from the 'luvvies' with whom he spent so much time in the 1980s to the taxi drivers who allowed their hero to travel free of charge across the capital. He also reached out to the disenfranchised; his controversial single 'Spasticus Autisticus' becoming an anthem for those among the disabled community who felt patronised and pitied by society.

Although undoubtedly an inspiration to thousands, the public's view of Ian was, in many ways, overly simplistic. The singer was far more of a mixed bag than the obituaries revealed. For a start, Ian wasn't, as he claimed in the early part of his career, a working-class lad from Essex. In fact, he was from Harrow, and enjoyed a more genteel, middle-class background. He was hothouse-schooled by his university-educated mother and aunties before studying at the Royal College of Art.

Ian was also a professional bully, who throughout his adult life manipulated his colleagues, both creatively and financially. At times an ugly drunk, Ian fell out with friends and colleagues on a regular basis, and seemed to take pride in stirring up confrontation. He also wasted much of his undoubted talent by disposing of his brilliant, and remarkably loyal, lieutenants, The Blockheads, for a decade and a half, and hiring other musicians as a cheaper option.

Ian's one-time manager, Peter Jenner, believes that by the early 1980s his former client had a professional death wish, which prevented Ian Dury And The Blockheads from 'becoming as big as The Rolling Stones'.

In Ian's defence, his formative years, which had such an influence on his personality, had been far from easy. Having contracted polio at the age of seven he was shunted into various unforgiving children's institutions for five years, where sexual abuse was rife and the principle of 'survival of the fittest' ruled. It is little wonder that, in his adult life, Ian used the survival skills he was forced to learn at such a tender age, to manipulate those around him.

At the same time Ian had a remarkably warm and generous side to his personality, as many of his friends and colleagues testify. He changed for the better the lives of many who crossed his path and, throughout his career, retained a deeply held, emotional commitment to the underprivileged.

Although I discuss in some detail how Ian's early years made him ruthless, and at times tyrannical, this book makes no claim to be a biography. As the title suggests, *Ian Dury And The Blockheads: Song By Song* deals primarily with music, and is as much concerned with the involvement and influence of Ian's formidable backing band as his own.

Indeed the writing of this book was prompted by The Blockheads themselves and I was able to speak to each of them at length, they having given generously of their time. While the Dury family have had no direct involvement in the project, they have kindly given it their backing.

The book describes the writing process of each of Ian's four albums with The Blockheads, in addition to his 1977 debut LP *New Boots And Panties*, which was written and recorded with band member Chaz Jankel. Hit singles 'What A Waste', 'Hit Me With Your Rhythm Stick' and 'Reasons To Be Cheerful' are also discussed in detail, along with Ian's controversial releases 'Sex And Drugs And Rock And Roll' and 'Spasticus Autisticus'. In order to explain the songwriting procedure fully, I have interviewed the co-writers of every track, both within and outside The Blockheads.

Song By Song explains in frank detail Ian's fractious relationship with his colleagues and how rows over money drove a wedge between himself and the band. The Blockheads' on-the-road antics, onstage punch-ups and frequent scrapes caused by Ian's heavy drinking are also examined, along with the tragic death of original drummer Charley Charles in 1990.

Over the years The Blockheads have been left frustrated at the failure of both the music business and the media to give them recognition for their crucial role in Ian's success. There is no doubt that, with the exception of his solo album *New Boots And Panties*, Ian's best material was written and performed with The Blockheads, and that his recording career outside the band was a resounding failure. Yet it was only towards the end of Ian's life that the star realised how much he needed his accomplished backing band, rekindling his recording partnership with them after a hiatus of 15 years.

Although the function of this book is primarily to examine the history of Ian and The Blockheads' songwriting career, I felt I should not ignore the singer's battle with cancer and his subsequent death. Accordingly, I have devoted an entire chapter to this period. The Blockheads' career since 2000 is also discussed in detail, the band having made the brave decision to continue recording and touring without their Svengali-like leader.

Ian Dury was in many ways a flawed genius, and certainly not the 'salt of the earth, diamond geezer' of media legend. Yet, like the majority of the public, I have been left with a tremendous amount of affection for Ian, despite never having had the privilege of meeting him. It's a tragedy that this intriguing wordsmith is no longer with us, particularly since he enjoyed such a return to form towards the end of his life. Ian's final two studio albums, *Mr Love Pants* and *Ten More Turnips From The Tip*, are awash with lyrics that most songwriters couldn't even dream of matching.

While writing this book I have been struck by how genuinely fond Ian's colleagues are of him. Despite his sometimes appalling behaviour, they do not seem to regret a single moment spent working with him, and I have found their feelings of warmth towards the singer contagious.

Ian's primary songwriting partner and musical soulmate, Chaz Jankel, told me that he believes Ian's spirit remains a constant presence within The Blockheads. Within seconds of Chaz making this statement, an incredible incident occurred. As we sat in his home studio Chaz began quoting from 'You're The Why', the track sung by The Blockheads at Ian's funeral. As he read the line 'Then like a ton of bricks the dawn descended' a sturdy bookshelf above his head collapsed at a deafening volume, showering books everywhere.

I remain convinced, despite my natural cynicism, that what we witnessed that day was indeed the presence of Ian's spirit.

I would like to take this opportunity to thank those people who agreed to be interviewed, namely The Blockheads themselves (Mickey Gallagher, Chaz Jankel, Norman Watt-Roy, Johnny Turnbull and Derek 'The Draw' Hussey), Wilko Johnson, Steve Nugent, Rod Melvin, Merlin Rhys-Jones, Peter Jenner and Laurie Latham. I'd also like to thank Lee Harris for smoothing my access to various interviewees and for his constant encouragement, Paul Phear and Joe Maryon for allowing me to pick their brains and rifle through their archives, Wreckless Eric and 'Simesy' for checking the accuracy of Ian's lyrics, Robert Goldstein, Robin Watson, Takeshi, the Blockheads archives and finally Ken Drury for transcribing interviews and proofreading.

1 From Kilburn To Billericay

It was the tragic death of rock 'n' roll casualty Gene Vincent on 12 October 1971 that kickstarted Ian Dury's transformation from brash art school teacher to 20th-century icon.

Vincent's 1956 international hit 'Be-Bop-A-Lula' left a deep imprint on the consciousness of 14-year-old Ian and, despite embracing a wide range of music over the following 15 years, his heart still belonged to Vincent and his booming Virginian vocals.

Ian's first serious dabblings in music took place at the Essex home of friend Alan Ritchie, joined by his old High Wycombe Royal Grammar School pal Ed Speight, an accomplished jazz guitarist, and Russell Hardy, a shy and retiring pianist. It was Hardy, in fact, who taught Ian how to sing, using a child's toy called a Pixiephone. The trio knocked out 50s rock 'n' roll numbers, with Ian playing basic drum rhythms and singing. Jazz percussionist Terry Day, saxophonist George Khan and bassist Charlie Hart completed the line-up, but the band drifted apart before it had made a single public appearance.

Having left his teaching position at Luton College of Technology Ian took a job at Canterbury College of Art in September 1970. He immediately set about forming a group, recruiting students Keith Lucas, Geoff Rigden, Chris Lucas and Humphrey Butler-Bowden (later christened Humphrey Ocean), and practising in Keith's digs.

The embryonic band had initially been regarded as merely a hobby, but when the recently rejuvenated 36-year-old Vincent died in his mother's arms of a bleeding ulcer, Ian decided to take the pastime a stage further.

Within weeks Ian had leant on Alan Upwood, the college's social secretary, sufficiently to secure a booking for his band at the Christmas dance. The band's moniker had been decided as long ago as 1969. While being driven through Kilburn by Russell, Ian declared that if he ever formed a band it would be called Kilburn And The High Roads.

Not content with being a one-gig wonder Ian secured a booking for his fledgling band at the Croydon School of Art, to take place one week before the Canterbury Christmas bash. Thus it was in Croydon on 5 December 1971 that, after a flurry of last-minute rehearsals, Kilburn And The High Roads made their debut performance. The line-up included Chris Lucas on drums, Keith Lucas (no relation) on lead guitar, Ian Smith on bass, Humphrey Ocean on rhythm guitar and a terrified Russell Hardy on piano.

A week later, augmented by Geoff Rigden on harmonica, Tony Edwards on bongos and Paul Tonkin on violin, the band belted out a string of 50s covers to their bemused peers at Canterbury, securing a £40 fee in the process. Kilburn And The High Roads were on their way.

December 1971 was indeed a busy month for Ian. Having moved with wife Betty and daughter Jemima to an old vicarage in Wingrave, Buckinghamshire, the Dury family was completed by the birth of Ian's second child, Baxter, on 18 December.

Incredibly, as Betty, aided by a midwife, gave birth to their son in the couple's upstairs bedroom, Ian's other new arrival, Kilburn And The High Roads, continued to rehearse their unusual pot-pourri of rock and jazz covers downstairs. At one stage Ian left the session to see his wife, before returning with the words, 'It's a boy, it's a boy.' He then picked up his microphone to carry on where he had left off.

A determined and single-minded Ian continued to drive the band forwards with the sheer force of his personality, though he claims never to have considered a recording career at this stage. Continuing his work as a full-time lecturer, Ian threw all his spare energy into making the Kilburns a success, a decision that ultimately had disastrous effects on his marriage. Speaking in a 1999 BBC documentary on his life, Ian said, 'The band was the end of our marriage, but not because I was out there getting drunk and taking drugs and meeting groupies but because I was never there basically.'[1]

As he strove to create the perfect band, Ian controlled proceedings with an iron grip, constantly tinkering with the line-up and firing a string of musicians, such as Ian Smith, Chris Lucas, Terry Day and Paul Tonkin.

As the revolving door of musicians gathered momentum, one arrival to the Kilburns camp in mid-1972 was to have a lasting impact on Ian's career. Davey

Payne, a 28-year-old unschooled but brilliant saxophonist, with a violent temper, had met Ian in 1970. Two years later, having watched Kilburn And The High Roads play in Canning Town, East London, Davey was invited on board.

Meanwhile the pub rock revolution had taken off, initiated by visionary promoter Dave Robinson. The Irishman, then managing Brinsley Schwarz, knew there were scores of talented musicians in London full of enthusiasm but unable to find an outlet for their talent. At the time British youth was enamoured with stadium glam rock, but Robinson quickly persuaded watering holes in the capital to hire live bands. In a short space of time groups like Dr Feelgood, Bees Make Honey, and Ducks Deluxe were fuelling the pub rock explosion. Kilburn And The High Roads were only too grateful to hitch a ride on the bandwagon.

After drummer Terry Day was fired in January 1973 Ian replaced him with black percussionist David Newton-Rohoman, yet another visually striking musician. As the result of a childhood accident David needed crutches to get to and from the stage. When the Kilburns played two sets a night David was forced to sit alone at his kit during the interval while his colleagues quenched their thirst at the bar.

Peter Erskine, a journalist for the *NME*, summed up the band's unusual appearance in an article in August 1975, three months after the band had split. He wrote, 'The band seemed to have been composed almost entirely of demobbed cripples in chip-stained Dannimacs and vulcanised slip-ons. They all had short hair – badly cut and partially grown out like ex-cons. They had a bass player called Humphrey Ocean who was nearly seven feet tall, a black drummer who had to be lowered manually onto his drum stool and a lead singer with a stiff leg, a face like Gene Vincent, and a withered hand encased in a black glove.'[2]

The appointment of four-foot-high Charlie Sinclair on bass in January 1974 added further to the band's mystique. According to Humphrey, now a celebrated artist, the combination of the band's freak show visual and unusual musical fusion was part of the Kilburns' appeal: 'I think the thing about the Kilburns was that people couldn't kind of walk past them without thinking "Oh, I've got to have another look", and at that point with an audience, you've got 'em.'[1]

As the Kilburns began building a loyal following, Ian's commitment to his day job dwindled and he was sacked for moonlighting with his band. But his dismissal only increased Ian's desire to break into the big time. One of those movers and shakers whom the energetic Robinson persuaded to watch the Kilburns was BBC Radio London presenter Charlie Gillett. Transfixed by what he saw, Gillett began plugging the band on his show before being asked by Ian to be their manager, alongside Gordon Nelki.

By mid-1973 the Kilburns' reputation had spread to other parts of Britain and in October came their first big break, supporting rock colossus The Who on the band's Quadrophenia UK tour. During the tour, Who guitarist Pete Townshend drunkenly invited Ian and the band to accompany them on their forthcoming American tour, but the offer didn't come to anything despite the Kilburns queuing for visas at the US Embassy.

Astonishingly, despite having never appeared on record, Ian's popularity as an underground singer was such that a three-page interview in worldwide soft-porn magazine *Penthouse* appeared in January 1974. Rave reviews in the music press also followed. In one memorable piece Will Stout of *Cirkus* magazine wrote, 'Dancing to the Kilburns is like being on the verge of shitting your pants and enjoying it! You can't stand still so you jerk around uncomfortably for a while, then you develop a system of easy flowing constant motions to keep your bowels from evacuating.'[3] Music-lovers who would fill London's pubs to the rafters to see the extraordinary musical ensemble understood the sentiment precisely.

As Ian continued to ring the changes in the Kilburns his home life also altered. By spring 1974 his marriage to Betty was over in all but name and he had left the family home to live with Denise Roudette at Oval Mansions, Kennington. Yet, although Ian had walked out on Betty and their two children, aged just five and two, his ex-wife remained firm friends with him until her death from cancer in 1994.

Having done the rounds of the major record companies, Gillett and Nelki negotiated a recording contract with Raft, a small division of Warner Brothers. Produced by Tony Ashton in Apple Studios the band recorded 12 tracks for the forthcoming album: 'You're More Than Fair', 'Crippled with Nerves', 'Pam's Moods', 'Upminster Kid', 'Billy Bentley', 'Patience (So What?)', 'The Roadette Song', 'The Call Up', 'Huffety Puff', 'Rough Kids', 'The Mumble Rumble And The Cocktail Rock' and 'The Badger And The Rabbit'.

The final recording, complete with unnecessary added strings, left Ian bitterly disappointed: 'It was shitty...because Tony Ashton, our producer, was drunk all the time and didn't know what we wanted anyway, or what we were after.'[4] Worse was to follow when Raft went bankrupt before the record's release. Warner Brothers offered every Raft artist a deal except the Kilburns, whose curious mix of English wit and menace was beyond an American label's comprehension.

Undeterred, Gillett and Nelki visited Virgin Records and were offered a deal, but bizarrely Ian refused to sign, citing his curious desire to be on the same label as Max Bygraves. His two managers immediately ended their relationship with the Kilburns by agreeing a separate deal with Virgin, based upon other bands they were working with.

As the Kilburns continued the London circuit slog Ian was hit with another bombshell when a disillusioned Russell Hardy, his primary writing partner, quit the band. With Tommy Roberts in tow as his new manager, Ian was given another bite of the cherry when Dawn, a division of Pye Records, offered him a deal to re-record the 12 songs from the aborted Raft sessions. But Ian desperately needed a pianist.

Fortunately, the resourceful Roberts had somebody in mind and popped into the Last Resort restaurant on the Fulham Road where former Moodies founder Rod Melvin was playing piano. After performing on the sessions Rod found himself a permanent member of Kilburn And The High Roads, a band he had previously seen perform at college.

'Ian was making a single first, so I played on "Rough Kids" and the b-side ("Billy Bentley"),' explained Rod. 'At the end of the session Ian asked me to join the band. The Kilburns already had gigs lined up, so I had to learn the set quickly. Then we went back in the studio to record the *Handsome* album.'

Two new songs, co-written by Ian and Rod, found their way on to *Handsome*. 'I had this tune which I already had words for,' said Rod, 'but because Ian's lyrics were so good I gave him the tune and he wrote "Broken Skin". Then he'd got a song called "Father" and we did a short companion song which we wrote together called "Thank you Mum", which has got a great lyric. It was about when you're a kid and the lyric went "Thank you mum, you dear old girl/ through thick and thin, you knit and purl/ You put witchhazel on my bruise/ Have you done your number twos?" On the recording I sang it and Ian came in with the line "Gotta fiver?", which was very funny.'

But when *Handsome* saw the light of day in June 1975 it was a flop, selling around 3,000 copies. Rod explained, 'I enjoyed it but the album didn't really sound like the Kilburns because the drummer was replaced, a lot of guitar solos were done by a session guy, and we had backing singers and a steel band. The album was very much the producer Hugh Murphy's take on The Kilburns. For some tracks it would have been better to have live recordings, but there were some good songs on them.'

The band continued to tour, although the failure of *Handsome* brought fears that the entire project was doomed. Rod remembers being on the road with affection and says the band's visual element remained compelling. He said, 'I had a reputation for putting earplugs in after gigs while the drummer was telling loads of jokes because I wanted some quiet. We looked a bit like a circus troupe, getting out of this minibus at services. The drummer was on crutches, Ian had a calliper, the bass player was very short, Davey Payne was quite an unusual chap, and it looked like a freak show. It looked great on stage.'

However, tensions in the band over money, or the lack of it, precipitated the hasty demise of Kilburn And The High Roads. 'By the time the album was made things were going wrong with the band. There was no money and people were getting pissed off, so it all began to fall apart,' said Rod. As the various band members went their separate ways Ian and Rod decamped to Ian's rented home at Oval Mansions, nicknamed 'Catshit Mansions' by its tenant, to write more songs.

'Ian had this whole pile of lyrics and when I went through them some were so rhythmically written, especially the "list" songs, that they dictated what the music should be, certainly with "What a Waste" and "England's Glory". Some of them were very condensed lyrics while others I couldn't really grasp. He had some great lyrics. One I particularly liked was called "All Kinds Of Naughty, All Kinds Of Nice".'

Rod's upbeat piano style fitted Ian's humorous lyrics neatly and the pair spent months writing new songs: 'One day I was looking out of his flat window at a guy unloading his car and Ian said, "He's one of my neighbours. He used to be in the rag trade, but he's now a drag artist." We were both howling with laughter and he wrote this hilarious lyric, which he gave me the next day, called "I've Left The Rag Trade To Join The Drag Trade". It's got lines like "For Chichi I'm a nutter, my tailoring's divine/ I'll make your trousers flutter, in something I've designed/ So goodbye rough trade, hello

powder puff trade/ I've hung up my shears, now I'm thrilling the queers."
On a subject like that Ian would immediately know the subject and get into
someone else's world.'

Feeling reinvigorated by his new writing partner, Ian took Rod to Dave
Robinson's studios at the Hope and Anchor to demo their new tracks. Ian recalled Ed Speight and recruited sax player John 'Irish' Earle, Malcolm Mortimer
on drums and Giorgi Dionisiev on bass. The new band was named Ian Dury
And The Kilburns and by the end of 1975 Ian was back on the road.

Yet disaster was to strike again for Ian when Rod made the dramatic
decision to quit music in early 1976 to join a religious church, the Scientologists:
'Some friends of mine were doing a course about personal awareness, so I
enrolled and found it very useful. I was smoking a lot of dope and needed to
sort myself out. I immediately stopped drinking and taking drugs, and
underwent counselling. In retrospect I could have done this at the same time
as working with Ian because I loved being in the band.'

Having lost two writing partners in quick succession Ian again needed a
speedy replacement, now that Ian Dury And The Kilburns were appearing
regularly at Dingwalls.

Meanwhile Dave Robinson, who had become Ian's manager, was on the
verge of setting up Stiff Records alongside partner Jake Riviera with a £400
loan from Dr Feelgood. Robinson decided he could no longer devote enough
time to 34-year-old Ian's increasingly desperate attempts to forge a career.
Instead he recommended Ian to dynamic management company Blackhill
Enterprises, run by Oxbridge graduates Peter Jenner and Andrew King, and
in February 1976 took his protégé to meet them.

Blackhill had been established in the mid-1960s when Jenner and King
helped propel Pink Floyd to international stardom. Among the leading artists
the company had successfully managed since then were the Edgar Broughton
Band and Kevin Ayers. Initially Ian was to be co-managed by Robinson and
Blackhill, but the idea quickly foundered. According to Peter Jenner, 'We said
we'd co-manage Ian with Dave but then we realised it wasn't going to work
and we suggested managing Ian ourselves. Dave agreed because he was going
off to start Stiff and he had his studio at the Hope and Anchor. So we started
looking after Ian and being his publisher.'

Ian still needed a new writing partner to replace the departed Rod Melvin
and it was Ed Speight who initiated matters by asking the manager of Maurice

Plaquat's piano store in Shepherd's Bush to keep his eyes open for a pianist. Within days a young musician, who had already tasted brief success and was hungry for more, decided to pay the shop a visit.

24-year-old Chaz Jankel had rejected a place at St Martin's School of Art in London to forge a musical career with hippy band Byzantium. Like Ian, Chaz did not come from a musical family, although his uncle by marriage was Joe Loss, whose light orchestra dominated big band music for almost 40 years. Uncle Joe encouraged his talented nephew to persevere with his piano and guitar playing, and at family parties advised Chaz's parents to nurture his talent. Intriguingly, one of the singers who worked with Loss was Ross McManus, whose son Declan was later to find fame under the name Elvis Costello.

After making two albums for A&M Records, *Byzantium* and *Seasons Changing*, Chaz had become bored with the band's musical direction and quit in 1973. He explained, 'There were musical differences. The rest of the band were more into stuff like the Grateful Dead whereas I was into Afro-American music. What were emerging at this time were bands like Sly And The Family Stone, Mandrill and War, which was more my scene. I had a wide range of taste, I liked stuff like Led Zeppelin, but I was really into groove-oriented music.'

Chaz continued to eke out a living playing piano in a bar in London's Berkeley Square, performing occasionally with Red Shoes, and getting session work with the likes of Small Faces singer Steve Marriott and Tim Hardin. 'Then one day I bought a Wurlitzer electric piano in Maurice Plaquat's and, having bought it, I left my telephone number with Mike, the manager, and asked him to give it to anyone who needed a keyboard player.

'Ed Speight was given my number by Mike and soon afterwards I got a call from him to say that Kilburn And The High Roads needed a piano player, and inviting me to watch them at The Nashville the following evening.' What Chaz witnessed that night electrified him: 'I was gobsmacked. Ian was very eccentric and wearing a Tommy Cooper fez, and the sax player was a dead ringer for Frank Zappa. It was the style of music as well, very edgy and theatrical, with lots of dark humour and energy. Punk had not really emerged at that point, so this was something completely new.

'Ian was the focal point, there's no doubt about it. Right up until the last gig of his life the audience's eyes were trained on Ian. Because he was so visual he could command an audience. That is the language for most of the punters. If they can't play an instrument then music is a weird science. Ian's style allowed them to be drawn into the world of the singer.'

As the band finished their set a mesmerised Chaz strode across the stage and pursued them towards the dressing room. 'I was about to go down the tunnel to see the band when a roadie stopped me in my tracks and told me to go round the proper way. So I hopped off the stage to go to the front entrance and there was Ian and the band, all sweating and taking off their T-shirts. It looked like a Turkish bath.'

But if Chaz was hoping for an instant rapport with the man who had captivated him for three hours, he was in for a rude awakening: 'I stood there waiting to speak to Ian, but he looked my way and said, "'ere mate, do I know you?" I said no, and he replied: "Well, fuck off then!" I didn't know what to do because I'd been invited. Just as I was backing off Ed Speight said, "Hello. Are you Chaz Jankel?" and then everything was OK.'

The next day Chaz attended rehearsals with the Kilburns and, having impressed, was invited into the fold. After playing around 25 further gigs the band disbanded, Ian's doctors advising him to come off the road for the good of his health. Chaz believes the band was 'coming to a natural conclusion' anyway. He said, 'It was tired and Ian was tired of it. I felt it had gone a little too suburban and didn't have enough meat on the bone. Ian traditionally had written with the keyboard player, and Ian and I found ourselves talking about writing music. We decided to write an album together, which I was very excited about.'

Despite being told to take things easy, Ian had no such intentions. His feelings of jealousy towards the punk bands, who from nowhere were getting attention, were allied to his fears that, at almost 35, time was running out for him to forge a successful career.

At the Kilburns' final performance on 17 June 1976 Ian's bitterness was compounded while watching one of the support bands, fronted by a young upstart taking off his own seemingly inimitable style. In a documentary filmed the year before Ian's death he recalled the incident: 'During the later part of the Kilburns, Malcolm McLaren would bring The Sex Pistols down to our gigs and at the very last gig...we were headlining at Walthamstow Assembly Rooms, and underneath us was The Stranglers and bottom of the bill was The Sex Pistols. I stood with Fred [Rowe], our handler, one either side of Malcolm

McLaren, whilst watching The Sex Pistols, who had safety pins, which was the sartorial elegance that I'd inspired. Leaning forwards and growling and holding the microphone just like I did was Johnny Rotten. Malcolm had got me one side and Fred the other going "What's all that about, Malcolm? He's copying me, isn't he?" Malcolm was there just squeaking.'[1]

Ian knew that time was not on his side but felt a fresh sense of optimism working alongside his new partner. Chaz visited Catshit Mansions regularly over the next six months, travelling from his parents' home in Stanmore, Middlesex. As Ian handed over lyrics, either printed on his manual typewriter or handwritten on large A3 sheets, Chaz composed music for what would become the bulk of *New Boots And Panties*.

He says, 'Without wishing to put a feather in my cap I was just the right sort of person for Ian to bounce off. I was tapping into a genre which most of the musicians he'd played with previously hadn't, and this gave him a broader musical spectrum to draw from. I think that they were more interested in rockabilly and English rock, whereas Ian was really into jazz, Charlie Mingus and heavyweight, black protest music.'

Chaz was not the only musician writing with Ian at this stage. Having agreed a generous publishing deal with Blackhill to write songs, Ian was keen to widen his pool of creative talent and called in Steve Nugent, a 26-year-old American he had met in the early days of Kilburn And The High Roads.

Steve, now a lecturer at Goldsmiths College, University of London, had come to London in 1972 to complete his PhD in Anthropology. Working as a book reviewer Steve had written an article for *Let It Rock* magazine about the Kilburns, whom he had watched regularly in North London. Ian's initial meeting with Steve wasn't a roaring success, as the American revealed: 'My article involved visiting Ian and his then wife and kids. Ian was quite a paranoid person and he was suspicious of an American journalist having some interest in him, so we didn't get on very well at first. But over time I became friends both with him and with Humphrey Ocean.'

In order to obtain a visa for a trip to Brazil, the long-haired Nugent roped in Ian as a makeshift hairdresser to make himself look more respectable. He remained in contact with Ocean and Charlie Gillett during his two years in the Amazon and on his return to Blighty rekindled his friendship with Ian.

The pair wrote six songs in Steve's house in Parliament Hill Fields, Ian travelling by bus from Kennington or being driven over by Denise. Steve recalls: 'Any songs Ian wrote he had to give to Blackhill. It was quite a generous publishing contract in terms of the split. I think Blackhill took a third, Ian took a third and the composer took a third. The advance was £25 a song.'

Ian and Steve assembled six songs, including 'Plaistow Patricia', 'Billericay Dickie', 'Blackmail Man', 'My Old Man' and 'Wifey', described by Steve as 'an unpleasant song about Ian's wife Betty'. 'Wifey' included the following vitriolic outburst: 'I offer you this band of gold/Now do exactly what you're told/Never whimper, moan or scold/Especially when we are old'.

The pair also wrote another song, the title of which remains a mystery. According to Steve, 'I can't remember what the sixth song was, but I do recall Ian saying it sounded like The Hollies, which was enough to put a stop to it.' The six tracks were recorded at Alvic Studios in Wimbledon over a period of less than a week. Steve played guitar, Chaz played bass, piano and guitar, while Ian shared duties on the drums with the studio's owners, whose first names were Al and Vic.

During the sessions a disgruntled Steve walked out, claiming (as others would do later) that Ian's belligerence was poisoning the atmosphere of the recordings. 'He was not terribly easy to work with in the sense that he'd watched too many American movies,' said Steve. 'He politicised everything so you either did it his way or not at all, and you'd get into a wrangle with him. I got fed up with being told what to do and how to play, without any reason being given by him. He was just being a little dictator. As the tape was running I said, "That's me leaving the room." Ian was a bully. I don't think anyone would deny that. That didn't exhaust his personality by any means, but he was a highly manipulative character.'

At this stage Peter Jenner and Andrew King were desperately attempting to interest major record companies in signing Ian. But in a business where new singers over the age of 22 were regarded as over the hill they had a hard task selling a 34-year-old, crippled, Ian Dury. However, with more than 20 songs already written, Ian's managers decided to send him and Chaz into a studio to lay down some demos.

The choice of Alvic Studios was highly fortuitous for Ian and Chaz. As attention turned to the recording of an album the pair decided they must recruit a rhythm section, believing the drums and bass laid down on their demos to be inadequate. It was Al, one half of the owners who gave their name to the studio, who suggested hiring Norman Watt-Roy and Charley Charles.

Norman had been born in February 1951 in Bombay, India, to English parents, who both served in the Royal Air Force. Following the collapse of the Raj as India gained independence from Britain, Norman's parents decided in November 1954 to return to England with their two young sons, Norman and Garth. Norman retains vivid memories of the three-week voyage to Southampton and recalls an incident in which the passengers thought the boat was sinking: 'We came over on a Polish ocean liner and my mum thought it was sinking because the alarm went off. She made us say a prayer in our cabins, but it turned out that the wrong alarm had gone. It should have been the one for "man overboard". It took 18 days from Bombay to Southampton. We landed in Southampton in November and when we arrived there was heavy snow. It was the first time myself or Garth had ever seen snow. We didn't even know what it was.'

A year after leaving school at 15 Norman went off to Germany with his older brother, a talented guitarist, to tour with show-bands. In the late 1960s the brothers made their recording debut in a band called The Living Daylights, laying down a single and an EP. After the group's dissolution Norman and Garth joined nine-piece soul band The Greatest Show On Earth, for whom they made two albums, *Horizons* and *The Going's Easy*. When The Greatest Show folded in 1971, Norman stopped working with his brother, who continues to play professionally to this day, and joined Scottish band Glencoe.

'I used to live in a commune with the woman who later became my wife, Patti, and her then husband,' said Norman. 'They let lots of Scottish groups stay in the house, including Glencoe and another group called Forever More. It was a very musical pad. Alan Gorrie, who went on to form The Average White Band, was with Glencoe, and they needed a bass player so I joined them.'

When Glencoe's guitarist left shortly afterwards it was Norman who made the move to recruit replacement Johnny Turnbull, who had recently been earning his corn in Bell & Arc with Graham Bell. An energetic young musician from Newcastle with striking good looks, Johnny had been playing guitar since he was nine and had spent the mid- to late 1960s gigging around the north-east. His CV included playing in Primitive Sect, The Chosen Few and underground hit Skip Bifferty, alongside future Blockheads colleague Mickey Gallagher. Deciding that London was the place to be to become successful, Skip Bifferty had moved to the capital in 1966 and secured a residency at the Marquee. The band was later renamed Heavy Jelly, but when it disintegrated in 1969 and Bell joined Every Which Way, Johnny and Mickey were recruited by Robbins Music as songwriters. The pair both had resonant voices and found their vocal talents employed in the hit 60s movie *Get Carter*, starring Michael Caine.

Norman had seen Johnny play in Skip Bifferty and decided he was the ideal man for Glencoe. He said, 'I knew where Johnny lived so I went round to his home in Reddington Road, Hampstead, with the drummer. I really wanted to play with Johnny because the guy we had before was more of a folk guitarist and we wanted to rock. Me and Johnny were in Glencoe for a while and we went to America when Miles Copeland was managing us. We did a couple of albums with CBS and Miles got us on some great tours, supporting The Steve Miller Band and BB King. We even played Madison Square Garden as support to Edgar Winter.'

Shortly before Copeland, who later went on to manage The Police, ended his association with the band, keyboard player Graham Maitland quit, citing domestic problems, and Johnny suggested bringing in his old songwriting partner Mickey, who had been playing with Peter Frampton in Frampton's Camel.

Mickey had enjoyed a fruitful career and at the age of 18 had been on the verge of joining 60s sensation The Animals as replacement for original keyboard player Alan Price. But having deputised for Price on a UK tour Mickey was left heartbroken when told he could not join the band, being regarded as too young by the other band members, who were all at least five years his senior.

The call from his old pal Johnny came at just the right moment for Mickey: 'Peter Frampton had decided to change from an English band to an American band so I found myself without a job. I'd met John in Newcastle when he was 16 and in a band called Primitive Sect. They were performing at the Quay Club, which is where I played for the club's resident band. He jumped out of the back of a van and shouted: "Oi Mickey. I've lost me tooth." I thought, "What a strange geezer coming up, acting as if he knew me." I was quite well known in Newcastle because I'd gone off with The Animals, so I suppose that's why he knew who I was.'

Glencoe, who had quickly become a three-piece outfit again when the drummer was sacked, were then introduced to Radio Caroline owner Ronan O'Rahilly. Mickey said, 'A friend of Norman's came along who used to look after Alice Cooper's snake and he introduced us to Ronan, who wanted to manage a band. He had a concept called "Loving Awareness" that he used to push on Radio Caroline. He wanted us to write songs that related to "Loving Awareness" and was prepared to give us some schooling in it.'

Ronan's philosophy involved ridding oneself of 'defensive awareness' and allowing one's mind to expand exponentially and consciously. According to Mickey, 'Ronan brought these gurus along, who we used to have sessions with. We found a rehearsal room in Chelsea, and went down there for about two years, just rehearsing. Ronan gave us 30 or 40 quid a week each on this retainer to do an album. In the meantime we did jingles for his station all about this concept of Loving Awareness.'

The band continued without a drummer for months and auditioned almost 100 candidates, including Artimus Pyle from Lynyrd Skynyrd. Johnny and Mickey were becoming impatient with Norman's search for the perfect drummer, but bowed to the bassist's desire to have a rhythm partner he was comfortable with. It was while watching television that Norman chanced across Charley Charles, the man who would become his musical soulmate for the next 16 years.

'I was watching *The Old Grey Whistle Test* and saw Charley playing with Link Wray. I thought to myself, "That's the kind of drummer I want." I got our manager Raff to track him down. I thought Charley must be American but it turned out he lived in Tooting and was doing a session for Link, who was playing Manchester Apollo that night. Raff rang round all the hotels and eventually got through to Charley. Link Wray was playing in Britain for a couple more weeks, and after that Charley didn't have a gig.

'Up until then we'd been using Simon Phillips, a friend of Johnny's, but he had so many commitments he couldn't do it full time. The day Charley came down for the audition Simon was there and we had this big octopus kit that divided in two, so we split up the two drummers. Charley was magnificent and Simon turned round and said, "That's your drummer, isn't it?" and we all agreed. We just hit it off straight away.'

Charley was 13 when the Charles family moved to London from Guyana. Having left Wandsworth Technical College, Charley (born Hugh) worked for a couple of years as a store detective for Woolworths in Whitechapel before joining the army. After postings in Germany and Singapore he bought himself out of the Forces in 1969 and toured the Far East with a band called

No Sweat. Returning to London in 1972 he began a successful stint as a session drummer.

Loving Awareness was now complete but the eccentric O'Rahilly would not countenance the recording of an album until he felt the band were spiritually and mentally in harmony. The foursome persuaded their mentor to send them to the States to make their eponymous LP. The band stayed in a house in Palm Springs on the edge of the desert for six weeks, where Mickey hired out Booker T's Hammond organ. During preparations for the trip the band discovered that travelling would not be straightforward with Ronan in charge. Mickey explained, 'To get into the States, Ronan made us take "musicians" off our passports. He gave us letters with different explanations of why we were travelling. I was supposed to be researching for a university in LA and had to dye my hair ginger. We didn't go through as a group. It was all over-the-top subterfuge, but we treated it as a game.'

O'Rahilly decided to launch the album from the same hotel in Amsterdam where John Lennon and Yoko Ono had staged their bed-in for peace. Mickey claims that O'Rahilly conned the hotel into allowing the band to use a hotel conference room free of charge, with a truly magnificent gesture: 'Ronan took all the out-takes from the album in a big canister and gave it to the hotel and said, "This is the finished record, keep that in your safe", instead of giving them money up front. They thought they had collateral, but what they had was actually bugger all.'

Not content with launching the album in one continent O'Rahilly also hired a room in the World Trade Center where he set up a half-hour satellite link-up with Amsterdam. 'All the journalists were bemused because they'd never heard of us,' said Mickey. Veteran 60s TV personality Simon Dee was hired as compère and the band walked in wearing crushed velvet suits made in different colours by avant-garde designers from The Fool.

The launch was a disaster. Mickey explained, 'Ronan didn't have a very good reputation because of Radio Caroline. He was keeping a low profile but some journalists realised we were connected. After the press call we went straight in taxis to the airport to England. It was the classic sting, but it did us no good at all. We'd signed a deal with Polygram to release the album in Holland but they were disgusted and refused to release it. When we got back to England Charley rang the factory that produced them and was told the records were to be thrown away, so he arranged for them to be shipped over to a squat I had in Shepherd's Bush. I woke up one morning to find a container lorry outside with huge pallets holding 15,000 albums. They were piled to the roof in my house. All the lads came round and took their share. Charley used to flog them on Willesden High Road wearing dark glasses. They go for about 20 or 30 quid on eBay nowadays.'

When Mickey suffered a broken hand Loving Awareness came off the road. O'Rahilly had lost Polygram's backing, so the band members resorted to session work to pay the bills. Norman and Charley regularly found work as a rhythm section and it was a session with the dynamic songwriting duo of Ian Dury and Chaz Jankel that would change their lives forever.

2 New Boots And Panties

Although desperate to make a hit record and secure the recognition he felt was his due, Ian knew from bitter experience the dangers of rushing into the studio unprepared. The disastrous abortion of the first Kilburns album and the subsequent flop of *Handsome* had instilled in Ian a healthy caution. As well as taking his time over the writing process with Chaz and Steve Nugent, Ian was content to wait until he found other musicians he felt could complement his work. Ian's management agreed.

'It took about a year for Ian to find a rhythm section,' said Peter Jenner. 'Ian said to me, "I'm not going to record anything until I find the right rhythm section", which I thought was a really smart view. He did some demos with Chaz but didn't record anything properly until he found Charley and Norman at Alvic.'

The sessions at Alvic were a revelation. Norman claims that he and Charley walked out of the first session open-mouthed. He said, 'Every time I looked at a lyric by Ian I thought, "This is fucking amazing"; I'd never heard anything like it. The first thing that got me was "Clevor Trever", 'cos it was talking in the way we talked, but was also like a poem. I knew Ian had something special. Musically, Chaz was obviously a great player, who made nice changes and wrote great chords. The music felt new, but it was the lyrics that set it apart.'

The foursome also clicked on a personal level, despite an unfortunate faux pas by Norman during a break from recording: 'We were sitting at a table and I didn't realise Ian had polio. He was very down to earth and I didn't feel any difficulty talking to him, so I said, "'ere, your head is really big for your body." He said, "Yeah, that's 'cos I got polio." He showed me his withered arm, then pointed to his head and said, "There's nothing wrong up here", and I said, "You're spot on, mate." He didn't take offence because he didn't want to be treated differently.'

The demos were of high quality, but Ian's managers continued to find it impossible to elicit the interest of record companies. Despairing at their failure, Jenner and King made the inspired decision to go ahead and make an album without a record deal, and then hawk around the finished product.

Jenner explained, 'Andrew and I tried to punt the demos around everywhere and nobody wanted to know because Ian Dury was 35 and he was a cripple. We had bought a share at the Workhouse Studio, so we thought "Bugger it. We'll make the record ourselves" because we loved the demos.'

The following week, Ian, Chaz, Norman and Charley decamped to the Workhouse Studio in London's Old Kent Road to begin recording what was to become *New Boots And Panties*. Ian's old friend Ed Speight was re-called for guitar overdubs, along with ex-Kilburns saxophonist Davey Payne. Blackhill owned a 50 per cent share in the Workhouse, along with 60s legend Manfred Mann. Eleven songs were recorded in 'dead time' while the studio lay empty, with production duties shared by Peter Jenner, Laurie Latham and Rick Walton.

Jenner was experienced in making hits, having produced a number of records for Harvest Records, including albums for Kevin Ayers and Roy Harper. Latham, however, was relatively green, although recognised in his field as an outstanding engineer. After working as an engineer on the number one single 'Blinded By The Light' by Manfred Mann's Earth Band, he had moved to America. But when Mann called to say Blackhill had bought half his studio, Latham found himself excited at the prospect of working with artists such as Ayers and Soup Machine, and returned to Britain.

What he hadn't banked on was working with the interesting little man who hobbled into the studio clutching a carrier bag full of lyrics. Latham said, 'I didn't know much about Ian to be honest. I knew very little about Kilburn And The High Roads and I had no idea what material we were going to be working on until Ian walked in. I just remember thinking he looked a really interesting character.'

The first song recorded at the Workhouse was Ian's controversial debut single 'Sex And Drugs And Rock And Roll'. The song was co-written by Chaz, who initially took much persuading to work on it. Whenever Chaz visited Ian at Catshit Mansions the singer would lay out a pile of lyrics for him to compose melodies to. According to Chaz, the lyric that always seemed to be on top of the pile was 'Sex And Drugs And Rock And Roll'.

'Whenever I saw the lyric in front of me I would be a bit blasé and say to Ian, "We all know about that already", and put it to one side while I looked at another lyric.' But eventually Ian's persistence paid off when he found a new way to attract his partner's attention: 'Ian almost never came up with musical ideas. He would usually have a rhythm, which was where we connected. He had what were almost like Zulu rhythms embedded in him. But on this occasion he came up with a riff which he hummed to me and it sounded great. I wrote the bridge and the chords that went round the lyrics, and all of a sudden we had a song.'

Efforts to get a record deal for Ian were far from easy, even after the recordings were completed. But eventually in August 1977 'Sex And Drugs And Rock And Roll' was released as Ian Dury's debut single. The song started with Charley sweeping his way imperiously across his octopus drum kit. Chaz's guitar riff then kicked in, his 330 Gibson blasting through Laurie Latham's small Selmer amp, which had a blown speaker, giving it its distorted sound.

The song was irresistibly catchy, and fans of Stevie Wonder, The Commodores, Earth, Wind And Fire and co might have been surprised to realise that it was a white band knocking out such an authentic African-American rhythm. The half-spoken, half-sung vocals delivered by a growling singer not far from middle age made the song stand out, but predictably the song was banned by the BBC, which believed that Ian was advocating hedonism among the nation's youth. This was a charge he vigorously denied.

'When we went on the Stiff tour after *New Boots* was released, "Sex And Drugs And Rock And Roll" became the tour anthem, although slightly against my will. I didn't write it to be an anthem, I wrote it to make a question mark about these three items. It seemed to fit together: sex and drugs and rock 'n' roll seemed to be quite user-friendly and also joined together in some diabolic alliance but I wrote it as a question, "Are you sure about this, is this all there is?"

'It's as though, sex and drugs and rock 'n' roll – we're programmed to like these things. If you go to work pulling a lever five days a week from nine to five, all you can think about Friday night and Saturday is sex and drugs and rock 'n' roll, but there's the National Gallery, there's Primrose Hill, there's Kenwood, there's other scenarios, swimming, there's a million things.'[5] However, the BBC's interpretation, although prissy, certainly has some validity when one examines the chorus: 'Sex and drugs and rock 'n' roll is all my brain and body needs/Sex and drugs and rock 'n' roll is very good indeed'.

The song remained a mainstay of Ian Dury's set for the remainder of his life, both with The Blockheads and when he went solo, Ian screeching the lyrics and breathing dirtily into the microphone to consummate effect. To this day the song's title remains a gift to tabloid headline writers. The phrase 'sex and drugs and rock 'n' roll' seems to have been around for aeons and few remember that it was Ian who brought it to the world. It would not be the last time one of his phrases imprinted itself on the nation's consciousness.

According to Norman, 'When Ian first showed us the lyrics in the studio we were falling about laughing. We couldn't believe that someone had the nerve to write a song like that, 'cos it's what everyone knew, but no one had said it before in a song, and he had the bottle to do it. Even today people say those words in that order. If he'd written a song called "Drugs And Sex And Rock And Roll" people would probably use that phrase instead.'

Despite the refusal by the BBC to play the song it was a massive underground hit and alerted the fans of punk bands like The Sex Pistols and The Clash that it wasn't just teenagers with safety pins through their noses who could deliver a song of rebellion. *NME* made it single of the week, but after selling 19,000 copies Stiff Records deleted the 45, upsetting both the music press and the record-buying public.

Months after the single had been released Chaz received one of the shocks of his life as he sat in Catshit Mansions preparing to begin a writing session: 'Ian went into the kitchen to make some coffee and put on a 60s record called "Change of the Century" by Ornette Coleman, with Don Cherry and Charlie Hayden. I was listening with half an ear, and about a minute into the song I heard the main riff for "Sex And Drugs" on a Charlie Hayden bass solo. I thought "Where have I heard that before?" Then it dawned on me. I was in shock and looked up to see Ian standing in the doorway carrying two cups of coffee with a grin from ear to ear. I said, "Oh my God, what have you done?"'

Ian allayed Chaz's fears by getting in touch with Cherry, who would later record and tour with Ian, Chaz and The Blockheads. Cherry, one of the world's leading trumpet players, sent Ian a postcard saying 'Do not worry. This is not our music.' Chaz later spent time tracing the origins of the song and believes the riff that Ian had purloined comes from New Orleans and may originally have been part of a French piece of music.

Ironically, Chaz has himself delved into 'Sex And Drugs And Rock And Roll' on his recent acoustic jazz album *Zoom*, using the song's bridge for a be-bop number he named 'Keep Your Silly Ways' after one of the lines from Ian's lyric.

The b-side of Ian's debut single was 'Razzle In My Pocket', a hilarious tale, supposedly true, of Ian as a teenage boy being caught stealing pornographic magazines: 'Instead of being sneaky I strolled inside, I put my thieving hand on something rude/I walked right out with a silhouette of nudes'. The story, carried along by Chaz's sumptuous guitar licks, ends with the chastised narrator returning the second stolen magazine to the owner, but leaving the shop 'with the Razzle in my pocket as second prize'. The song was recorded at the Alvic Studios session and featured just two musicians: Chaz on guitar and bass, and Ian on drums.

The opening track of *New Boots And Panties* was 'Wake Up And Make Love With Me', which was to become the first song in the set for most Ian Dury And The Blockheads gigs. It was another Dury/Jankel effort and broke one of the conventional rules of songwriting.

Chaz recalls the moment when the song took shape: 'Ian had a friend called Smart Mart, who was round at Catshit Mansions with his Venezuelan girlfriend one night as we were playing around with 'Wake Up'. I remember bouncing ideas off her and coming to the conclusion that just because you had eight bars of music it didn't mean you had to go immediately to the next bit and change course. Instead we built on a rhythm and added more layers on top, creating a momentum. It was a whole different thing prevalent in black music.

'We let the groove build up, which was something I had never heard other white groups doing. The song had a beat that accompanied the melody. It was more that way inclined rather than starting with a very heavy bass line and groove. I was building from the bottom up rather than from the top down, so to speak.'

According to Norman the lyric for 'Wake Up' is based on Ian's relationship with Denise Roudette, with whom he was living at the time. Although beginning with the innuendo-laden line 'I come awake with a gift for womankind', the song is exceptionally warm and affectionate. Chaz describes the song as 'very personal and very tactile. The singer Dido touches that same mood in her lyric writing. There is almost a conversational style, which makes it very intimate.'

In fact, a chance remark about the song by Ian's former co-manager Gordon Nelki changed the entire way Ian looked at his writing. Ian had recorded a demo of the track with Chaz and a bass player called Kuma at Livingstone Studios in Barnet, in which he had sung with the North Atlantic drawl that so dominated the music scene: 'I played it to Gordon Nelki and he said, "Oh, doing the old Barry White, are ya?" I went home and I thought "I've got to do this another way." I lived with this acute embarrassment of "Who was I trying to be?" So I changed the lyric to make it funny. The only way I can be seductive is if somebody was laughing, I couldn't come steaming in on a cloud of angel dust, going "Hey baby", so I did it again in English and I really like the lyric.'[6]

Nelki's jibe so pained Ian that the singer revolutionised his singing style. No longer would he attempt to sing with an American accent, he would just be himself, and to devastating effect.

Lyrics such as 'I cup your areolas' were replaced by more quaint lines such as 'What happens next is private, it's also very rude'. The song challenged the typical male-oriented view of sex in song, with the dominant man finding himself transformed into the submissive partner. Lines such as 'I'll go and get the post and make some tea and toast' were unheard of in rock 'n' roll songs.

The jazz pianist Geoff Castle, a friend of Ed Speight, was called in to play Moog synthesiser, a part that co-producer Laurie Latham regarded as a crucial ingredient. Castle would later hook up with Ian in his backing band The Music Students after The Blockheads had been cast aside.

Most of the current Blockheads cite 'Wake Up' as one of their favourite songs to perform live, although since Ian's death it has been removed from their set. Mickey, in particular, relished the opportunity to play a song in E flat minor, an unusual key for a keyboard player. The band used the instrumental beginning to great effect on stage. Chaz would start quietly on piano before Norman and Charley kicked off the song's rhythm. As the opening bars were repeated an indeterminate number of times, the crowd would reach fever pitch as they awaited the arrival of the Messianic figure of Ian.

Despite Ian's insistence that singles and LPs were completely separate entities Stiff released the album's second song 'Sweet Gene Vincent' on 45 in November 1977. Vincent and his backing band The Blue Caps had been the first rockers to stop Ian in his tracks and divert his interest away from jazz.

The American's adult life was a scriptwriter's dream, fusing rapid success with a catalogue of tragedies of Shakespearean proportions. In July 1955 the 20-year-old Vincent was knocked off his motorbike by a woman driver who had gone through a red light. His left leg was smashed to smithereens, but he and his adoring mother somehow persuaded the doctors not to amputate.

For the rest of his life Vincent, christened Vincent Eugene Craddock, walked with a distinct limp, his left leg protected by a steel brace. Yet within a year of the accident Gene and The Blue Caps had been signed up by Capitol Records, recording a string of hits on both sides of the Atlantic. Most 50s music fans would remember 'Be-Bop-A-Lula', but Vincent's biggest UK hits were 'Blue Jean Bop', 'My Heart' and 'Pistol Packin' Mama', all reaching the top 20 between 1956 and 1960.

But in April 1960 tragedy was again to befall Vincent while leaving a gig in Bristol with Eddie Cochran and the latter's girlfriend Sharon Sheeley. Their taxi left the road and smashed into a cement post while travelling through nearby Chippenham. Cochran died and a traumatised Vincent suffered more injuries to his withered left leg. By the mid-60s his drinking was out of control and he found himself addicted to painkillers. Having returned to America to sort himself out, a rejuvenated Vincent made a brief comeback in Britain in 1971, but fell ill again and returned to the States. By October he was dead from a bleeding ulcer. His last words to his mother in the family's Californian home were 'You can call the ambulance now, mum.'

In his 1974 *Penthouse* interview Ian admits to crying whenever he played 'Be-Bop-A-Lula' as an adolescent, but says Vincent's wearing of a leg brace was purely coincidental to his appeal. He said, 'Gene Vincent got to me more than anybody, he was in a special little category because it was what I wanted to be as a singer. The way he could fly about. I didn't know he was crippled at the time so that didn't have anything to do with it. It was his head, the shape of his head because it was quite opposite from mine... It was when he was wearin' plaid and pale blue hair. The face, the beauty of it.'[7]

According to Mickey Gallagher, Ian's microphone style was heavily influenced by Vincent: 'He really determined Ian's microphone style. The way Ian used to hang on to the microphone was very Gene Vincent-like. Ian got a lot of inspiration from him.'

'Sweet Gene Vincent' begins as a mournful ballad. Ian's opening, unaccompanied line 'Blue Gene baby' is followed by Chaz, unhurried and economical on guitar and piano. As Norman joins proceedings with an understated bass line, the first minute sees Ian gently lamenting the loss of the 'skinny white sailor...with some Thunderbird wine and a black handkerchief' before the song grinds slowly to a halt. Four notes from Chaz's piano burst out like gunfire, followed by Ian growling 'Who, who, who slapped John?', a reference to a Vincent song title. The number then explodes into a rock 'n' roll celebration of Ian's hero with 'lazy skin and ashtray eyes, and perforated pride'.

Chaz Jankel credits the idea of dramatically changing the pace of the song to Ian: 'He wanted to start off slow and then get faster, and I came up with the melody and the chords. "Sweet Gene Vincent" was fairly easy to put together because it was driven entirely by the lyric and Ian had a clear idea of how he wanted it slow and then to pick up. We used this device again later on.'

Ian's lyric displays his intimate knowledge of his subject, describing The Blue Caps performing at 'the Sock Hop Ball in the Union Hall', watched by 'duck-tail Danny dragging uncanny Annie', an example of Ian's superlative use of alliteration. Even the seemingly throwaway lines tell a story: 'you lay the pistol down' a reference to the singer's bizarre habit of waving guns in the studio, a hobby that once terrified The Beatles when working alongside him in Hamburg.

Ian had certainly done his research, reading two biographies on Vincent before sitting down to write the song over a period of six weeks. When he eventually handed over his lyric to Chaz in Catshit Mansions the composer balked, saying that it would probably take 15 minutes to sing in its present format. Going back to the drawing board Ian chopped at least two-thirds of the lyric and handed it back to his collaborator. In later years Blockheads guitarist Johnny Turnbull would recall stumbling across the discarded lyrics in Ian's flat and believing them to be just as impressive as those that the writer had retained.

As with 'Wake Up', 'Sweet Gene' remained a mainstay of Ian's live set throughout his career, and was indeed performed at his last gig at the London Palladium in February 2000. 'It was always fantastic to do live,' says Mickey. 'At the beginning of the song the anticipation of what was going to happen next used to really excite the crowd. It was always the second or third last song in our set, when everything was building up to a climax. It was also quite useful for us onstage because the slow bit at the start meant we could have a breather and wipe the sweat off our brow before the main song kicked in.'

The single went down a storm with the music press, but disappointingly failed to chart. For the b-side Ian recorded the marvellous Kilburns number 'You're More Than Fair'. Sung in a mock-Jamaican accent Ian charts his seduction of a young maiden in his home. His debauchery begins with the enchanting couplet 'You got a gorgeous bum, why don't you come to my house and meet my mum.'

Throughout the song Ian gets more brave with his enchanted partner, informing her that he wants to squeeze her 'titties' in his front hall. Making his way up the stairs Ian tells the girl he wishes to 'caress your clitoris as we reach the toilet'. Eventually, Ian has persuaded her to 'taste the pudding...on the roof'. Ian's heavy breathing, displayed to such effect on 'Sex And Drugs And Rock And Roll', is accompanied by some solid saxophone by Davey Payne, and Chaz skanking on guitar.

The deliciously carnal 'I'm Partial To Your Abracadabra' was, perhaps surprisingly, Ian's least favourite song on *New Boots And Panties*. On a re-release of the album, Ian gave an interview on the origin of each song with Blockheads' media guru Kozmo Vinyl. 'Abracadabra' was the one song on which Ian declined to comment.

Chaz, who wrote the music for 'Abracadabra', says one of the reasons for Ian's dismissal of the track was that he found it difficult to sing. The music was more uneven melodically than other songs on the album and Ian had to stretch his vocal chords to meet the notes. 'Ian felt very nervous about his vocals at this point,' explained Chaz. If you listen to the record you can hear, for instance, that he was struggling with the line "The panties sends it up right the wall". I had written a lot of improvisational licks into the melody and he tried his best to do them, but you could see him struggling like hell at times. He was very self-conscious about it and found it particularly difficult to sing it live.'

According to both Mickey and Chaz, every band member enjoyed playing the song, but it became one of the first from *New Boots And Panties* to be dropped from the set and was not reinstated until after Ian's death. Johnny Turnbull, whose voice was often used to bolster Ian's vocals, now sings 'Abracadabra' whenever The Blockheads include it in their set.

'We all loved it,' explained Mickey. 'It was a great song, but because Ian found it rather trite for his tastes it went straight out of the set. Chaz's guitar playing is just fantastic, it's just one note but it's beautiful. He's a great, all-round musician and should be very proud of this album.' The song was later revitalised by Paul McCartney's tremendous version on the 2001 release of *Brand New Boots And Panties*.

Chaz also has his doubts about the song, which he recalls only just made the cut when the batch of recordings was whittled down to ten. '"Abracadabra" was quite lucky to get on the album because it was much more melodic than Ian's average song. I brought the melody to him, which wasn't the way we tended to work: 80 per cent of the time we wrote together Ian would have the lyric first; only around 20 per cent of our songs came from me initiating a piece of music and giving it to him to write to. When I gave him the piece of music he had the opening line, "I'm partial to your abracadabra" and, as I recall, he then worked it with my melody.

'It was a bit too singalong and didn't quite have the gravitas of the other work we did together. But on the album it served its purpose and sits well as track three. It was the best way of getting from "Sweet Gene Vincent" to "My Old Man".'

Ian's lyric continued his method of writing about sex in a way previously unheard of in song. Although less graphic than 'Wake Up And Make Love With Me', the words are more cheeky, the second verse describing his growing erection and his girlfriend's teasing touch: 'Please please stop it, it likes it/Tickles it to death in a way/These lovely boots exist to drive it round the twist/The call of nature must be obeyed.'

Towards the end of the song Ian describes his eventual ejaculation in terms that could easily pass the censor's eye: 'There's been a manifestation/Nature made it answer the call/It simply can't resist boots and pants like this/Abracadabra for all.'

'Ian loved writing in double entendres,' said Chaz. 'You could say that about "Hit Me With Your Rhythm Stick", as well. I think he liked to create mystery. Writing "Abracadabra" was when I first became aware of it.'

'My Old Man', an ode to Ian's father, was undoubtedly the most personal song on *New Boots*. William Dury was a one-time boxer who had his nose broken three times in the ring. Brought up in humble surroundings, William followed in his father's footsteps by becoming a London bus driver. As Ian's tribute to him pointed out, he was a working-class man who 'knew where he belonged'.

Speaking about his father in a television documentary Ian remarked, 'My old man's dad was a bus driver, and I think his grandfather was a bus driver at a time when a bus driver was seen for a working boy as a really good gig, which it probably was.'[1]

A proud man, William felt angry that he had been deprived of a decent education, knowing he was intellectually bright, but aware that the opportunities for people of his generation mainly existed for the middle and upper classes. A handsome man, William met his future bride, Margaret Walker, in a social club in Harrow. Margaret, known to friends as Peggy, was a university-educated young woman when she met her suitor.

Her parents, John and Mary Walker, had moved from Donegal on the Irish border in the 1920s to the lush English countryside of Cornwall. John Walker, a doctor, subsequently set up a medical practice in the fishing village of Mevagissey. While living in Cornwall the family home for Peggy, her brother William, and sisters Elizabeth and Mary, was an idyllic eight-bedroom house, in startling contrast to the humble upbringing of her husband.

Encouraged by their parents to pursue an education, all three of the Walker girls enrolled at university, with Peggy deciding to follow in her father's footsteps and undertake medical training. Having moved to London she took up work as a health visitor. Her husband, by contrast, left school at 13 with only a rudimentary education.

The clash of the couple's differing upbringing and education did little for the long-term health of their marriage, as Ian himself confessed: 'There was a point where my mum, because she was at university and she'd had this middle-class upbringing, she could dig him out with the verbals to the extent that he'd lose the plot and get very angry. I think that created quite a little bit of the old tension that existed between them. My dad and my mum split up. It didn't spring off as a natural relationship.'[1]

Ian was born an only child on 12 May 1942, not in Upminster as has often been claimed, but in the genteel Middlesex suburb of Harrow. In the early part of his career, Ian chose to give his birthplace to interviewers as Upminster, believing that to admit to coming from Harrow might dent the laddish, working-class 'salt of the earth' image he had so carefully cultivated.

Before his parents' split in 1946, when Ian was just four, the family briefly moved to Switzerland. William had undertaken an intensive training programme with Rolls-Royce and had qualified as a driver for wealthy businessmen, or as Ian sang 'Later on he drove a Roller/Chauffeuring for foreign men/Dropped his aitches on occasion/said, "Cor blimey" now and then'. It was a job he relished: 'My dad was, I know, very proud of his skills as a bus driver and after that as a chauffeur. He wasn't thinking it was a demeaning occupation, although he never let anyone call him Billy, he always had to be Dury.'[1]

When Peggy took Ian back to England to settle in the village of Cranham, bordering Upminster in Essex, her marriage to William was over in all but name. The Walker family hadn't approved of the union from the start. According to Ian, 'At the Kilcadden connections there was a feeling of that, for sure. My mum's dad was the brother of Aunt Janet and Uncle Arthur, he became a doctor and got out. He didn't want to be a farmer, so a doctor's daughter and a bus driver's son would have been [disapproved of] anyway.'[1]

Although William remained a doting father to Ian, visiting him regularly when he was sent off to Chailey Heritage Craft School, their relationship went through a sticky patch for a number of years. In Chaz's words 'Ian's dad was not happy with the way in which Ian was leading his life, and disapproved of his hippy, art student lifestyle. Basically they severed all contact for many years and I think Ian's view of his dad was tainted by this for quite a long time. He loved his dad, but it was from a distance.'

Eventually the two were reconciled, a fact brought out starkly in the last verse of 'My Old Man': 'Seven years went out the window, we met as one to one/Died before we'd done much talking/Relations had begun/All the while we thought about each other/All the best mate from your son/All the best mate from your son/My old man'.

Sadly William died in his bedsit in Victoria, central London, in March 1968, having suffered a bout of emphysema, after waiting at Heathrow Airport in the pouring rain for his businessman boss. Upon the receipt of £2,000 from William's will Ian and his wife Betty decided they could afford to have a baby, and so it was just over nine months later, on 4 January 1969, that Jemima Dury came into the world. 'We got weaving straight away basically,' joked Ian.[1]

Ian insisted that despite the song's emotional content, he never found singing about his father upsetting: 'I sometimes cry when I'm doing "Sweet Gene Vincent" live because I get swept away with the chords and I really want it to come across as a sad thing, but I don't cry when I do "My Old Man" because it is something that is part of me, so it's not a tragedy anymore.' [6]

Ian said he had been forced to couch the lyric in deference to his mother: 'Because my parents were separated I had to write it in such a way that my mum didn't feel it was her worry, her problem, so it was about me and my relationship with him bearing in mind mum's feelings. There are a few bits and pieces I didn't put in there, [but] not that he was a rogue or anything.' [6]

'My Old Man' was the first track on *New Boots And Panties* to come out of Ian's writing session with Steve Nugent. The American says that of the four tracks he co-wrote, this was the one most modified in the recording, crediting Ed Speight's guitar overdub with installing the swinging sound of the song. By contrast, the original demo had owed more to Steve's taste in folk music.

Norman's counter-melody on the bass, developed at the Alvic demos, was another key ingredient. 'On "My Old Man" it was a basic groove on two chords,' he explained. 'The choice was for me to either play the roots of those chords or make a little tune up, which I thought would be better. I loved players like Chuck Rainey, the giants of bass who would create a melody in its own right. I loved that approach, so whenever I thought it would work in a song I used to try and write a counter-melody to the melody. I always think this makes it more interesting rather than just playing the root note. Not just more interesting for people to listen to, but for me to get off on as well.'

During gigs the song was used regularly as the first encore, with Ian allowing Norman the chance to take the glory alone. While the rest of the band waited in the wings, Ian often sent out Norman on his own to start off the song with his celebrated bass riff. As his introduction neared its completion Norman would sometimes glance around to see that none of his colleagues were alongside him. 'Ian would be standing there laughing, so I'd have to carry on alone and do a solo, which was great 'cos it gave me the chance to play. Ian would do that with Charley as well. He'd say "Charley, go out and start 'Reasons'", and he'd tell the rest of us not to go on. After a while Charley would realise no one was coming out, so he'd be able to play a solo.'

Various members of 80s icons, Madness, many of whom were brought up watching Kilburn And The High Roads in dingy North London boozers, cite 'My Old Man' as one of the songs that most influenced them. Lead singer Suggs paid tribute to Ian in a 1999 Radio 2 documentary about the singer, claiming that he inspired Madness to realise that they could sing about London, rather than having to pretend to be from across the Atlantic.

'He seemed more like a poet than a rock 'n' roll artist. That inspired Madness to go down that route without actually having to know anything about the music business. We didn't understand the process of making records…[but] we had seen Ian Dury do it, somebody with polio, and you just saw all the possibilities for people who didn't necessarily look like rock stars.'[8]

Suggs went on to admit that Madness's classic first two albums, *One Step Beyond* and *Absolutely* contained far more Cockney patter than there would have been otherwise, as a result of the band members listening to Ian Dury. The song 'In The Middle Of The Night', from 1979's stunning debut *One Step Beyond*, is perhaps the most striking example of this. A cheeky tale of 'knicker thief, underwear taker' George who enters gardens after dark and rifles through women's smalls hanging on the line before finding himself exposed on the front page of 'the Currant Bun', it is pure Ian Dury.

But Ian's attempts to portray himself as genuinely working class did not always endear him to his colleagues, particularly keyboard player Mickey Gallagher: 'In moments of pique I would say to Ian, "You are making your career out of singing about a class that I am from and you are not." It did not go down well with him, but it was true. Apart from the institutionalisation, his roots were essentially in Middle England. His mother and his aunts were all highly educated. I didn't come from that background. My mum and dad knew that education was important, but couldn't afford it. I had to get out to work as soon as possible.

'Johnny and myself and Norman are all from working-class backgrounds, and this was always something we could use on Ian without getting any comeback. Joe Strummer was exactly the same – singing about being from the streets. He wasn't from the fucking streets, he was the son of a diplomat. Shane MacGowan is another who had an educated and privileged background. I've always thought that it was easier for people like that to sing about the fact that they have suffered, when they haven't.'

But if Ian's working-class credentials were in doubt, his feelings for the working man were not. A passionate socialist who despised what he regarded as the ruling class's abuse of privilege, Ian was very protective of those who found themselves in similar employment to that of his father. Steve Nugent recalls an ugly incident at a dinner party, probably in the 1980s, at the home of American poet/songwriter Fran Landesman, when Ian's defence of the working man got somewhat out of hand.

Sitting down to eat with them was caustic columnist Julie Burchill, who tried to goad Ian by describing him and Chaz as 'the Richard Burton and Elizabeth Taylor of rock', because of their compulsive pattern of separation followed by reconciliation.

Ian did not rise to the bait on this occasion, but when a Hollywood director dropped in on the party, leaving his chauffeur outside, Steve says the singer erupted: 'This fellow was telling very funny stories hour after hour, and it was a good evening. But then Ian started laying into him because his driver was sitting out in the car. He drew analogies with his father. It was completely overblown. The chap said, "That's the guy's job. He's driving my car." Ian would say this kind of thing and you could either rise to the bait or ignore it. To me that kind of behaviour is interesting, but you don't want it every day.'

The final song on side one was 'Billericay Dickie', which drew heavily on Ian's fascination with music hall. Two of his heroes were Max Wall and Max Miller, their irreverent and frequently outrageous acts inspiring many of Ian's lyrics for Kilburn And The High Roads, most notably on 'England's Glory'.

'Billericay Dickie' saw Ian in the role of narrator, listing Dickie's sexual conquests across the county of Essex in a series of filthy rhymes: 'Had a love affair with Nina in the back of my Cortina/A seasoned-up hyena could not have been more obscener' was but one example as Dickie swept through the county, taking in, among others, randy Sandy, Janet from 'quite near the Isle of Thanet', a 'charming shag from Shoeburyness', and 'a nice bit of posh from Burnham-on-Crouch'. Part of the song's appeal was Ian's liberal use of English place names. The young residents of Essex had never heard anyone sing about the towns and villages where they lived, and this helped make *New Boots And Panties* a groundbreaking record.

By doing this, Ian comprehensively shattered the myth that writing about England was unsexy, as Mott The Hoople singer Ian Hunter had once claimed, when explaining why he never sang about his native Walthamstow. Self-confessed Ian Dury fan Billy Bragg later used the technique to great effect on the song 'A13', a parody of rock standard 'Route 66'. Bragg's song, containing references to Essex towns such as Hadleigh, Leigh-on-Sea, Thundersley, Grays, Thurrock and Southend, may not have been attempted had it not been for Ian's 'Billericay Dickie'.

A great people-watcher, Ian based the lyric on the alleged sexual exploits of his friends, once explaining, 'He's somebody we probably all know from our youth. If you've got a circle of friends one of them's a braggart and one of them's a comedian and sometimes it's both the same and Billericay Dickie is a sort of observation of a few swag artists that I've known, and none of them being about me.

'I used to know a geezer who was really adept, he'd get on a tube train and I'd be with him and he would see some pretty face and he'd just smile and the girl would smile because he was so cooled out, and I was double envious of him but every night he used to wash his willy with salt, so there is a sting in the tail.'[6]

Considering the song's unashamedly English feel, it is somewhat of a surprise that it was the American Steve Nugent to whom Ian turned to write the music. As Steve himself admits, 'I was pretty insensitive to the lyric. I've never been to Billericay. I know there's a place called Essex but the specific references to places in Essex were not part of any mental landscape of mine at all. It was just a story.'

Steve's way of interpreting the lyrics was to let the words sit on top of a very basic musical arrangement with big chords: 'My playing is pretty folk derived, so it's open chords, nothing very complicated. There's no modulation in any of the songs I wrote with Ian, they're all pretty straightforward. Ian was obsessed with American black music and jazz, so that was always his aesthetic focal point, combined with his interest in being a contemporary lyricist.

'There was always an implied meter in Ian's songs, less so with "Blackmail Man", which could have gone a number of ways.'

Steve was surprised when, on the release of the album, he discovered that Chaz had been given an equal share of the royalties for Billericay: 'I don't think if you listen to the original demo it's that different from the record. But it's no big deal.' Chaz, on the other hand, says he 'put a little descending line through the chords, a minor diminished thing I put on top of the existing song'.

Whatever the truth of the matter the song was a classic of its time, full of catchy, but simple hooks, and with one of the funniest lyrics the record-buying public had ever heard. It subsequently earned Ian a huge following in Essex, becoming, as Mickey put it, 'the cab driver's favourite'. He added, '"Billericay Dickie" encompassed a whole generation's experience of encounters with the opposite sex, in a way that simply hadn't been done before.'

The song also contained a nice example of one of those unplanned incidents in the studio that make it on to a record. The cheerful whistling accompanying the final verse was an off-the-cuff addition from Charley Charles, who absent-mindedly began whistling the tune in the studio. Ian realised that it would add to the chirpiness of his 'oompah' song and implored his trio of producers to add it to the record.

A subsequent feature of the song when played live was the performance – or more accurately, non-performance – of maverick saxophonist Davey Payne. Finding himself redundant on the stage without a single note to play, Davey decided the best way to gain attention was to stand like a statue, challenging the audience to look his way, which they frequently did. He did the same when the band played 'Sweet Gene Vincent'.

Speaking in an *NME* interview in 1979 Davey explained that the idea had come from Ian: 'I sat down during those numbers ("Billericay Dickie" and "Sweet Gene Vincent") in Amsterdam and almost fell asleep. Ian said, "You might as well just stand there – it'll be really heavy." And I enjoy that. I try and get into the songs' characters. Sometimes my mind wanders but other times I look at my feet and think of myself as Gene Vincent or imagine myself to be Billericay Dickie. But if I'm tired, I just take it easy.' [9]

Davey's impression of a waxwork became a strong feature of The Blockheads' live performance. Often the band would find themselves staring at the seemingly lifeless musician as they played and having returned their eyes to their instruments would frequently look up to find Davey doing exactly the same thing, but on the other side of the stage.

Despite the appeal of the lyric to a generation of jack the lads, Ian claimed that 'Billericay Dickie' was not a celebration of that culture, instead believing the chief character to be a rather pathetic figure. He said, 'The last couple of verses were more poignant, more sad and more obvious that he was boasting [and] is actually a bit pathetic, but I never developed it that far on the record. But there is a tragedy in there in the fact that he's all mouth and trousers, although he probably may go swagging a lot. He does a lot of pulling but really he gets the push.'[6]

The deliberately mis-spelt 'Clevor Trever' was another successful attempt by Ian to push back the boundaries of songwriting. Singing in his adopted working-class dialect, Ian manipulated the English language beautifully, peppering the lyric with wave upon wave of delicious Cockney patter. The mispronounced first line of the chorus, 'Knock me down wiv a fevva, Clevor Trever', remains one of his fans' favourites.

A tongue-twister from start to finish, the song is a paradox, full of apparently nonsensical statements delivered at high speed: 'And it ain't not having one thing nor not another neither either, is it anything whatever'. Barely pausing for breath, the second verse sees poor Trever bemoaning his luck at finding his words constantly misinterpreted: 'Just 'cos I ain't never said, no, nothing worth saying, never ever, never, never ever/Things have got read into what I never said til me mouth becomes me head which ain't not all that clever'. One of Ian's most imaginative songs, by the end of 'Clevor Trever', the listener is left to question Trever's inarticulacy or, as Chaz puts it, 'It made you ask yourself, "Is Trevor a divvie or not?"'

Ian had originally written the lyric for a young protégé, whom he had recently befriended. A former art student himself, Eric Goulden was 22 when he walked drunkenly into Stiff's offices in Alexander Street in late 1976 with a tape of his music. Nick Lowe, who had recently gone solo after the collapse of Brinsley Schwarz, was already working with the fledgling label. He remembers the shambolic Eric walking past the office trying to conquer his nerves and enter the building. Having visited the local pub to instil some Dutch courage, Eric eventually overcame his fears and handed over a tape, with the immortal words 'I'm one of those cunts that comes in and brings in their tape', before leaving the building.

Eric was surprised when, days later, he received a phone call from Jake Riviera and in a fit of embarrassment told the Stiff co-owner he could record over the cassette if he so desired. When Riviera stopped him mid-flow with the offer to release one of Eric's songs as a single he was staggered. Produced by Nick Lowe, 'Whole Wide World' became an underground hit for Eric, although he had to wait almost a year, until August 1977, for it to be released, under his new name, Wreckless Eric.

An avid fan of Kilburn And The High Roads from his art school days in Hull, Eric even recorded a cover version of one of the band's numbers 'Rough Kids' on his 1978 album *Wreckless Eric*. In early 1977 he was introduced to his hero backstage at a Graham Parker And The Rumour gig at the Victoria Palace Theatre. Within days he found himself sitting in Catshit Mansions as Ian and Chaz honed 'Sweet Gene Vincent'.

Eric soon became firm friends with Ian and also with Denise, who began visiting his Wandsworth flat with her bass guitar. The pair quickly built up a musical rapport and began writing songs together. Incredibly, despite throwing so much energy into his new solo career, the tireless Ian found time to become Wreckless Eric's drummer, a role he continued to occupy throughout the momentous Stiff tour.

According to Chaz the final line of 'Clevor Trever' – 'Also it takes much longer to get up north the slow way' – was a statement that Eric had made on more than one occasion: 'Eric does talk a bit like that. He is very bright but can go off at a tangent at any moment. He's a typical art student, very lateral. You might ask him a question and ten minutes later he'd still be speaking, but what he was saying would have nothing to do with the question you'd asked. It was like he'd landed in another country mid-sentence.'

Having written the song, Ian decided he liked it so much that he could no longer countenance handing it over. Although written for Eric, Ian claims the lyric was not ostensibly about his newfound friend. He said, 'I originally wrote hoping that Wreckless Eric was going to sing it, not because it's about Wreckless Eric but because he'd be able to express what it's about, I thought probably better than me.

'It's about memories of people, of places where I've been, like in Chailey, [where] there'd be people there born with parts of their mind that were affected and they couldn't necessarily have a normal conversation with them. So it's about somebody who knows that there's a limitation within his abilities to express himself. And yet he knows also that he is expressing himself because he knows he's not making sense. Therefore the nonsense is describing him accurately.'[6]

Chaz's stuttering guitar riff was the perfect accompaniment to Ian's irregular lyric and his solo towards the end was simply masterful. Fellow Blockhead

Mickey Gallagher remains in awe of it: 'It's wonderful. So economical and right in the pocket. The attitude is "If you can do it with one note, why move?" Chaz has always been one of the guitarist's favourite musicians because of his approach. Chaz's guitar playing is always in a hurry, but never seems to be panicking. Johnny, who is such a good guitarist, will dive in, screaming very effectively and Chaz has a different approach, which is why they complement each other so well.'

Musically, 'Clevor Trever' is the funkiest number on the album, a world away from other artists who were making their name on the new wave scene. Much of the credit for the song's funk vibe goes to the rhythm section of Norman and Charley. It was the first song the pair played through with Ian and Chaz down at Alvic, as the bass player explains.

'It was just a simple groove basically, and as soon as they played it to us we picked up on the groove of it and the heart of it. When Ian and Chaz heard us playing to it they loved the tightness we had and left us to our own devices.'

Laurie Latham credits his co-producer Peter Jenner with bringing the rhythm section of Charley and Norman to the fore on *New Boots And Panties*: 'Peter was very conscious of personalising that funky, solid rhythm section, and making sure that was an angle.' For his part, Jenner says that without Charley and Norman, the album would not have been a success, 'although equally they wouldn't have had the success they did if they had never met Ian'.

Norman and Charley were the perfect foil, vindicating the former's decision to look patiently for a drummer as Loving Awareness began to drift. Charley's playing was steady and minimalistic, his timekeeping almost military in its efficiency. At the same time his sense of rhythm was supremely funky. His partner's awareness and instinctive feel for a wide variety of songs allied to an exceptional ability to create groovy counter-melodies on bass fitted perfectly with Charley. They were a potent combination.

'If I Was With A Woman' heralded the beginning of the album's dark side. Its vitriolic lyric tells the story of a hate-filled misogynist explaining his desire to domineer over his partner, making her upset and confused, 'specially when she did not want me to'.

The narrator uses mental torture to control his victim, pretending to love her, offering his indifference and refusing to ask her questions, although 'if she did not want me to I would'. Ian himself admitted that the lyrics were 'horrendous' in places: 'It was written on the rebound from an argument with a woman, so it says horrendous things. The first impression you might get is of a very bitter person. It's a song of hate.'[10]

Despite its hard-edged lyric, the accompanying music is melodic, influenced largely by co-writer Chaz's love of American funk and jazz. The gentle chords he plays on the piano are the perfect antidote to the angry words spouted by the singer, although his understated guitar bubbling under the surface gives off a definite air of menace.

After an effortless guitar solo by Chaz two-thirds of the way through, Ian gives the lyric a clever twist: 'I've been with a woman, she took away my spirit/No woman's coming close to me again'. In the space of two lines Ian has overturned the listener's antipathy. The narrator is now unmasked as an emasculated and humiliated wreck, deserving of sympathy, and whose previous rants were a vain attempt at self-protection.

The song reaches its climax with Ian singing 'Look at them laughing'. The band then sing the word 'laughing' repeatedly in discordant harmony that is gradually distorted by a harmoniser. The effect is to conjure up the image of an ever-increasing circle of mocking women tormenting the downtrodden man. Some listeners found this part of the record unbearable, as Chaz recalls.

'My sister was working in an animation department in London at the time this record came out. They used to play the record a lot and one girl was so insecure she actually had to leave the office every time it came on because whenever she heard 'Look at them laughing' she thought everyone was laughing about her. So she had to sit in the toilet for the duration of that song and then come out again.'

Ian's relationships with women were certainly not straightforward. Ian's minder Fred 'Spider' Rowe recalls breaking up physical fights between him and Denise, his girlfriend at the time the song was written. Chaz was another who witnessed violence between the pair: 'I was working with him when she was chucking knives at him and had a pair of scissors ready. I have to say that he was such a wind-up merchant he was lucky he lasted as long as he did. I don't want to bad-mouth him, but Ian had the most vicious tongue if he wanted.'

Steve Nugent says he was often bemused by Ian's choice in women: 'He had a string of dysfunctional girlfriends who were students to the old master. He was trying to teach them something about life. It was really that awful.

Some of them were quite nice, but it always seemed a little bit weird and kind of inappropriate.'

In later years Ian's relationship with a girlfriend named Belinda took on similarly violent overtones. Uncontrollable rows between the two are said to have broken out in restaurants and bars, and on one occasion the police were called to Ian's Hammersmith flat.

Mickey's view of Ian was of a man who was fond of the opposite sex, but only when they focused on him: 'Ian liked women but misogyny got in the way if the woman's attention was not towards him.'

Ian had previously written 'I Made Mary Cry', a song so threatening that it made 'If I Was With A Woman' sound like Chris de Burgh's 'Lady In Red'. The lyric, albeit purely tongue in cheek, was based around attacking a woman in a bus shelter: 'I made Mary cry in a lonely bus shelter/I put in my laundry tongs in the back of her leg/Severed a hamstring in the lonely bus shelter/I paid no attention but I made Mary beg'. The song featured in Ian's set with The Blockheads throughout 1977 and 1978, the singer taking out a knife mid-song and running it along his face menacingly.

'When I first heard "Made Mary Cry" I thought "Urgh",' said Mickey. 'It gave me a shiver up my back. But all's fair in love and war. It was a great piece of artistic licence.'

In Ian's words 'Blockheads' is 'about looking out of the window at the Oval, where I used to live. On Sunday at a pub called the Cricketers, these persons with freckled shoulders used to come out and get into orange and black motorcars, rev up and drive off, all making a terrible racket. I used to see them as a group that I really didn't want to mingle with.'[6]

The lyric is a stinging criticism of 'yob culture', with Ian delighting in his withering put-downs of those 'Blockheads' that he saw from the safety of his flat: 'You must have seen parties of Blockheads, with blotched and lagered skin/ Blockheads with food particles in their teeth, what a horrible state they're in.'

Although not averse to raucous and drunken behaviour himself, Ian disapproved of the mindlessness he saw in many of the day's youth. As Chaz explains, 'Ian was a very passionate person, with a big heart. Whenever anyone showed off by being macho or was uncaring Ian would get annoyed. He found the sort of senseless yobbo antics quite appalling. Don't forget, Ian was quite defenceless. He could only defend himself with his mouth, his wit. Therefore violence was anathema to him. He wanted to incite people but not to the point where they would nut each other. He wanted the incitement to be thoughtful, making people think about their lives but not to be violent.'

As the song reaches its crescendo and Ian completes his metamorphosis into a blockhead, his backing musicians chip in with the football-terrace-like chant of 'Oi oi'. A passionate anti-racist, Ian was horrified when the shout brought out another side to his almost exclusively male audience: 'We used "Oi oi" on that and that's subsequently been made into some horrible racist thing, but "Oi oi" was used at West Ham football ground in the East End before the war as a war cry, you know, "Up the Hammers, Oi oi." The East End of London is where they beat Moseley in his marches and the East End of London has always been open racially.'[6]

It was in the studios at Alvic where a chance remark by the then session drummer Charley Charles was to encourage Ian to make a small, yet significant, change to the lyric. As he sat marking a lyric sheet to work out his drum parts Charley stumbled across the line 'They've got womanly breasts under pale mauve vests/Shoes like dead pigs' noses'.

According to Ian, Charley was wearing 'a pale mauve tank top with white piping with Lois written across the front in white taped letters and a pair of jeans that if you pulled them hard enough would occupy the space of about an acre, the sign of a post-war boom in cotton, plus a pair of shoes with a four-inch Cuban heel with a great cluster of two-tone leather on the front.'[6] Or in other words, a 'pale mauve vest' and 'shoes like dead pigs' noses'.

The crestfallen drummer turned to Ian and said ''ere Ian. This geezer's dressed just like me.' As those assembled in the studio fell about laughing, Ian decided to change the last line of the song to 'You're all blockheads too'. This alteration deflected from the hectoring tone of the song. He later confessed, 'I wrote a song about them, but then thought "Who am I to criticise them?" So at the end I put "You're all blockheads too" to try to absolve myself from the venom. It was easier to hate them knowing we're all part of the same hideous pageant.'[10]

Following Ian's rant against British 'laddishness' came the most startling four seconds of the album. Most of the million or so punters who bought the LP will remember their sense of shock the first time they heard Ian's unaccompanied introduction to 'Plaistow Patricia': 'Arseholes, bastards, fucking cunts and pricks'.

Ian explained, 'I put a string of pink and blue swear words to try and clear them out of my way, to put all the swearing I could think of in one contained sentence, so it was no longer a problem to me whether I was swearing in a lyric or not. Since everybody does it I can't see why we can't do it as a poem or lyric if we want to.' [6]

Some of his friends were aghast, thinking the use of such shock tactics might backfire, but others realised that it was a canny way of securing the 'geezer' vote. Mickey admits, 'This was one of those songs that gave Ian the hardcore bloke audience. It's not a song very complimentary to women and one that my wife hated. But all the blokes loved that introduction. For kids at school this was the song that you bought the album for. Whack it up on full volume in your bedroom, so that your mum and dad could hear "Arseholes, bastards, fucking cunts and pricks".'

The generation gap between parents and children in the 1970s was undoubtedly larger than it is today. Many of those with children had been brought up on jazz, swing bands and rat pack crooners like Frank Sinatra, Dean Martin and Jerry Lewis. This was a world away from the music of 1977, when Second World War heroes shook their walking sticks in disgust as The Sex Pistols marred Her Majesty's Silver Jubilee celebrations with their alternative version of 'God Save the Queen'. In 2004 such a song would barely raise an eyebrow among modern parents. The supremely talented comic Peter Kay made the point memorably in his 2000 stand-up video *Live at the Tower*, foreseeing a time when grandma asks to hear 'Smack My Bitch Up' by Prodigy, because 'she loves a bit of that'.

Chaz recalls the moment he proudly played *New Boots And Panties* to his father days after the mixing had been completed: 'I played the tape to my parents after Sunday lunch one day. He was typical of his generation, my dad, who had fought for the liberty of my generation, and here was us lot, long-haired hippies, hanging around smoking dope, and not doing very much with their lives.

'I sat there waiting for "Arseholes, bastards, fucking cunts and pricks" to come up, and watched him. Not one muscle moved, he just sat there po-faced. At the end of the album he walked out on to the lawn and I followed him outside like a reporter, to listen to his every word. He stretched out and said: "I don't know what they see in this bloke. It will never sell." I used to quote him regularly on that and gave him plenty of stick over the years.'

More than a quarter of century later, with swearing increasingly finding its way into mainstream English, the tirade of swear words remains shocking, particularly the use of the word 'cunts'. As we listened to the song in The Blockheads office in Harlow, both myself and Mickey cringed as a middle-aged sandwich lady popped her head round the door with her wares, just as Ian's outburst came blaring from the stereo.

The song itself sees Ian telling the story of Patricia, a downtrodden young woman who becomes hooked on heroin and goes on the game: 'A lawless brat from a council flat, oh oh/A little bit of this and a little bit of that, oh, oh/Dirty tricks'.

Ironically Ian had once dated a woman from Plaistow called Patricia Few while a student at the Royal College of Art, Patricia accompanied him to jazz clubs and stayed at his home, although their relationship foundered fairly quickly. It would seem more than likely that the name 'Plaistow Patricia' was taken from his one-time lover, although the story itself was an invention and nothing to do with either her or her lifestyle.

The tale was inspired by Ian's knowledge of the murky world of hard drugs in the 1960s. As a student he would go to Soho to score some dope, and one day was horrified to come across a room full of junkies out for the count. Although Class A drugs were not part of Ian's recreational habits, he'd once known a girl who died of a heroin overdose aged 17. This incident helped fuel Ian's detestation of hard drugs, something that was noticed by producer Laurie Latham.

'Ian was really anti-cocaine. If he caught anybody having a nifty line they'd have been out on their ear. At the time of recording *Do It Yourself* Ian said, "No one is to take cocaine. It turns you into a fascist." I understood exactly what he meant because when people take it they think they know everything.'

The girl's descent into drug addiction begins with her getting pregnant at 15 and living with her child in a council flat: 'She turned the corner before she turned fifteen/She got into a mess on the NHS, oh oh'. As her world collapses Patricia loses her looks, her body ravaged by heroin: 'Her tits had dropped, her arse was getting spread/She lost some teeth, she nearly lost the thread'.

In the song's original manifestation Patricia dies by walking into the River Thames, but as he had done on 'Blockheads', Ian decided to put a twist in the tale and rescue his character. 'An affair began with Charlie Chan' and her Chinese saviour sends Patricia to Switzerland to receive a new supply of blood: 'The finest grains for my lady's veins'. She ends up owning 'a showroom down the Mile End Road' and presumably lives happily ever after, with Ian's endorsement 'Go on, girl' ringing in her ears. In Ian's words, 'Patricia had to not die, she had to survive and be active because so many people don't.'⁶

The semi-screaming vocal was difficult to replicate live and as he got older Ian found 'Plaistow Patricia' increasingly problematic because it drained so much of his energy. The song was accordingly dumped from the set, along with the similarly ranting 'Blockheads'.

Again, it was the urbane American Steve Nugent to whom Ian turned for the music to 'Plaistow Patricia' after Chaz refused to work on it. In an interview with the *NME* Chaz explained why: 'A lot of Ian's words are in the form of rhyming couplets and sometimes you can't actually put a melody to it, as in the case of "Plaistow Patricia", which I refused to write the music for as I didn't really get off on the words. I thought any song that starts off "Arseholes, bastards, fucking cunts and pricks" is not exactly going to be a major number one world hit. But that's beside the point, the point being that because there was only one way of singing the words – blaaagh! blaaagh! blaaagh! You could only put the simplest music behind it.'⁹

Despite his lack of awareness of the East End of London, 'from the Mile End Road to the Matchstick, Becontree', Steve's composition fitted the song neatly. He explained, '"Plaistow Patricia" was pretty straightforward because it was such a raucous lyric. It came together quickly and sounded pretty much the same on record as it did on our demo.'

The music is dominated from the beginning by Davey Payne's unschooled, eccentric saxophone playing. As the song begins at a slow pace, a plodding guitar riff is accompanied by a basic one-beat-to-the-bar drumbeat while Ian sets the scene. As the pace quickens dramatically, it is Davey and Charley who take centre stage, with Chaz bashing out open chords on guitar. Davey's increasingly manic playing conjures up an appropriate sense of mental distortion as the song fades out.

The album climaxes with the frenzied thrash of 'Blackmail Man', a diatribe against the racists that Ian so despised. In a vitriolic display of raw emotion Ian attacks the ignorance of racists by utilising the same rhyming slang they use to dismiss people of a different nationality. The song begins by Ian identifying himself with 'an Irish cripple', 'a Scottish Jew', 'a buckle my shoe', 'a dead fish coon' and 'a pikey Greek'. He even uses the term 'a raspberry ripple', the slang used to describe disabled people such as himself.

The clever title 'Blackmail Man' could also be interpreted as 'black male man', an alternative surely not lost on the wordsmith himself. In addition, the use of the term 'I'll put the black on you', meaning putting a curse on the racists, was another example of Ian's spellbinding use of the English language.

Ian's colleagues all attest to Ian's disdain for what he saw as artificial divisions within society, be they on the grounds of class, disability or race. In Chaz's view 'Ian could not stand pretentiousness or arrogance of any kind, and he absolutely despised racism. I'm Jewish and he kind of felt a kindred spirit with me, because of the persecution of the Jews and the disabled in Nazi Germany. I rarely spoke about politics with him, but his politics infused his passion. He liked people to know how he felt.'

Chaz believes Ian used his in-built sense of anger as a writing tool: 'Ian had a lot of anger within himself, which he could vent through his lyrics. Ian liked talking about people who were living on the edge, Plaistow Patricia being one other example. He stuck up for the disenfranchised side of the population, people you don't usually hear about, that have been sidelined by the government and don't fit neatly into a box. Those were the sort of people which Ian felt a kindred spirit with, because of his background.'

Steve Nugent agrees, saying, 'A lot of his anger came from the fact that he felt he had to struggle out of being institutionalised. Being physically marked as somebody who was different, someone who was not able to do what a lot of people were able to do, which was to get up and move across the room easily or get on a bus without worrying about falling off.'

Mickey Gallagher offers an alternative view of Ian's songwriting. Although agreeing that Ian was passionate in his defence of minorities, Mickey believes Ian had an actor's ability to switch on his emotions at a moment's notice, a tool he used to great effect on 'Blackmail Man': 'He could easily get into that really evil side of a character's nature and enjoyed playing the part of somebody who was a horrible thug. Ian could do that for real, hence he could write songs like this and deliver them with force. I don't know of anybody else who could write a song like that.'

After the release of the more gentle *Do It Yourself*, 'Blackmail Man' was a song that Ian quickly dispensed with in the live arena, despite the wishes of the band. 'We did some great live takes of this that were longer than on the record,' says Mickey. 'The remit for Charley was to go as fast as he could, and we would try and keep up with him. Charley's drumming, as usual, was phenomenal, despite this song's unrelenting pace.'

Again, the track contained a lyric that was extremely difficult to sing, requiring Ian to become increasingly hysterical, shouting himself hoarse until the music crashed into a painful mess of feedback and discordant guitar. Until the release of *Mr Love Pants* in 1998 none of Ian's records were accompanied by lyric sheets, and when the *Brand New Boots And Panties* tribute was compiled in 2001 a section of the final verse was deemed indecipherable.

Ian described the song as 'an attempt at making something extremely raucous for the sake of raucousness. In the Kilburns there were a couple of songs that we did that were out and out blatant screams and extremely lovely, good fun to do. But somewhere a bit of class exists and Charley can't play bad drums whatever you ask him to play.'[6]

The album took less than three weeks to record, with Ian and Chaz working to strict conditions laid down by Peter Jenner, the most senior of the production trio. It was Jenner's decision to stick to no more than two overdubs per track that kept the LP's sound tight and raw. Wearing his manager's hat Jenner was also the person most able to arbitrate with Ian in the studio.

Although relatively green about technical matters in the studio, Ian was certainly forthright in his opinions. The singer's attitude was not helped by the design of the Workhouse, which contained a narrow staircase leading to the control room. Always uncomfortable with hauling himself up flights of stairs it would take Ian a considerable time to reach the control room, using his walking stick as a prop and mouthing profanities as he went. In Laurie Latham's words, 'The Workhouse was the worst place in the world for him to work.'

Latham is generous in his praise of Peter Jenner, claiming that his role was crucial to the success of *New Boots*: 'Peter's whole input was underrated. He was an old-fashioned producer, sitting there rolling joints, but he did oversee the whole thing. It's sad that he seems to have been written out of the equation somewhat regarding this album.'

Jenner himself describes his role as that of 'an old-fashioned vibe producer, someone who'd sit there and make sure everybody was happy, and that there was a good vibe and spirit. I think I was quite good at it because I did make a lot of good records. It's so important to have a good atmosphere in the studio. I would take a view of the sound, and I'd make the odd suggestion and Laurie would play with it. Laurie was a great engineer, so he did what he did very well and I sat and admired it.'

New Boots And Panties is rightly regarded as one of the seminal albums of the new wave era, capturing the raw vitality of Ian and Chaz's writing partnership perfectly. It seems incredible that in spite of the high esteem in which the LP is now held, Ian's management company, Blackhill, found it almost impossible to garner the interest of a record company. All the majors rejected the completed masterpiece, still refusing to believe that Ian Dury was a sellable commodity.

Ironically, the answer was lying at Blackhill's feet, quite literally. Stiff Records had recently become Blackhill's tenants at 32 Alexander Street, Bayswater, setting up an office in the basement of the three-floor house. The fledgling record company had already signed up Elvis Costello from nowhere and was making waves with the likes of The Damned, Dave Edmunds and Nick Lowe on its roster.

Listening to the recording, Dave Robinson and Jake Riviera were astonished to hear that the ten tracks were still unallocated. Blessing his good fortune, Robinson immediately offered his former client Ian Dury a three-album deal. According to Jenner, 'Stiff wanted them because Jake and Dave were both serious fans and Ian was absolutely right for Stiff. I couldn't imagine anybody more like a Stiff artist than Ian Dury, a guy who'd been famous but hadn't yet achieved anything.'

The album's title was chosen from a list of 20 drawn up by Ian and run past the energetic 23-year-old Kozmo Vinyl. It was inspired by a photograph taken for the LP's front cover by Chris Gabrin, who had taken Ian out and about in London in search of a shot that would best illustrate Ian's urban mystique. While strolling through Victoria, Ian suggested a photograph of himself outside an intriguing shop that had previously caught his eye while waiting for a bus. Having secured the permission of the shop's owner, who told them 'I didn't see ya, and I didn't 'ear ya', Ian posed in between a row of Dr Martens boots and a window display of women's underwear. As Gabrin began firing off a roll of film, Ian's five-year-old son Baxter, who was visiting his father, wandered into the frame, with his hands in his pocket. It was a perfect shot.

Released on 30 September 1977, *New Boots And Panties* was received ecstatically by the music inkies. The *NME*'s Roy Carr paid Ian the ultimate compliment of being a superior writer to Ray Davies of The Kinks, who had written stories of urban poverty with aplomb on songs like 'Dead End Street'. He wrote, 'Davies has dallied with a similar approach, but Dury has none of the self-conscious pretensions that Davies exposed in his Flash Harry caricature. Ian Dury feels no need to adopt a transatlantic voice to comply with his subject matter, preferring to deliver ribald and bittersweet monologues in the tone of voice he was born with.'

Allan Jones of the *Melody Maker* was equally fulsome in his praise, claiming the 'tense, harrowing account of urban degradation' conveyed the 'desperation and squalor of social conditions' in a way that put his new wave/punk contemporaries to shame. *Sounds* magazine joined the throng of journalists heaping praise on Ian, giving the album a five-star rating.

Of those involved in the recording only Ian expected *New Boots And Panties* to sell a million copies. 'The whole record had a really good sound, but I didn't think it would do as well as it did,' said Latham. 'I don't think any of us did. I ended up in *Music Week*'s top ten producers for two years on the basis of that record, which was incredible because beforehand I wasn't really an out-and-out producer. I'd only been an engineer.'

Chaz puts the album's success down to its simplicity, an ironic confession given the glossy shine he put on the album's follow-up, *Do It Yourself*: 'Someone told me the other day that they thought *New Boots And Panties* was the best album ever, that it sounded perfect, which is a hell of a compliment. We weren't aware of that at the time. We just tried to make tight music because we did not have the extravagance of spending a lot of time on it. So we kept it fairly stripped down.'

3 Stiff Me, Hype Me Up The Charts

Just three days after *New Boots And Panties* was unleashed on an unsuspecting public Ian went on the road for the first time since disbanding the Kilburns. Stiff Records had set up a nationwide tour for five of its most highly rated new artists: Ian, Elvis Costello, Larry Wallis, Nick Lowe and Wreckless Eric. The idea was inspired by the 1975 Naughty Rhythms Tour, which saw pub rock outfits Dr Feelgood, Kokomo and Chilli Willi & The Red Hot Peppers going on the road together. Stiff's co-owners Dave and Jake realised the immense potential for publicity in having five acts on the same tour and hired a private coach to whisk the 18 musicians involved across the length and breadth of the country.

As the tour approached Ian was left with something of a conundrum. He and Chaz had been gift-wrapped their dream rhythm section, but knew they needed an extra guitarist and keyboard player. Chaz, after all, only had one pair of hands. But what promised to be a painstaking search for two more musicians to augment their line-up was over almost as soon as it began. Charley and Norman explained to Ian that they had been working with Johnny Turnbull and Mickey Gallagher for the past three years in Loving Awareness. Ian and Chaz duly invited the pair into the fold, realising astutely that a band that had been working together for three years would be a tight, compact outfit. In fact, they wouldn't really be a new band at all.

Both Johnny and Mickey had been impressed with the extracts from *New Boots And Panties* that their friends had played them and were more than happy to accept their places on the tour bus. Mickey explained, 'I remember when Charley and Norman played us "Sex And Drugs And Rock And Roll" we couldn't stop laughing because it was so funny. The next thing we were being asked to go on the Stiff tour, so we met Ian under the arches somewhere in Kennington, near to where he had a rehearsal place. I was introduced to

Ian, who in fact was the two things I didn't like. He was an art student and I didn't like art students. He was also a Cockney and, being a northerner, I didn't like them either. But when I read his lyrics I cracked up and thought, "This guy's really got something."'

Johnny was similarly taken with Ian's songs, particularly the lyrics to 'Billericay Dickie'. The guitarist believes Ian may have visited Ronan O'Rahilly seeking permission to use the four members of Loving Awareness and that money may have changed hands. 'If it's true, then they would obviously have been talking money because we had a debt to Ronan, as we had before to Miles Copeland after we left Glencoe.'

Having rehearsed for the Stiff tour, the four members of Ian and Chaz's new backing band negotiated a salary of £75 a week for the tour's five-week duration. According to Mickey, 'We tried to get 100 quid a week, but Dave Robinson said, "It's your best shot", so we accepted it, with the agreement that when things got better we'd get 100 quid a week.'

The band's line-up was completed by Davey Payne. Although a long-standing member of the Kilburns and having played on *New Boots And Panties*, Davey's major commitment was as part of Wreckless Eric's band. Ian Dury on drums and Denise Roudette on bass completed Eric's combo, which created a minor problem for the tour organisers. Ian would clearly need a break between Eric's set and his own, so this had to be built in to Stiff's plans every night.

At 4pm on 3 October, Stiff's five hottest acts and their respective backing bands boarded the coach outside the label's office and began the relatively short journey to High Wycombe Town Hall in Buckinghamshire. Mickey recalls vividly his first experience of playing with Ian: 'After the gig I told Ian that I couldn't concentrate for laughing. I'd never seen anything like it in my life. He went on wearing a white suit with stains on it and a plastic fried egg on his shoulder. It was all art school stuff. The rest of us had all come from bands that were very serious and here was a guy who was actually performing and just using music as a medium.'

Before the tour began it was widely expected that Elvis Costello and his newly formed backing band The Attractions would be the best received of the five acts. After all, Elvis's debut album, *My Aim Is True*, had been in the shops for three months and had received good publicity. But it was the unknown Ian Dury and his as yet unnamed band who would steal the show night after night.

Mickey recalls how Ian enjoyed the air of mystery surrounding his colleagues as they boarded the bus that first day: 'We were complete strangers, the black sheep sitting very quietly at the back of the bus, whereas everyone else was joking and being laddish. Ian loved this air of mystique. We'd played together for three or four years so we were really tight and everyone else thought we'd just formed to go on this tour. Elvis's band were there and they thought they were superior, but when we went on and started playing everyone thought "Bloody hell, they're good."'

The other band members echo Mickey's recollections, with Norman adding, 'That's what helped us on the Stiff tour because everyone else had formed new bands for the tour, whereas we were already tight. We were pissing over the other bands.'

As the 25-date tour took shape, Ian and Elvis took turns as the headline act and quickly formed a mutual antagonism. According to Mickey, Ian used the animosity between the two artists as a tool to gee himself up: 'If things were peaceful and nice Ian didn't like it. There had to be some tension to get him going, and if it wasn't there he'd create it.'

Chaz believes part of the conflict came from the fact that Ian, at ten years older than Elvis, did not respect his rival as an artist: 'I think that Ian felt he had a real agenda to sing about and thought, "What does Elvis Costello know about life?"' The two singers barely spoke, although whenever Ian closed the show with 'Sex And Drugs And Rock And Roll' Costello, along with the other ten artists and musicians, would come onstage and join in. Television footage of the tour includes the incredible sight of three drummers sitting at different kits on the stage playing to the song.

Costello had surprised both his record company and his public by ignoring almost all the material from his successful album, and concentrating instead on new songs not yet recorded and a batch of covers. Strangely, considering his antipathy towards Ian, one of those covers was the Kilburn And The High Roads number 'The Roadette Song'.

As the audience became disappointed with Costello's performance, what followed was almost inevitable, as Chaz recalls: 'Elvis Costello thought he was the bee's knees and he and Ian would fight to see who was top dog. They were alternating as top of the bill, but then one night we went on first and played so well that the audience's energy was drained. There was nothing left for Elvis to tap into, so he said that we could top the bill from then on.'

Johnny retains some sympathy for Costello, believing that his performance was hindered by the choice of tour venues: 'The gigs were a mixture of some echoey halls and some really good university halls. Elvis never sounded good in echoey halls. You really had to listen carefully to his lyrics, whereas Ian's were banner headlines like "Sex And Drugs And Rock And Roll". There wasn't much that could go wrong with that, which is why we raised the roof.'

As the tour reached its climax, its anthem had undeniably become 'Sex And Drugs And Rock And Roll', which was appropriate considering the offstage behaviour of many of the artists. The subsequent tour video, *Stiffs Live Stiffs Tour '77*, showed the aggressive backstage mauling of a woman by one of The Attractions, drug-taking on the coach, and extensive all-day drinking. According to Johnny, 'The Stiff tour was mad. People like Dave Edmunds and Nick Lowe were a breed apart and started the "24-Hour Club", which consisted of various people staying up all night drinking. I wasn't into that too much.'

It was during the tour that Ian's backing band was finally named 'The Blockheads', after a gig in the Midlands. The young Kozmo Vinyl, a jack the lad with the gift of the gab, was employed as the show's compère by Stiff and each night introduced the band under a different name. 'He used to introduce us as all sorts of things, like "Ian Dury And The Readers' Wives",' recalls Mickey. 'Then one night he said: "Ladies and gentlemen, this is Ian Dury And The Blockheads."' As the band relaxed backstage Norman piped up, ''ere, we're The Blockheads, aren't we?' The name stuck.

Kozmo was a massive fan of Ian from his Kilburns days and became the band's PR mouthpiece. 'He was a young lad, interested in journalism, and hung about Fleet Street with the Danny Bakers,' says Mickey. 'He was a very mouthy and opinionated West Ham supporter and became our link to PR.'

'He was a right spiv,' agrees Chaz. 'He used to wear loud suits and did outrageous things to get us attention. He was a cocky dickie and Ian liked that. Ian usually liked people to be quite submissive around him, which is what generally happened. But if he found someone with whom he could have a laugh he would put up with it. Quite a lot of jousting took place between them.'

The tour was a huge success, propelling Ian to nationwide fame and on to the front cover of the inkies. Five weeks on the road had also created a strong bond between his musicians and, when the coach rolled back in to London on 5 November, Loving Awareness had become The Blockheads in name and also in attitude. Johnny explains, 'One by one we all changed. When we had been Loving Awareness we were all dressed by The Fool from Apple and by the end of the tour we dressed like punks. At the start I looked like I was in The Bee Gees, with a big beard. I remember getting to Aberystwyth and coming down one day after shaving the beard off, but having kept the moustache. Everyone was laughing so I went upstairs and shaved the 'tache off too.'

Wishing to capitalise on the band's momentum, Blackhill set up the Dirty Dozen Tour, comprising 12 nights across the UK. Davey Payne defected full-time from Wreckless Eric, leaving the latter with a sour taste in his mouth. But Davey's existing commitments to Eric meant that he missed The Blockheads' first tour, and Ian was forced to delve into his Kilburns past for a replacement. As Mickey explained, 'We brought in John Earle from The Rumour Brass, a very funny geezer and lovely sax player, schooled in Tamla, but he wasn't really what Ian wanted. Ian liked Davey's approach because Davey was not a schooled sax player, he was a bit off the wall, a Salvador Dali with his playing. He'd paint with the sax, but his playing was beautiful and his timing was great.'

With their reputation spreading like wildfire, Ian and The Blockheads found themselves invited on a six-week tour of the United States, supporting former Velvet Underground frontman Lou Reed. Having completed a highly successful UK tour, Norman, Charley, Mickey, Davey and Johnny felt they were due a rise in wages and demanded the magic figure of £100 a week. In a compromise Blackhill offered them £90 a week plus a small percentage of the American sales of 'Sex And Drugs And Rock And Roll'. The subsequent banning of the record stateside rendered the second part of the agreement useless.

Mickey says he now regrets the decision he and his colleagues made not to seek a written agreement with Blackhill, instead relying on a verbal contract. He believes the Loving Awareness quartet felt 'damaged by the music business and the different managers we'd had' and were cagey about being bound to contracts. 'We didn't sign anything with the management because at the time it was lucrative enough not to, but as our fame grew it became detrimental because everything became about Ian. We wanted to go to the States anyway. At the time we weren't resentful because Ian deserved it, but we were a little miffed that they wouldn't give us 100 quid a week.'

The band members were understandably nervous about playing second fiddle to an American audience whom they feared might not understand them. Just as worrying was the prospect of undertaking the tour without Chaz, who, not for the last time, had tired of Ian's offstage antics.

Speaking in an interview in the *NME* in 1980, after yet another departure, Chaz revealed his unhappiness with certain parts of life with Ian: 'Ian is a strong personality. He's very charming, very forceful and charismatic. He knows it too and can use that facility to hedge someone into doing something they actually don't honestly wish to do. Ian, I've found – and this says as much about my weakness and his strengths and isn't anything to do with malice – Ian at times to be very, very threatening.' [11]

Although briefly shaken by Chaz's departure the band were buoyed by a string of telegrams from Blighty wishing them well. One of the telegrams was from Elvis Costello and Jake Riviera at Stiff, proving that the Irish singer was not one to bear grudges. Another was sent by The Who's irrepressible guitarist Pete Townshend, the man who had originally promised to take Ian's music across the Atlantic.

The tour comprised 28 dates, although The Blockheads were required to play two sets at each gig before retiring, exhausted, to their 12-bed coach.

The first four dates of the tour, from 26–29 March 1978, were at the famous Roxy club in Los Angeles. It had become apparent even at this early stage that Lou Reed was not going to be anything like a genial host and a fractious relationship between the American and Ian quickly developed. The tension was not eased by two famous visitors who arrived backstage before the fourth night at the Roxy.

Rolling Stones drummer Charlie Watts had been a friend of Ian's since 1962 and had asked his friend, guitarist Ronnie Wood, staying in LA at the time, to drop in on Ian and show his support. Shortly before The Blockheads' set Ronnie arrived, along with Faces colleague Rod Stewart. Having been warmly welcomed by Ian and the band, the two rockers were keen to find out how Lou Reed, by now in the middle of his period of heroin addiction, was behaving.

According to Norman, 'They asked us "How's this Lou Reed geezer treating you?" and Ian said, "He ain't spoken to us yet, he ain't said a fucking word." With that they said something to the effect of "Don't worry, we'll sort him out." Nothing more was said and we forgot about it. That evening

Lou goes onstage after we've had a blinding gig, picks up his guitar and begins strumming and it's right out of tune. He took it off and picked up one of the four other guitars behind him, but that was out of tune as well. Each one he picked up was the same and he stood there sneering at his roadie while saying to the audience "I'll come back in 20 minutes when the guitars are in tune."

'He went offstage fuming and we found out later it was Ronnie and Rod who had sneaked into the guitar room and twiddled the knobs on the guitars. Ever since that gig Lou thought it was us who'd done it and that made things even worse. It was nothing to do with us; it was Ronnie and Rod's little way of teaching Lou a lesson, telling him not to mess with us London boys.' After the show Ian, accompanied by Kozmo, went back to Wood's house to eat beans on toast before getting back on the road.

As the tour progressed it was Ian Dury And The Blockheads, as opposed to Lou Reed, who were taking all the plaudits. 'Lou was really cool and laid back with his LA band,' says Mickey. 'The Blockheads went on and blew them off the stage many nights, with our energy and ability. His band had ability but they didn't know how to project it like we did.'

Reed deliberately kept his distance from his backing musicians, walking around venues accompanied by burly minders and barely speaking to anyone, even his own band. Norman claims Reed's musicians had nothing good to say about their boss, who had even banned them from performing with his eccentric English support act.

'Their relationship was one where Lou was very much the boss and they were just employed musicians. The two girl singers really liked The Blockheads and watched our set, along with the rest of the band, nearly every night. They wanted to come and do backing vocals with us, but Lou told them if they did he'd give them the boot. I don't know Lou, I never really spoke to him, but he had a heavy period of heroin addiction, and I think that was why he was like it.'

By the final third of the tour Reed was said to be enraged by the attention being heaped on Ian and his band. 'All the reviews were talking about us more than Lou,' says Norman. 'In Toronto Peter Jenner showed us a national newspaper with the headline "Cockney boy wipes the floor with Lou Reed". He was getting really pissed off, 'cos he was doing us a really big favour taking us on the road. He should have been getting praise for bringing an unknown British act as good as us to America, which is what he was doing, and instead he was getting slated, with people saying how good we were, and that Lou was rubbish.'

As the mutual disdain between Reed and his support act intensified, The Blockheads resorted to ever more blatant acts of sabotage to irk their moody host. Reed had got into the habit of whipping his fans into a frenzy by delaying his entrance to the stage. As the clock struck 10:30, the time he was due to perform, a solitary red spotlight would be trained on his microphone. As the chants of 'Lou... Lou' intensified, the hero of the hour would often wait until 11 o'clock before walking out, by which time the audience was ready to burst.

Having cottoned on to Reed's plan, Ian spotted an opportunity to instigate a change in the proceedings after his band completed its set at the Tower Theatre in Philadelphia. The next gig was the following evening in New Jersey, so the band had already packed up their equipment in order to make a quick getaway. As they prepared to leave the venue the band discovered that the only way out was via the stage.

By this time Ian had befriended a burly African-American policewoman who offered to usher them across the stage. Seizing his opportunity to upset Reed, Ian informed the officer that the band were not yet ready to leave. Ian succeeded in delaying their departure until five minutes to eleven and, accompanied by the unsuspecting policewoman, led The Blockheads across the stage in the dark. The audience, assuming that Reed was finally gracing them with his presence, erupted. The grinning English invaders left the stage the other side, waving as they went. The red-hot passion of the audience had been defused in an instant, leaving Reed spitting feathers.

The tour reached its conclusion at the Bottom Line in New York on 3 May. Chaz had returned to the fold for the final night and remembers being shocked at how jaded his colleagues looked: 'I arrived in New York for the last gig of the tour and they looked ashen-faced. They were completely drained.'

Reinvigorated by the arrival of his writing partner, Ian plotted an even more audacious act of vengeance against Lou Reed. Towards the end of The Blockheads' set Ian decided to make a speech, one that is remembered with glee by Norman: 'Ian told the audience that as it was our last show with Lou he wanted to thank him for looking after us and how the tour wouldn't have been possible without him. Next up in the set was "Plaistow Patricia", so Ian then said, "I'd like to dedicate the next song to Lou... Arseholes, bastards, fucking cunts and pricks." Everybody fell about laughing.'

Everybody except Lou Reed, that is, who told the band's minder Fred Rowe that the remark had cost Ian a box of champagne. Whether such a riposte would have upset the beaming Ian is extremely debatable.

Despite the huge success of the tour Ian decided that he never wanted to return to play in America. Mickey claims that this was because The Blockheads' music had gone down better than Ian's lyrics. He claimed, 'Ian was very colloquially English and that confused the shit out of loads of Americans, who were saying, "What's he talking about?" The band got a lot of recognition and attention, and the upshot was that Ian never wanted to go back to America. He always regarded it as "Romford at right angles". We wanted to get back there as they loved us but he wouldn't go back, which was very disappointing.'

On their return to Britain the tired band had just a week to recuperate before launching a 26-date UK tour, starting at Birmingham Odeon on 11 May. Ian Dury And The Blockheads were fast becoming the nation's hottest act.

The previous month, while the band was in the States, Stiff had released the first ever Ian Dury And The Blockheads single, 'What A Waste'. The almost constant demands of gigging and press interviews since the end of the Stiff tour had meant that Ian had not had time to write any more songs. Stiff was desperate to capitalise on the band's growing reputation with a new release and before he stepped on the plane to America persuaded Ian to dust down a song that he had written more than two years earlier.

'What A Waste' had been composed with Rod Melvin at the latter's London home before his departure 'into the mystic', as Ian had put it. It was a well-crafted song, with a lyric describing various possibilities of a working man's life. In his second interview with *Penthouse* magazine, in 1984, Ian said he had written the song in an attempt to make a factory worker question his employment and look further afield. He said, 'I didn't want to say what they were doing was wrong, but ask a question, so that it went in almost subconsciously. I later made a film with this guy – a half Cornish half Nigerian playwright from the Isle of Dogs called Tunde Ecole. Very exotic geezer. At the party after he'd shown this diploma film for Beaconsfield Film School, he told me he'd stopped working in a factory after he heard that song, and said to himself "Yeah, I could have been a fucking playwright." I actually did burst into tears, 'cos I was pissed. But I was also really glad to hear it.'[12]

Melvin, who had demoed the song with Ian at Dave Robinson's studio at the Hope and Anchor, said that Ian's lyric demanded a simple accompaniment: 'With Ian's delivery it worked having minimal chords, just having a groove going on that he could float the lyrics on and where the melody wasn't jumping all over the place. Ian loved drumming and was very good at writing rhythmically, and "What A Waste" immediately suggested a rhythm. At the time I'd been working with Brian Eno and he'd told me about a song he'd written on two chords called "Babies on Fire", and I liked this idea. So a lot of "What A Waste" is only two chords until you get to the chorus, which is a more conventional pop song. The arrangement was quite minimal at the time. It didn't have the bass pattern or anything like that.'

When the band, minus Chaz, started recording the song they felt it was too simplistic, and incorporated some material they had written for Loving Awareness which had never seen the light of day. Johnny explained, 'The middle bit, the instrumental package, was from a Loving Awareness out-take. We married all those bits together and improved the song, because it wasn't really happening on the Kilburns version. What we did was make it more musical and Mickey added all the synthesised saxes, the soprano and sax synth, and that gave it a good sound.

'Me and Mickey used to do a lot of lead lines together on Loving Awareness where it was his synth and my guitar synth, called a high flat. We used to cook up passages where we played the lead together and it was just Charley and Norman on the bottom, and me and Mickey pretending we were two fine sax players. That fitted really well on "What a Waste".'

Although Chaz was at the time no longer officially a Blockhead, Ian called him into the studio as 'quality control', not yet feeling confident enough to work alone with his new colleagues. Mickey believes that although Ian recognised good music, he disliked being in a room where musicians were talking. This was because 'he was out of his depth when were talking about chords and progressions and stuff like that'. With his right-hand man Chaz at his side, Ian felt more at ease. Chaz listened to the arrangement and made a couple of suggestions, including the use of a rhythmic organ.

Melvin graciously accepts that the band had improved the arrangement of the song, but says Ian never asked for his permission to use the track. He joked, 'I didn't know "What A Waste" was being recorded until I saw it in the *Melody Maker*, so I had to go and buy a copy from a record shop and see if my name was on it. Fortunately it was.'

The single, which contained 'Wake Up And Make Love With Me' on the b-side, was a great success, giving Ian not just his first chart entry, but his first top ten hit. After six weeks in the chart it peaked at number nine, the first of what were to be the three top ten hits of Ian's career.

As Ian's success became mainstream his previous record company, Warner, cynically decided to cash in by digging out the Kilburn And The High Roads back catalogue and giving it a fresh airing. The release of *Wotabunch* would have been fresher still had they allowed Ian to re-record the tracks with The Blockheads, a suggestion he made to them in vain. The album featured nine of the songs from *Handsome*, namely 'The Call Up', 'Crippled With Nerves', 'Patience (So What?)', 'Upminster Kid', 'Rough Kids', 'The Roadette Song', 'The Badger And The Rabbit', 'The Mumble Rumble And The Cocktail Rock' and 'Pam's Moods'. 'You're More Than Fair', 'Billy Bentley' and 'Huffety Puff' were added.

Making sure nobody missed the point, the album was released under the name 'Kilburn And The High Roads Featuring Ian Dury.' 'Billy Bentley' was also released as a single, but Ian's refusal to promote it meant that it failed to chart. Desperate for a slice of the action, another record company, Bonaparte, issued a five-track EP entitled 'The Best Of Kilburn And The High Roads Featuring Ian Dury'. This also sank without trace. Not wanting to miss out, Pye Records re-released both *Handsome* and a 10-inch record called *Upminster Kids* containing eight tracks. It is little wonder that when his manager Peter Jenner asked him to record some Kilburns numbers for the follow-up album to *New Boots And Panties* Ian declined to do so.

After the success of 'What A Waste' Blackhill urged Ian to come up with a follow-up single, despite his already heavy workload. Joining up with Chaz, who by this time had returned full-time to The Blockheads, the pair constructed a number of songs in Ian's new rented home in Rolvendon, Kent, but one in particular stood out, entitled 'Hit Me With Your Rhythm Stick'. The song showed a gentler side to Ian than had been seen on *New Boots And Panties*, with a witty lyric about people across the world wanting to be hit with his 'rhythm stick': 'In the deserts of Sudan/And the gardens of Japan/From Milan to Yucatan/Every woman, every man. Hit me with your rhythm stick/Hit me, hit me.'

The origins of 'Hit Me With Your Rhythm Stick' are disputed. Ian said he and Chaz wrote the song in about half an hour, a claim backed up by his writing partner. According to Chaz, 'I was jamming with Ian in his living room, me with a keyboard and Ian on his Roland drum machine. We'd got a great funk vibe going, a kind of Latin/funky vibe, and the next day when I came back I had a new idea, having listened to "Wake Up And Make Love With Me" the previous night. Ian had moved the drum kit and piano outside into his garage and when I showed him what I'd done he went off into the house and fetched the lyrics he'd written. He then left me and went back in the house. Within half an hour I'd written the intro and incorporated his verses and choruses into it. When Ian heard it he loved it. The next day we got the others down and they really got off on it, and within a few days we were recording it in the studio.'

Johnny Turnbull has a different version, claiming that Ian already had the idea for the lyric during the band's tour of the States six months previously: 'We were going round America and all Ian had was "Hit me with your rhythm stick, hit me, hit me". In hotels and radio stations we'd go through swing doors together. Ian would be at the front saying, "Hit me with your rhythm stick", with his stick in the air and we'd all be saying "Hit me". Someone would say "A beefburger, and a chips and a beans" and somebody else would say "and a nice cup of tea" or "a nice bit of toast". Everyone who saw us do it loved it and it wasn't even a song then. The lyrics were changing all the time. "It's nice to be a lunatic" used to be "It don't take arithmetic", so they were all slightly different, but Ian had a map in his head of what he wanted.'

According to Johnny, Ian was changing his lyrics up to the moment the band entered the studio. He cites the recording of 'Rhythm Stick' as one of his most enjoyable days spent in the studio: 'I had great fun with my first guitar synth, with the wah-wah that went backwards through the whole sweep. It was like a glorified pedal board really, with circuitry on it. I'd just got a boogie amp from The Who's company, one of the first ones in the country. We did all the sound effects with me and Mickey on the Hammond, with a wah-wah guitar synth following the words "Hit me". We recorded loads and Laurie mixed the best ones in.'

The song's three verses each included a phrase in both German and French, adding a quirky edge, and probably a few more sales in Europe. In the first verse he exclaimed, 'Je t'adore, ich liebe dich', in the second 'Das ist gut, c'est fantastique' and in the final verse 'C'est si bon, ist es nicht'. Each time Ian followed it up with 'Hit me! Hit me! Hit me!' in the style of a camp Nazi officer. Ian also made references to various people in his life. Norman believes the line 'From Bombay to Santa Fe' was inserted as a reference to his own birthplace in the Indian city. One-time Kilburns drummer Terry Day also claims that 'It's nice to be a lunatic' was inspired by an impromptu music session undertaken by the pair with paint brushes while studying at Walthamstow. A lecturer from downstairs, enraged by the noise, steamed into the room and said that Ian and Terry 'ought to be locked up in a lunatic asylum', a quote that the pair enjoyed reciting for many months.

There was no doubt that the song's suggestive title and chorus greatly appealed to the British public's sense of humour. Laurie Latham, in the producer's chair again, agrees: 'I thought the lyric would catch people's imagination. Sometimes in a pop song it's a guitar hook or saxophone solo but occasionally it's an infectious lyric. There was a feeling generally that "Rhythm Stick" would do really well.'

Another element considered vital to the song's appeal was Norman's extraordinary bass riff of 16 notes to the bar: 'I was listening and playing the roots of the chords but it was a bit boring and there was a lot of space I could fill. That's where I started doubling it up and make it 16s, so it would interest me and add a little flavour. Chaz had the riff and the hook line on the piano, so I bubbled around it. As soon as he heard it Chaz loved it. As musicians you know when things are right. If you listen to the bass line on "Rhythm Stick" it's playing a little melody around the chords that are changing.'

Another strong feature of 'Rhythm Stick' was Davey's audacious double saxophone solo in the middle. Watching Davey playing two saxophones at once for eight bars became a feature of every subsequent Blockheads gig until his expulsion from the band in 1998.

Having completed the recording Chaz dashed to the telephone to call his mother and inform her 'I've just recorded my first number one.' It was a feeling shared by everyone in the band. Speaking in a 1999 Channel 5 documentary on his life, Ian said, 'I thought it was brilliant. I knew it would be number one. We all knew it would be number one. It wasn't just the record. Don't forget the vibes on us at the time was a once in a lifetime [thing] and once is enough as well, thanks. But it was amazing. You couldn't walk out of the door. I'd get climbed on, so we were extremely popular, and the record was bloody good.'[5]

Mickey also believed the song would reach the top of the charts: 'We knew when we recorded it that it was good and we were the darlings of the press at the time, so the timing was right. We knew we'd have a number one sooner or later and this one had an aura about it. We recorded at least 11 takes and were sick of it by the end but Ian pushed us and pushed us. The longer you do it the more jaded it gets. I don't know what Ian was trying to squeeze out of us but at the end of the day he thought the second take was best.'

Mickey's criticism is refuted by Laurie Latham, who said, 'I know what he means, but I think that's how you make records. This whole notion that you can go in and get a snapshot is something I don't agree with. There are always exceptions to the rule. People will quote you that "The House Of The Rising Sun" was recorded in two hours, and every time the story is told the time diminishes. If you think of all the classic records that you like, chances are they took a long time and a lot of crafting. That's why in the end people started owning the means of production and getting their own studios. Ian was very knowledgeable about music and was a great record fan. You can always go back and use stuff. You can say take two was better after all, but I think Ian was absolutely right in pursuing it.'

One area on which Mickey and Laurie agree is their slight sense of disappointment at the record's mix. Mickey thinks the song sounds 'cramped', and dominated by the piano and Ian's voice, at the expense of Norman's bubbling bass line. 'Everybody talks about that bass line,' agrees Laurie, 'but the mix ended up a bit of a consensus. I wish I had been able to mix it on my own and I think it would have been better. I don't think the bass was loud enough. You can't hear it in the foreground, although that's possibly what makes people talk about it so much.'

The flip side to the track was the memorably titled 'There Ain't Half Been Some Clever Bastards', a song almost as well loved as 'Hit Me'. Indeed, many Blockheads fans claim that when they bought the record on 45 they played the b-side more often than the single itself. The song, co-written with Russell Hardy, was yet another of Ian's music-hall pastiches about all sorts of 'clever bastards' littered through popular culture and science.

The first verse concerned a 20th-century British entertainment legend who, coincidentally, may have lived in a house in Switzerland whose previous occupants were a family by the name of Dury: 'Noel Coward was a charmer/As a writer he was Brahma/Velvet jackets and pyjamas/The Gay Divorce and other dramas'.

In an article in *Mojo* in 1998 Ian said, 'We [Ian and his mother and father] lived in a little village called Les Avons, near Montreux. Noel Coward went to live in the same place in 1958 and I think it was the same house, called the Villa Christian. I was there ten years before Noel Coward! He probably found some of my old notes and knocked out a couple of musicals on the strength of it, the old bastard!' [13]

Using the Cockney slang that he had utilised so effectively on 'Billericay Dickie' Ian described artist Vincent Van Gogh as being a 'pencil squeezer' who produced some 'eye-ball pleasers'. Leonardo de Vinci was dismissed as merely 'an Italian geezer' while scientific genius Albert Einstein's work was simplified in the following way: 'Einstein can't be classed as witless/He claimed atoms were the littlest/When you did a bit of splittiness/Frightened everybody shitless'.

Although another example of Ian swearing on record, and in this case including a profanity in a song title, 'Clever Bastards' never comes across as offensive. Ian had an almost unique ability to make swearing acceptable, because his lyrics were so funny. Norman recalls explaining this phenomenon to his church-going mother: 'My mum used to say to me, "I like your songs, but why does Ian have to swear so much?" I said, "Because it makes people like you talk about him." He had a way of saying something that would make you laugh, so people didn't mind the swearing.

'I remember sending my mum a copy of *New Boots And Panties* and I put a note in saying, "Whatever you do, don't play side two, song four because the priest may be round." I could imagine her saying to him, "Here's my son's new album" and him being faced with "Plaistow Patricia". Of course that was the first track she listened to.'

Mickey says the lack of pressure felt by the band while recording b-sides was one of the reasons why Ian and The Blockheads recorded so many memorable ones: 'I loved the b-sides we did. They often come away as throwaway lyrics because they are the b-sides, but they were great. Who'd write a song about "clever bastards"? The sentiment is fantastic. People do think clever people are "lucky bleeders". This was music hall but done in a funky way. With b-sides the pressure was off as we'd usually already knocked out the single. This was banged out in one or two takes and when you listen back it comes across easy. A lovely song, delivered with aplomb.'

Sadly, the continued demise of the single as a marketable entity has made the b-side practically non-existent, having for many years been a unique channel for bands to experiment with styles and recording techniques.

Mickey fondly recalls 'Clever Bastards' as the first time he managed to squeeze one of his solos on to vinyl: 'I did this solo live as we recorded the track. I jammed it, which is what we do as Blockheads – we feel the movement and play to it. I knew that particular part had no lyric so I just stepped in and played a solo before anyone else did. I was well pleased. Ian and Chaz were so into the project that it didn't really occur to them, but getting a squeeze at a solo used to matter to us Blockheads.'

'Hit Me With Your Rhythm Stick' was released on 23 November 1978, but Ian and The Blockheads would have to wait more than two months for the song to top the chart. For five straight weeks from late December 1978 the song remained stuck at number two as The Village People's 'YMCA' held top spot. But just as it seemed their hopes were to be dashed, 'Rhythm Stick' leapfrogged to the top on 27 January 1979. Members of the band remember hearing the news as if it were yesterday.

Norman and Johnny were sat in a van with Charley outside the Kilburn State Cinema, now a bingo hall, for a Blockheads gig that evening. Norman said, 'Me and Charley arrived there for the soundcheck and that night it was the new chart at six o'clock. We kept hearing the presenter saying, "Is it a new number one?" When they eventually announced we were number one we shouted "Yesssss!" and ran in to the soundcheck and the others had heard it in there on a transistor. It was a great feeling. It does get to you. I was 26 at the time and remember phoning my mum to tell her.'

Mickey was still driving to the gig when he heard the news on his car radio. 'I was driving along the Embankment and listening to the radio when the presenter said, "He's made it, he's number one. Ian Dury", and I was ecstatic. It was an amazing feeling.'

For that week's appearance on *Top Of The Pops* the band decided to celebrate in style by visiting a Moss Bros store and renting dinner suits. After the record's introduction by the Hairy Cornflake, presenter Dave Lee Travis, the public were greeted by the unprecedented sight of Ian and the band in tuxedos and dickie bows.

Perhaps inevitably, after its slow ascension to the top spot, 'Hit Me With Your Rhythm Stick' was number one for just a week, being replaced seven days later by Blondie's 'Heart Of Glass'. According to Mickey, a feeling of anti-climax among the band members quickly followed: 'The next week we thought, "We've had a number one, so now we've got to get our second one." When you have a number one there's a momentary sense of elation and then a fear sets in. The pressure's on and there's not a lot of time to revel in it.'

Revelling in their number one success was certainly not an option for either Ian or The Blockheads. With almost a year and a half having passed since the release of *New Boots And Panties* the pressure was now on to release a follow-up album.

4 Do It Yourself

The groundwork for Ian's second album was laid in his new rented home in the genteel Kent village of Rolvendon. In late 1978 Ian's six colleagues converged on his new pad to begin writing the first Ian Dury And The Blockheads album, as opposed to one by Ian Dury, Chaz Jankel and a handful of session musicians. This change inspired Ian to include all The Blockheads in the writing process, rather than rely solely on his tried and trusted partnership with Chaz.

Ian's management tried in vain to persuade their client to dust down some of his barely known Kilburns numbers and re-record them with his new band, a process that would, if nothing else, have been quicker and less expensive. Still smarting at the decision by his previous record company to cash in on the Kilburns back catalogue, Ian refused point blank. Peter Jenner explained, 'We'd be saying to Ian, "Why don't you do England's Glory?" It's such a great song. That was a fucking hit record in the making, but he wouldn't do it. He increasingly wouldn't listen to anyone, except that he would kowtow to Chaz with bad grace.'

Another person left disappointed at this stage was Steve Nugent. Having contributed to the success of *New Boots And Panties*, Steve had expected to be given the chance to continue writing with Ian, but with the formation of The Blockheads he was shunted into the sidings: 'I was pretty much squeezed out of the writing once The Blockheads were assembled. By that point I was employed as a lecturer, but I still spent time working with music and I found it somewhat frustrating that I was not included in the songwriting. Of course, I can see why it happened because Ian had to keep The Blockheads going. They were all great musicians and it would have been very hard to bring in another musician who wasn't part of the group to contribute material.'

The band were pleased to be involved in the writing process, something they had got a brief taste of during the recording of 'What A Waste', and enjoyed their 'open house' invitation to stay with Ian at Rolvendon, where they had access to a heated swimming pool and landscaped gardens. But if any band members thought they were in for an easy ride, they were in for a sharp shock. Ian believed his group would work best in isolation and split them into different rooms where they were provided with separate lyrics each, to work on in isolation.

Mickey believes that this strict way of working typified Ian's 'Protestant work ethic', a philosophy that was alien to his more laid-back colleagues: 'Ian was the result of institutions from the age of seven, so that's the way he worked, with a very Protestant work ethic. If it didn't bleed and it wasn't hard then it wasn't worth it in Ian's head. You couldn't just say "I've got this idea" and then record it. We were there for about a week and Ian would wander around the rooms like a teacher saying "How ya doing?" We were all bemused but we pandered to the geezer.'

Johnny has a similar view of the writing methods imposed by Ian: 'We would go through the mill a little bit. He was quite fastidious if he had a beat or rhythm in mind and if it didn't meet that mark he would say, "It's got to be faster." Ian didn't like the easy escape, like "This music goes with that lyric." He would mention some obscure jazzer who you'd never heard of and then leave you. It seemed a bit strange at first being put in another room with a lyric but we all wanted to get on the writer's list and to write songs with him 'cos his words were so fucking good.'

One of the songs to come from the Rolvendon sessions was 'Hit Me With Your Rhythm Stick', but Ian stubbornly refused to include it on the album. His policy of separating singles from albums as a point of principle was opposed by his band and management, but encouraged by Kozmo Vinyl. Despite his management arguing that a successful single would help increase sales, Ian countered by saying that to include a single on an album would be forcing his fans to pay for the same song twice.

The song on *Do It Yourself* that most cried out for an outing in the charts was the opener, 'Inbetweenies'. The bones of the song's musical structure had been composed by Chaz while working with his friend Philip Bagenal in Bagenal's basement in Bermondsey, South London. Chaz regarded most of the music he had written there as unsuitable for Ian because of its Latin flavour, but felt differently about this particular piece, and accordingly brought it to Rolvendon.

Ian liked the music immediately, although he found it difficult to write the accompanying lyric, instinctively preferring to write to his own rhythm, as opposed to a pre-ordained piece of music. As Chaz records, '"Inbetweenies" was quite tough for Ian to write because it was setting him in a landscape. He was not in the driving seat here. He was also coming in on the second beat of the bar. It was as if he was commenting on the music, which is something he did not like to do. But he threw himself in at the deep end and wrote a fine lyric.'

The song helped to develop The Blockheads' unique sound, with each band member contributing musical ideas to the pot. Mickey's keyboards became a strong feature of the band's sound, with his new pride and joy, a Hammond organ, allowing him to create a multi-layered effect, 'as opposed to the thin Farfisa sound that I used on the Stiff tour. The Hammond brings a cultured sound to the band, a layer that you can then add other sophisticated instruments like the Fender Rhodes electric piano to. I was also getting into synths at this time.'

Reflecting the more polished production that Ian wanted to move towards, 'Inbetweenies' was unrecognisable from the songs on *New Boots And Panties*, with its jazz-inflected piano solos and gentle pace allied to a soothing vocal delivery. According to Mickey, Ian's close ally Kozmo was horrified when he first heard the song, particularly the two chords that heralded the album's introduction: 'When Kozmo heard the demo, he turned to Ian and said, "Ian, is your next album really going to start 'der dum'?", which said it all. In retrospect, I don't know whether it was the right album to do after *New Boots And Panties*. I don't mean the songs, because they were great, but in the more sophisticated way they were approached in the recording studio.'

The title to 'Inbetweenies' and its suggestive lyrics are believed to relate to the issue of bisexuality: 'A body likes to be near the bone/Oh Nancy, Leslie, Jack and Joan/I die when I'm alone'. It was certainly a subject that Ian was fascinated by, as his colleagues testify. According to Chaz, 'Generally speaking, I think Ian was happier in men's company. I did once think he might be bisexual because he liked younger male company, but I later dismissed the idea. He would relate to the gang element, with himself as the gang boss. It empowered him. I've chatted about it recently with my wife Elaine, but he certainly wasn't gay. I just think he was very, very happy in male company.

'More so than with men, the women in Ian's life would very much have to appreciate him for the way he was. A lot of the time the women in his life would be very quiet and introverted. Many of those girls who were attracted to Ian looked like broken birds. It was as if they had a broken wing and they came to Ian and in time that wing would mend. I saw that a lot of girls who were attracted to Ian were emotionally very insecure and Ian would make them feel fantastic about themselves. And once he had gained their confidence the rollercoaster would start.'

When asked about the subject of potential bisexuality Mickey simply expressed his view that Ian was 'certainly aware of his feminine side and was androgynous in his own way'.

'Inbetweenies' saw the rest of the band, and in particular Johnny, making a contribution on backing vocals for the first time. As their career progressed the band were credited on record with the affectionate nickname 'The Breezeblocks' when providing backing contributions. From the third verse onwards the band sang the song's title in between Ian's lines. Ian, by contrast, never utters the word 'Inbetweenies' at any stage of the song. In the last verse, The Breezeblocks exchanged 'Inbetweenies, Inbetweenies' for 'Barney Beenies, ultra marinees' as a tribute to Stiff's inspirational in-house artist Barney Bubbles.

The then 36-year-old Bubbles, real-name Colin Fulcher, had helped Jake Riviera decide on the Stiff 'look' back in 1976 and was renowned for his innovative design work. Bubbles, who at one stage had his own office in Stiff's basement below the company's leaky toilet, was the brains behind the extraordinary range of promotional gimmicks that accompanied the release of *Do It Yourself.*

The album was released in 12 different sleeves around the country, each a different style of home wallpaper made by Crown. The design company, which agreed to sponsor the *Do It Yourself* tour, even covered the band's stages with wallpaper.

The dozen separate LP covers were a marketing man's dream, with The Blockheads' large contingent of committed fans competing to snap up as many as they could. As Johnny recalls, 'As well as there being 12 in Britain there were other ones released in Holland and France... When we got over there we'd have all these people at gigs coming up with wallpaper covers that we'd never seen and asking us to sign them. In Britain people would actually travel to different towns to try and complete their collection.'

Other examples of Barney's work were badges donned with individual band members' names. Again Blockheads' fans would try and collect each one. 'You'd hear people saying "Davey's badges are a bit scarce, someone must be hoarding them",' joked Johnny. 'Barney was coming up with so many ideas, it was fantastic. He made small things you'd find in a Christmas cracker, which were given away, small earrings in the shape of a pot of paint with a paintbrush sticking out of it, and the word "Blockhead" on it in garish colours. I liked that arty sort of stuff and it fitted the title *Do It Yourself*.'

Bubbles was also the brains behind the famous Blockheads 'clock face' logo, a design the band still uses today. Tragically, the designer, having endured a three-year battle with depression, took his life on 14 November 1983.

Ian, a former art student of some repute, who counted famous artists such as Peter Blake among his friends, paid the following tribute to Bubbles: 'Barney was easily the most incredible designer I'd ever come across. His vision was fantastic. It really did impress me... He was righteous. He didn't have the faults, or the ego and he made me feel second class. I wanted his approval in a strange kind of way. I wanted the acceptance.'[14]

The basis for the album's next song, 'Quiet', was cooked up by Johnny, Charley, Norman and Mickey during a songwriting session for Loving Awareness. The foursome wrote the music in the mid-1970s at Mickey's home in Shepherd's Bush, where he had a small studio. Originally it was destined to be an instrumental, but was put on the back burner, having been excluded from the band's eponymous album.

The lyrics were influenced by one of Ian's school teachers, as he admitted to *Smash Hits* in 1979: 'It's about a guy who used to teach me. He used to say, "I'll come over there and bang a few heads." It's about the teaching profession for sure, about the dangers of it in a way. If you point it out too much it becomes ridiculous, you become what I'm complaining about. It's really just a small amount of ridicule. I heard that 60 per cent of all teachers in England are maladjusted. It's gonna end up with the teachers becoming the students and the students becoming the teachers. The teachers are going to realise how much help they need from the students. Children of eight years old now know more than people of 48 years old.'[15]

Ian, who had taught at art school, delivered the lyric in the style of an old-fashioned schoolteacher dressed in cape and gown: 'Quiet! Or else there will be measures/Quiet! Stop this unholy row/Quiet! Shut up, you little treasures/Quiet! When you've been told, and how.'

According to Mickey, Ian was a fan of the St Trinian's films, and in particular the headmaster played with such aplomb by actor Alistair Sim: 'He'd quote phrases from the St Trinian's films by Sim, who used to say things to the kids like "Come along...some of you." This lyric is in Sim's style. "Quiet! Shut up, you little treasures".'

The backing vocals on the track were a string of childish phrases, such as 'Plop plops', 'Big jobs', and 'Wee wees', delivered by The Breezeblocks in the manner of a naughty six year old. As Mickey joked, 'It wasn't a sexy lyric to sing, but humorous. Little boys loved it. My two boys did, and they were six or seven then. That was the kind of audience it appealed to.'

Underneath the jovial lyrics of 'Quiet' lay another song heavily influenced by Ian and Chaz's shared love of jazz. Chaz and Mickey's piano and keyboards dominated, while Norman's bass bubbled away with a trademark counter-melody. Revelling in the freedom given by Ian to experiment, Davey played a backward reverb on the sax solo, a trick that reminded Johnny of one of his heroes, Frank Zappa: 'It made the sound sort of shimmer before Davey played a note, which I'd heard of, but had never been in a room when it was done. I thought that was pretty cool and I was into kind of "Zappa-ish" sounds where you'd put a sax through a pedal and make it play a harmony or speed it up to make it sound squeaky. I remember holding the tape machine and chalking a mark on the tape, and then turning it over and counting Davey in. He just played and then we turned the tape over again and it was playing backwards. I think Laurie Latham instigated that.'

'Don't Ask Me' follows, a jaunty number with a lyric that Chaz believes to have been based upon him: 'If Ian asked me a question I'd sometimes say "Don't ask me", not because I was being evasive but because I knew there was a certain amount of responsibility involved. If Ian asked me a question about something important and I wasn't sure of the answer I'd say "Don't ask me."

'Maybe I picked this up from my Jewish heritage. It was done in that sort of Jewish way with upturned palms. The last lyric Ian ever gave me was called "It's All Going In The Book", which I never actually managed to write any music to. That lyric was a little dig at my Jewish character but in a friendly, warm way. He would use a character as a basis for a song and then develop it further, which is what happened with "Plaistow Patricia" and "Billericay Dickie". He would take an aspect of somebody as a source of inspiration and then carry along in his own whimsy.'

Asked about specific lyrical references to himself, Chaz picked out one in particular: 'Ian thought I was a bit dozy at times and used to say "Don't be a doughnut", which I was sure was the basis for the first line, "'ere I stand with a doughnut for a brain". Sometimes if I'd written a melody for him to sing, he'd get me to sing it first so he could pitch the notes. He wanted me to sing this when we demoed it, but there was no way I was going to start singing "'ere I stand with a doughnut for a brain", so he had to sing it himself.

'"I should worry if the weather spoils the trade" is like he's saying that I'd become hardened to whether I hurt people or not. This was a reference to the fact that I didn't mind ruffling feathers in the studio and making a scene to get my own way. "I'm a crumb and I'm in your lemonade" was Ian's way of saying I was the fly in his ointment. I might only be a "crumb", but I'd got in the way of his flavour.'

The track also contained further examples of The Blockheads' musical experimentation. Although the seven band members had now been working together for almost 18 months, they were still relative strangers in terms of creating music together, having spent most of that time on the road. The dual role of Chaz meant that The Blockheads had, in effect, two guitarists and two keyboard players, a luxury that allowed them to change their sound or approach to a song easily.

For 'Don't Ask Me' a TR808 Roland rhythm box was played in to Charley's headphones, but mixed down so low it could barely be heard on the recording. Johnny says the band got much mileage out of this machine: 'It was like early playing on to a loop, but more rhythmical, which worked well on "Don't Ask Me". The TR808 had lots of brightly coloured buttons you could press, like samba, bosanova, tango, all these old-fashioned rhythms. I think this is what Sly And The Family Stone used on their early records. It also had a really good bass drum sound in it, so we would use it to get the final tempo, and play it as a click track for Charley.'

Mickey's ARP was used to harmonise a synth sound alongside Davey's sax, creating the impression of a two-pronged horn section, while Chaz and

Johnny joined together mid-song to play harmony guitars. 'We did a lot of playing with dual guitars at this time,' said Johnny. 'It was the idiom of the time, but not a lot of it made it on to the records. In the room when we were recording this track it seemed to have a lot more bollocks than on the vinyl and that's all down to the mix, which we didn't have much say on. We put in long hours and chipped in with our sixpenn'orth but I don't think a lot of it was listened to.'

Mickey was also disappointed at the recorded version of 'Don't Ask Me', claiming 'it sounds as if it was recorded in the bathroom. It's very echoey. This was Chaz's early beginnings as a producer and in retrospect some mistakes were made.'

Upon his return to The Blockheads after the making of 'What A Waste', Chaz had demanded a more hands-on role in the studio, taking on the Ian-inspired title of MD (musical director) and working alongside, rather than under, the co-producer of *New Boots And Panties*, Laurie Latham. In the sleeve notes to *Do It Yourself* Latham's role was downgraded to that of 'recording engineer', highlighting Ian's disdain for what he saw as the inflated status of producers. At the same time Ian's co-manager Peter Jenner stepped aside from his studio role, a position he was more than happy to forsake.

'I liked being a producer, but I'd also started a family and it was becoming harder to produce and so I had to stop. I had secretly told myself that once I'd had a hit I would give up and after the success of "Rhythm Stick" and *New Boots And Panties* I was willing to leave the studio behind.' A quarter of a century on, Jenner believes his decision to step aside was a grave error.

'Chaz wanted to be the producer and I was happy to back down, but I think it was a terrible mistake in hindsight because Chaz is a great musician but this made *Do It Yourself* more musical. I'm not a musician but I can relate to how important Ian's voice was and it didn't worry me if it was out of tune, whereas all these musicians would get terribly upset. They mixed down the vocals so you could hear their great music because that's all they were interested in. They recorded the vocals really quickly and would rather spend a day on guitar overdubs, and I think it was a classic case of musicians not realising what a pop record's about. That sounds incredibly patronising, but you have to realise that pop records are not just about music, they're about communication. In Ian's case his communication was the vocal and lyrics.'

Latham found himself constantly frustrated by Ian's policy of production by committee, wanting the opportunity to produce the album alone and give it a clear direction. Without the regimented control applied by Jenner on the wonderfully economical *New Boots And Panties* Latham found himself competing with Ian, Chaz, various band members and Ian's two live sound engineers in an effort to steer the ship.

He said, 'We recorded the first album in under a month and it's got a great groove, but the second album was an absolute nightmare. Peter Jenner wasn't there and I think instead of letting me have more say Ian went with safety in numbers, which I felt was completely the wrong way of going about it. I'd done the first album and they should have let me get on with it. You don't need that many chiefs. Every overdub became a big debate.

'I used to think, "Who are all these people chipping in?" There was lots of whispering in corners going on and in different rooms. Even with a cocaine ban imposed by Ian there was still this air of paranoia.'

In addition, Latham believed that Ian was badly prepared and was rewriting songs with The Blockheads throughout their time in the Workhouse. 'This kind of thing is OK if you own the studio and you're using it as a writing tool but if the meter's ticking away and you're paying for time it's not the best way of making an album.'

'Sink My Boats' was the first song that Ian and Chaz had ever written together, but the pair had deemed that it was not hard-edged enough to make the cut for *New Boots And Panties*. Indeed, Norman remembers it as one of the 20 or so tracks that he and Charley had demoed at Alvic, along with the never-to-be-released 'Something's Gonna Happen In The Winter'.

According to Chaz, the lyric was inspired by an unintentionally humorous domestic argument between Ian and first wife Betty in the couple's bathroom: 'He told me that he was sitting in the bath and Betty came in and dropped soap on his floating boats! That is absolutely true. The weird thing about Ian's lyrics is that sometimes they have to be taken literally. But it's so bizarre.'

This extraordinary tale is backed up by Johnny: 'I remember hearing about his first wife coming in and sinking his rubber duck in the bath and Ian getting pissed off. But I seem to remember him telling me about a Woody Allen film, which involved something similar. Ian drew his inspiration from many quarters. He was into odd books, films, and wild and wacky poets, and listened to a lot of jazz. Later in his life he finished off a WH Davies poem, called "Leisure", which was used on the Centreparcs advert. Ian wrote another verse and we recorded it on the album of a jazz harmonica player. Ian read it and I sang the chorus.'

Both Johnny and Chaz believe that the bathroom incident was merely the inspiration for the song, and that the lyrics did not apply solely to his relationship with Betty. Johnny said, 'He was singing about various girlfriends that had come and gone. Some of them were still lingering as friends, the romance was over but they were still in his life. They were all characters, a bit Dickensian sometimes. He did remind me of a kind of a nice Bill Sykes, when he was a bit mad. I got such a Victorian, Dickensian vibe from him sometimes, this jack the lad who was middle-class educated but pretending that he wasn't. It was way over my head the way he was using words. I'd never even heard of the word "blandishment" that he used in "Sink My Boats". It's not a word you tend to hear in rock 'n' roll songs.'

Chaz believes the lyric may have taken Ian years to write, because he had so many songs under construction at any time, all being added to his enormous pile of neatly written A3 sheets: 'To write a good lyric could take Ian years. Sometimes he would put things on hold because he couldn't find a context for a lyric. He got a lot of inspiration from having friends round. They would sit in his music room having a few drinks and "jazz woodbines", and listening to records. If somebody came up with a phrase that he liked – for instance, "Jack Shit George" – he'd write it down and use it some time later.'

'Sink My Boats' was certainly a world away from Ian's harsh words for the opposite sex in earlier tracks, such as 'If I Was With A Woman' and 'I Made Mary Cry': 'I've got the feeling but I ain't got the skill/And I don't like your suggestion/Will you still love me when I'm over the hill?/Is another stupid question'.

Ian was determined to break new ground, and pushed himself into singing melodies rather than delivering the growling, semi-spoken vocals that had become his forte. Not a natural note-singer, Ian felt pressurised to hit a higher range of notes, having been voted Male Vocalist of the Year 1978 by one of the inkies. Mickey explains, 'Ian wanted to push himself and made a good fist of it but was always shaky when trying to hit those high notes. These were the days when there were no machines to retune your vocals, so it was all down to performance. It was not always pleasant to listen to and certainly not pleasant to watch his facial expressions as he tried.'

Notable on 'Sink My Boats' were the discordant backing harmonies, with The Breezeblocks' vocals put through a harmoniser by Latham, giving off a quirky falsetto effect in the style of The Beach Boys. 'Harmonisers were a relatively new invention,' explained Johnny. 'We could put the signal through it and dial the harmony, and we thought on this song the stranger we could make it sound the better. I can't remember what the interval was, but we dialled a fourth and a fifth together and it sounded terrific. We could never re-create it live.'

The innovative Davey played his outstanding solo through a sax synthesiser, basically a microphone on the end of his instrument connected to an electronic signal box, giving the song a freeform feel. 'It was a sound man's nightmare,' said Mickey. 'Davey sometimes used to over-use it onstage because it's the sort of sound you only want to hear once or twice. Any more and it becomes too much. But it works on that song and it was always fun for us to play.' Mickey himself used his ARP at the end of the track, simulating the sound of an aeroplane plummeting to earth.

'Waiting For Your Taxi' was one song that neither Chaz nor Ian could possibly have countenanced on *New Boots And Panties*. Described by Johnny as 'the ultimate filler track', 'Taxi' had a lyric containing just two lines: 'Waiting for your taxi/Which taxi never comes'.

The lyrics were delivered by Ian in a mock Jamaican dialect, as he had done so memorably on 'You're More Than Fair'. 'Ian loved dialects and different parlance,' said Chaz. 'He liked imitating Jamaican street slang, hence the phrase "Hit me with your rhythm stick", which is very much a black slang phrase. A lot of the phrases he adopted were basically black, jazz slang.'

The music was experimental in the extreme, based, in Mickey's words, on a 'very simple, inane idea' – someone trying to hail a cab. The idea was dreamed up by Ian and Chaz at 11:30pm on New Year's Eve 1978 while holidaying in the Bahamas. Rather than rely on a library tape to get the sound of a taxi, Chaz and Ian went to the flat of sound monitor Chris Warwick in the bustling central London area of Bayswater. Using a Nagra tape recorder hung out of Warwick's window they recorded the distinctive sound of various taxis' diesel engines, in addition to the voices of cab drivers and customers.

In the studio the band played along to a click track, created on Mickey's ARP Odyssey, an early synthesiser that was smaller than a Moog. It was an instrument that the keyboard player often wore onstage with a guitar strap.

Describing the technique he used on 'Taxi', Mickey said, 'There is a sequence going through which is from the ARP, a random "sample and hold" all the way through. It was playing with a sequence before the days of sampling. We got an electronic pulse going and looped it, which gave us a rhythm track.'

Although it was possible for Mickey to generate the rhythm track live on his ARP, 'Waiting For Your Taxi' did not stay in the band's set for long. Chaz recalls members of the audience almost vomiting because the track's synth bass seemed to permeate their entire body: 'We tried doing it live a couple of times and it went horribly wrong. We were using a very heavy bass Moog synthesiser on it and I remember it was uncomfortable the amount of bass we used to use on that track live.

'Members of the audience came up to us afterwards looking really worried and said: "Fantastic gig, but what was that awful bass on 'Taxi?' It suddenly went so loud." We were using a synth that actually went down an octave lower than the bass guitar. It was fairly heavy and if you listen to *Do It Yourself* loud you can hear that the bass synth on "Taxi" was mixed too high.'

Mickey, however, says that when the band played it at the Hammersmith Odeon during their seven-day stint there, the song worked superbly: 'It was very spectacular and visual. All the "stops" were great and we had the lights going crazy.'

The 'stops' were a series of gaps of various lengths where the music stopped completely, helping to create a mood of endlessly waiting for a cab. 'Ian wanted all the gaps to be different, so we had to write them all down for when we played live,' remembered Johnny. 'The first gap might have been six beats, then it was eight, then twelve, then ten. It was all over the place and we couldn't wait for the middle bit of the solo because we wanted to funk it up like Sly. There were little "and" beats everywhere because I had this Teewah auto-wah and it clipped the sound and made it all staccato and funky. When it got to the solo there was a change of key and we just rode away with Davey's sax.'

The song hung on a simple blues-type riff. 'Davey's horns gradually built up through the song, which was influenced by my love of Sly And The Family Stone,' said Chaz. 'It was a funky little riff really that was crying out for a basic lyric, which Ian put on.'

Laurie Latham remembers an incident while recording 'Taxi', which reflected the disarray in which the album was laid down: 'We were using these Poly Moog synthesisers on "Taxi", and I remember coming in to find that three of them had been hired by different people because there had been no coordination. So much money was wasted on that sort of thing. Apart from anything else, this album desperately needed a producer solely to oversee the budget.'

As Ian and Chaz began to clash repeatedly in the studio the latter took the brave step of banning his partner from there, a decision for which Mickey claims Ian never forgave him. But Chaz, a sensitive man who dislikes conflict, found it impossible to put up with Ian's egotistical outbursts and obstructive behaviour.

'In the studio he knew what he should be doing, but he'd often do completely the opposite, which was quite frustrating. One day I said to him, "Ian, I think it would be a good idea if you stayed away for a little while." I don't know how I summoned the courage to do it when I think about it now. There followed the longest silence I can ever remember before Ian replied, "I don't fucking believe it. I've just been asked to stay away from my own fucking album."

'He did indeed stay away, before creeping back in later in the recording. It wasn't that I minded his being there but he had been such a distraction. That is why the record does sound different in a lot of respects.'

According to Mickey, Ian 'could be really nasty' at this time and despite handing over the reins of the record to Chaz, had only done so 'on the surface'. When Ian tried to reassert control over proceedings, conflict between the two was inevitable. 'Chaz is a marshmallow, really sensitive and you have to be careful with your humour,' explained Mickey. 'Sometimes it builds up and after about six months Chaz will say "Here, that wasn't a very nice thing to say."'

Latham was another who found Ian's outbursts increasingly difficult to handle and admitted becoming a nervous wreck during the recordings. He recalls full-blown shouting matches and various people storming out of the studio, claiming that most present were forced to resort to taking 'serious ganja' to calm their nerves.

He remembers in detail the fallout from Chaz's brave decision to banish Ian from the studio: 'Before he left Ian went round to everyone individually and told them they shouldn't be working in the music business and allocated them various jobs which he said they should be doing. He went up to Norman and said, "You should be working for London Underground" and similar things to everybody else. Then I could hear him shuffling up behind me at the mixing desk. He crushed up a whole packet of McVitie's Digestive biscuits and threw them all over me and the desk. It took days to clean up, between the EQs and down the faders. It was all in my hair as well. I was so freaked out and was very relieved when he walked out of the door.'

Towards the end of Ian's life, when the pair were working at RAK Studios on Ian's final batch of recordings, Latham recalled the story to the singer, by now a far more mellow and level-headed studio animal: 'Ian laughed his head off when I told him.'

Latham claims that he had originally found Ian 'a pleasure to work with' on *New Boots And Panties*, but that his personality had changed by the time *Do It Yourself* was being laid down. He said, 'Ian was tricky working with and cantankerous, there's no point pretending otherwise. Some of my worst moments in the studio ever were with Ian. When I'm making records nowadays and someone is stressed by an argument I think "God, mate. You should have been here with Ian if you want to know what bad vibes in the studio are like."'

Side two began with the hilarious 'This Is What We Find', like 'Inbetweenies' a definite contender for release as a single, if Ian would have allowed it. One of Ian's funniest lyrics, the song is peppered with witty observations on the mundane nature of people's lives in Britain, and tapping into Ian's extensive knowledge of crude slang. The first verse sees 'Forty-year-old housewife Mrs Elizabeth Walk of Lambeth Walk' who had 'a husband who was jubblified with only half a stalk'.

In the first of an unusual series of euphemisms, Ian reflects on Mrs Walker taking 'an overdose of Omo', Ian's nickname for cocaine. Even more outrageously Ian was able to mention the taboo of female masturbation: 'Could have been watching Frankie Vaughan on the telly and giving herself a scratch.'

In his next verse Ian brings us 'single bachelor with little dog, Tony Green of Turnham Green', and entertains the listener with an extraordinary outburst of toilet humour of which the writers of satirical comic *Viz* would be proud: 'Cos the mongrel laid a cable in the sandpit of the playground of the park where they had been/And with a bit of tissue he wiped its bum-hole clean/A bit of claggy on the waggy'. Tom's mutt is later revealed to have laid his cable 'on the Golden Hind', the ship sailed in by Sir Francis Drake. At the time a replica of the ship was on display alongside Ian's beloved Southend Pier.

Mid-song the narrator switches language briefly, delivering a line in Latin, 'O vanitatus vanitatum/Which of us happy in this life?/Which of us has our desire, or having it, is gratified?' According to Johnny, 'I don't think Ian spoke Latin but the way he delivered the line made it sound like he could. There's a spooky bit on the end of one of our new songs that I sing called "Feel the Funk", and it's coming out of a weird solo and the band told me to say something, so I said, "O vanitatus vanitatum" as a little tribute to Ian.'

Ian's next character is the cuckolded 'home improvement expert Harold Hill of Harold Hill, of do-it-yourself dexterity and double-glazing skill'. Poor Harold comes home one day 'to find another gentleman's kippers in the grill/ So sanded off his winkle with his Black and Decker drill'. Rarely, if ever, has the sexual act been described in such an imaginative way on a pop record. 'If he had an epitaph it should be that, shouldn't it?' exclaimed Chaz. 'It's Ian at his most brilliant and his most grotesque.' Epitaph or no epitaph, the song helped propel Ian into the *Oxford Book of Quotations* with the line 'The hope that springs eternal/Springs right up your behind'.

'This Is What We Find' signalled the beginning of a long and fruitful writing partnership between Ian and Mickey. Having spent so much time with Ian over the previous 18 months the keyboard player had begun to understand what Ian wanted musically. Mickey found the composition, another music hall pastiche, almost embarrassingly easy to write: 'When I gave Ian the music he was impressed that I could write the tune to order and that he did not have to change anything.

'The lyric and the music fitted like a hand in a glove. I found it very easy to write. I just thought of the "Carry On" films and gave Ian a simple melody to sing because when he gave me the lyric he had been speaking it, as opposed to singing. To be honest, we were all screaming out for a big funky track to be able to write with him, but those always seemed to go to Chaz, and the rest of us would get the oompah songs.'

Despite its outrageous content most of the lyrics would probably have passed the BBC censor if the song had been released as a single, the depths of Ian's lyrical depravity being intelligently shrouded. But if Mickey had harboured any hopes of making some money from radio play, they were shattered by a needlessly crude line, reminiscent of Ian's opening line to Plaistow Patricia: 'Hello, Mrs Wood, this boy looks familiar, they used to call him Robin Hood/Now he's robbin' fuckin' Shit Cunt'.

Mickey moaned, 'This was the kind of song that Benny Hill could have covered, except for that bloody line. It was very disappointing when you were writing songs with Ian because he had this reputation for being blue with his lyrics. And you always knew that if he put swear words in it wasn't going to be played on the radio. If you deliberately put something like that in a song it's like burning £1,000.'

After Davey plays out with a sax riff uncannily similar to Benny Hill's theme tune, the song segues into 'Uneasy Sunny Day Hotsy Totsy'. The unusual title was another example of Ian's use of West Indian parlance and its lyric was a revolutionary call to arms to those dissatisfied with life in late 1970s Britain: 'Open up the nicks/Close down the schools/The law is a prick/Not fit to write the rules, it's time that the babies kept quiet'

In Chaz's opinion, 'Uneasy Sunny Day' is an 'exposition of Ian's political stance. He cared deeply about humanity and was always looking out for the disenfranchised. The song suggests a warning that there is a potential revolution in the air, although the line "Melt the guns/Dismantle the bombs" is showing that he favoured peaceful revolution, as opposed to violence.'

Again, Ian had made the deliberate decision to use swearing as a way of shocking the listener. The first verse, 'Bankrupt the banks/Withhold the rent/Shitters are a wank/And the landlord's bent', ensured that PRS statements would be non-existent for the co-writer, in this case Johnny. 'I knew I wasn't gonna get double-glazing out of that song,' he chuckled.

Mickey says that despite their joy at being included in the songwriting process The Blockheads quickly became 'very sensitive' about Ian swearing to their compositions: 'Ian was blasé about it and would say, "If the script requires it then the script requires it." I used to think "Why doesn't he swear on Chaz's songs?" There was always an element of that.'

Chaz's retort is simple: 'Why didn't Ian swear on my songs? Because I told him to take it out! I didn't want it in my songs, hence there were a lot of metaphors going on in many lyrics. I think he felt he was a bit more under manners with me and respected my input. He'd had hits with me and we had a proven formula, and he knew that. He was a socialist but he liked to live well. He knew he needed to make a few bob.'

Despite the obvious frustration at Ian's seemingly deliberate decision to sabotage any hope of their making money from songwriting, the various band members preferred not to challenge their master. As Johnny explained,

'It never created any resentment towards Chaz because we were too busy getting on with it. If I think about it now, I might agree that it was totally unfair the way the words were dished out and I was given the fillers, but I never complained. If Ian was putting a lyric to one of my tunes I was quite happy that they had seen the light of day in a finished formula and people were playing them.'

The structure of the lyric to 'Uneasy' did not make things easy for Johnny: 'I couldn't see a way to marry the verses and the choruses and at the time I had written something more "rocky" but Ian didn't want it like that. He wanted it a bit more disconnected with no musical passages to break it up. Ian seemed to like that abrupt change between the verse and the "Uneasy" bit. They're so different, in different keys and with different beats, but it worked because we segued it from the song before. The words are so bizarre anyway that it didn't matter that it was so disjointed.'

'Mischief', a title that could describe Ian's whole outlook on life, is a song about youthful bad behaviour, allied to a rocking beat, dominated by distorted guitar licks and jazz piano chords. For the second time on the album the listener is introduced to a host of exquisite suburban characters, on this occasion all male. In the first verse we meet Ricky, who 'loves a kicking' and 'wants to join the Guards' and then Barry, who 'breaks the windows of his broken home'. In a withering put-down Barry's reasoning for his crime is dismissed by Ian: 'Have a guess? His tiny mind's been scarred'.

Lest anyone forget, Ian had spent much of his childhood hidden away in unforgiving institutions, and was more than justified in poking fun in this way. Indeed, the traumas of Ian's childhood clearly influenced much of the song, in particular the couplet 'Jack and Stan are tossing pals like monkeys in the zoo/When they got caught by Gonad Gibbs they had to wank him too'.

Speaking to the *NME* in 1978 Ian recalled the horrors of sexual abuse among fellow inmates at Chailey Heritage School: 'I've been incarcerated for quite a long time myself, that's why I am like I am, a hard case. I 'ad my liberty taken away for five years from the age of seven to the age of twelve. I know what it feels like. I was doin' things like wanking geezers off at the age of eight 'cos they made me. Geezers who only 'ad one leg or an arm missing or fuckin' nuts and bolts missing – and I never thought it was at all freaky. I was just doin' what was 'appening. Know what I mean? My mind didn't get scrambled.'[16]

Among the other social outcasts in the song are Lionel and Roger. Lionel 'touches women when they're walking through the park' and 'goes in people's gardens nicking laundry in the dark' while Roger, whose 'dad's a shipping clerk' leaves a 'sleeper across the District Line'. Returning to the topic of highly charged teenage boys, depicted so well in 'Razzle In My Pocket', Ian visualises a group of lusting lads boasting about their sexual conquests: 'She's got crinkly hair underneath her underwear'. Ian's childish delivery only adds to the hilarity of the scene.

The schoolboy pranks celebrated by the narrator range from the naughty, like taking a pigeon into the cinema, to the downright criminal: 'Let's go and kill some kiosks, start a few more fires, could this be mischief?'

'Mischief' also includes a mistake made by Ian, accommodated in the song by Chaz and Laurie Latham, because of its charm. During one take in the studio Ian sang the line 'He failed his interview' too early and, immediately realising his error, reacted by saying 'Oh yeah.' Ian's unplanned ad lib was left on the recording, with The Breezeblocks' backing vocals 'Failed his interview' filling the hole where Ian should have delivered his line. The effect was to make the lyric sound like a conversational interchange and worked brilliantly.

The basic riff for 'Mischief' had been written years earlier by Johnny in his Loving Awareness days and developed by Mickey and Charley. Having witnessed Ian's habit of rejecting music that had already been constructed without the sweat demanded by his Protestant work ethic, the band kept schtum about its origins. 'It was fair enough,' explained Mickey. 'If we'd owned up it wouldn't have mattered to Ian that we had a song that fitted perfectly. He would have said, "Oh no, it has to be tailor-made." Rather than go through all that rigmarole and try and prove your point it was better left unsaid, so we got this one by him.'

After getting the skeleton of the music past Ian, the band constructed a middle eight and chorus, creating another perfect marriage between lyrics and music. Johnny played his guitar through a high-fly synthesiser, which helped to bend his notes. By this stage The Blockheads were beginning to really enjoy themselves. Mickey believes this was because, for the first time, 'We weren't under instruction on these songs because we had brought them to the table, whereas on things that Chaz and Ian had written we were very much under orders.'

The song draws to a close with Ian repeatedly issuing a frantic apology, 'I'm sorry I done it'. His penance becomes louder and more manic until it segues neatly into the similarly manic 'Dance Of The Screamers'.

'Screamers' is described neatly as 'punk jazz' by co-writer Chaz, an incongruous fusion between a primal vocal delivery and Latin funk music: 'The song creates a frisson because of its imbalance. I played a comfortable, Latin funk piece, but in its context it seems right. If it didn't have Ian screaming it might have sounded bland, but in its context it's an underscore for screaming. It is like a parallel world but the rhythm is holding him and me together.'

The track begins with a funky rhythmic vibe, allied to a light, jazzy piano melody. But just as the hearer settles down for some easy listening Ian butts in, singing 'So I'm screaming this to you/From the last place in the queue', the lines separated by the first of several ear-piercing yelps.

The lyrics strongly suggest the influence of Ian's five-year virtual incarceration, consisting of 18 months in Black Notley Hospital near Braintree, Essex, followed by three and a half years in Chailey Heritage School. Over this period Ian became accustomed to the daily horrors suffered by children with disabilities far worse than his own. Speaking in the 1999 BBC documentary on his life, Ian painted a vivid picture of life at Black Notley, where the severely disabled would scream through the night. Ian admitted that his sympathy, and that of the other children trying to get to sleep, depended almost entirely upon whether they liked the child or not.

He said, 'When you're a kid you're very open to whatever's going on, you're with a peer group, with people who are just the same as you or in different states or even worse, and you don't consider them anything different from what's normal... You're only judging whether they're a nice person or not and there are some real shockers and there are some real smashing ones and sometimes the really smashing ones can't even communicate at all.

'I was in bed next to a geezer, he had a device where he could turn a page of a book and he was in very, very bad pain and everybody liked him and yet he hardly communicated with anybody but everybody liked him, they thought he was a top geezer. At night the pain used to make him cry and scream and you'd sleep through it. You'd get used to it, and because you liked him you didn't resent it. Now there was other people in there who you didn't like who were horrible people who might be crying and screaming and you fucking hated them, you really loathed them for doing that.' [1]

The song's chorus articulates the desire of the severely disabled to break through the ignorance of able-bodied people and to be treated as an equal: 'I really think you'd like me given half the chance/And since we ain't got that I'll do the screamers' dance'.

Throughout the lyrics Ian explains the whole gamut of disabilities, from those who 'were born like this' to others, like himself, whose disability struck 'by the yard', or in other words, due to illness or injury. Ian describes those whose appearance could be unsettling: 'Some of us are ugly, angel/Some of us are only small'. His sympathetic, and at times provocative, lyric also mentions those with mental disabilities, who 'never quite caught the bus'.

'I think that for some disabled people the only way they can express themselves is through screaming and dancing,' explained Chaz. 'The lyric is saying that for some people screaming is the only way of getting their point of view heard. That is what rock 'n' roll is all about. It's a different form of screaming for attention.'

As Ian's career developed, and he began singing more frequently about life as a disabled person, he attracted a hardcore following of people who could identify directly with his lyrics. According to Mickey, 'Ian provided a vehicle for a lot of people's frustrations. He was writing about those who'd never had songs written about them before. Take the line "It's hard to be a hero, handsome/When you've had your helmet cracked". A lot of people who had experienced those things that Ian sang about started coming to our gigs and came backstage for autographs. You'd hear people saying "He's writing about me, he identifies with me."'

Chaz also believes that the difficult studio atmosphere during the recording of *Do It Yourself* added to the tension of the song: 'This was actually recorded under pretty strained conditions. The whole song is about screaming and you can't divorce it from the time it was made and what the conditions were. We'd been touring persistently and we were tired when making this record. We'd get pissed off with each other pretty quickly, so this song was Ian's way of reacting to that tension.'

Listening to Ian's screams does not evoke pleasant memories for his colleagues, who wince at the recollection of being left practically deafened in the studio. Indeed, Johnny has original monitor mixes in which the screams were even louder and says that at one point Ian's cries became so loud that he cracked a microphone, rendering it useless.

'Ian had this ability to produce a scream and a note at the same time, so it was in fact two notes,' said Johnny. 'On a lot of Gregorian chant music the singer opens their mouth and two notes come out. I don't know how they do it, but it's something that happens in the throat box, giving a note and an overtone to it. When Ian was doing this on "Screamers" he made such a horrible racket he broke a real valve microphone. It completely shattered inside. When we were playing in the studio we could hear Ian in our headphones and it was unbearable. You couldn't hear the music you were playing. His screaming is still very loud on the record but I can tell you it's not as painful as it was in the studio.'

After Ian completes his lyric the final minute and a half is dedicated to The Blockheads' impeccable fast-paced funk grooves. 'Davey was screaming on the sax through pedals that make him sound like he's playing a cheese grater,' said Johnny. 'Yet below that there's Norman and me funking away on these riffs that are like sped up a Chic track, or a Nile Rodgers dance track. Chaz flips out at the end with octaves apart on the piano, really going for it, like it was a really serious funk track, but speeded up.' Alongside was Mickey's moody synthesiser chords, giving a reminder of the song's serious subject matter.

The album draws to a close with 'Lullaby for Franc(i)es', an uncharacteristically gentle love song, with a rich, reggae vibe. 'Lullaby' has similar undertones to the opener, 'Inbetweenies', with its dual-gender title that could be sung to a male (Francis), a female (Frances), or indeed an adult or child. The track's origins began with a melody composed by Chaz on his acoustic guitar, to which Ian added the lyric. Although undoubtedly melodic, the song's soft texture made it relatively easy for Ian to sing over. With 1979 heralding the revival of ska music, and bands like Madness, The Specials, and The Beat storming the UK charts, 'Lullaby for Franc(i)es' drew from similar inspiration, with Johnny skanking on guitar and Chaz and Mickey playing restrained, basic chords. Mickey believes the recording to have the best overall sound of the ten songs on *Do It Yourself*: 'It may have taken him to the end of the album in order to get it right, but Chaz got it right on this one.'

The song's title is certainly apt, evoking images of the narrator gently singing someone to sleep with the soothing chorus, 'Go to sleep now Franc(i)es/You've done all you can for the day/Safe and sound, that's a promise/You'll be welcome in the Milky Way/Tumbledown, tired and true/Spirit to restore/A balance is due/Go to sleep now Franc(i)es/Close your eyes'.

One of Ian's warmest lyrics, he dedicated the song to Charley Charles at the series of benefit concerts for the drummer at the Town & Country Club in September 1990. Although Ian decided not to swap the name 'Charley' for 'Franc(i)es', the turning of the spotlight on to a 30-foot-high photograph of Charley at the back of the stage meant there was barely a dry eye in the house. At the song's conclusion Johnny added an off-the-cuff musical ad lib that engineered a subtle mood change in the room.

'The room was very emotional and at the end when it just goes out on an "E" I started playing a famous old reggae riff and it fitted perfectly. We sailed out on that which meant the mood wasn't too sad in the end, and the audience floated out in another dimension. Whenever I play that song now I always end with a reggae riff that reminds you of something from your past.'

'Lullaby' remained a popular feature of gigs with Ian for many years, being the perfect final encore. The Blockheads have recently considered re-calling it to the band's set, but have decided that with a wealth of new material there simply isn't enough room at present for it to be accommodated.

In the early 1980s the band regularly plugged a 'sleep machine' owned by Chaz into the PA in an attempt to calm any over-refreshed members of the audience. Chaz explained, 'I'd bought a sleep machine, which was a small device to be put under your pillow that simulated the sea and rain, all calming effects. We used to put it in the PA system so that our audience would go home chilled out and we wouldn't have to deal with any riots. But it probably wasn't switched on in Madrid.'

The fateful night in Madrid to which Chaz refers took place during the *Do It Yourself* tour, when the inclusion of 'Lullaby' in the set provided a stir for all the wrong reasons. On the previous number Davey had been playing tenor sax and wanted to exchange it for his alto for the introduction of 'Lullaby'. According to Norman, Chaz had a habit of counting the song in before Davey had managed to complete the switch and claims the sax player had warned Chaz three or four times before the show not to repeat the mistake. Caught up in the mood of what had been a thrilling performance Chaz forgot the request and counted the band in almost immediately after the previous song's conclusion. Davey's response was instant – and brutal.

'I had been playing for about 15 seconds and suddenly I felt a hand on my head,' remembered Chaz. 'I turned round and there was Davey Payne about a foot away. He got hold of my head and said, "If you ever do that again I'll kill you." I said, "Do what?" and he replied "Bring a number in before I am ready." Then, bang, from out of nowhere he head-butts me. Then he came for me with his fists, but I managed to block it and walloped him right in the eye. The rest of the band were watching; I could see Charley looking on at right angles but still playing, he didn't drop a stitch. This was all going off and then Ian's minder Spider finally catches on to what is happening and dragged Davey off and sent him to the dressing room.

'Ian came over to the Hammond where I'd resumed playing. I could see he was gutted by what had happened but was still somehow managing to sing with his head bowed. He was a sensitive guy and didn't like what he'd seen.'

Although at the time horrified at the assault by one colleague on another Mickey now laughs when he remembers the audience's reaction to the fight: 'We had carried on playing through the song in stately fashion and managed to get off the stage but afterwards everybody was coming up to us and saying "What a phenomenal stage act. What a concept." Looking back it must have looked very funny, with us playing this majestic, beautiful lullaby with a full-scale fight happening between two of the band onstage.'

With his head throbbing, and dripping with blood, Chaz was sent by Spider into a room containing a contrite Davey and his wife, the rest of the band being forbidden from entering. 'I went over to get some water to wash the blood off my face, not knowing what to expect. Davey was hovering around and said, "I'm sorry, Chaz. I don't know what's happening to me."'

But if Chaz had thought things couldn't get any worse for him, he was in for a rude awakening. Having been given a strong painkiller by Spider, Chaz slipped into a mammoth sleep, only waking at 1pm the following day, an hour after the rest of the band had checked out and started their journey up to Barcelona. 'I phoned down to reception and asked whether The Blockheads were still in the hotel, only to be told that they had checked out at midday. I put the phone down and realised I'd been abandoned. The band had checked out and I'd been head-butted. I was sitting there thinking, "What the fuck is going on in my life?"

'I had just enough money to get a plane back to England, but I felt that something was not right, that they couldn't have left me on purpose so I made my way to Barcelona. The upshot of it was that I had been travelling with a girlfriend who had booked a hotel room the previous afternoon in her name, which I didn't know about. When a roadie was sent to get me, he asked which room Mr Jankel was in and was given this girl's room number. He saw that nobody was sleeping in it, so thought I'd checked out in a huff, and they proceeded to the next gig.

'I caught a plane to Barcelona and when I arrived at the gig Kozmo saw me and looked as if he'd seen a ghost. I got in the dressing room and it was a dark, shadowy room, and there's all the band getting ready to go onstage, and in the corner was Davey, looking sorry for himself. He'd been sent to Coventry and had a swollen eye from where I'd hit him, that proceeded to become more swollen and purple over the next few days.'

It was not to be the last time that the powder keg that was Davey's temper erupted onstage, with painful consequences for a colleague. According to Chaz, Davey's behaviour bordered on the schizophrenic, but Ian, who regarded the sax man as his foil onstage, was anxious that he did *not* receive any treatment: 'I remember after one incident talking to Ian about Davey getting help and he said, "We've talked about him having some sort of treatment but I don't think it would be a good idea because it might take the edge off his playing."'

On the other hand, Chaz also believes Ian felt responsible for Davey, having known him since 1972: 'Ian felt he owed Davey a favour, so he never wanted to just chuck him out, especially as he'd been there right from the beginning in Kilburn And The High Roads.' In addition, Davey's off-the-wall, unschooled playing style, combined with his stage manner, and weird and wonderful costumes made him a hugely popular member of the band. Chaz admits, 'On stage he was very exciting to look at. He put a lot of thought into what he wore, much more so than the other Blockheads. He was extremely visual and had that edge of madness where anything could happen at any time, which Ian shared. The rest of us were more middle class musos, which I think is why Ian wanted him in the band.'

Mickey shares this view, remembering fondly Davey's penchant for travelling with an old suitcase, which contained all manner of props and costumes, mirrors and toys: 'Davey was a fantastic showman. One night at Hammersmith the curtain went back and Davey appeared wearing a huge Indian head-dress and birthday candles stuck to his leather jacket with mirrors reflecting them. When the curtain went back he looked as if he was ablaze. Davey really knew how to make an entrance.'

Ian had a similar style, wearing a bizarre assortment of items bought from joke shops and walking onstage with a carrier bag full of tricks to entertain the crowd. During the set Ian would pull various items out of his bag, as well as throwing scarves in the air and pretending to eat handkerchiefs.

Johnny recalls one night at the Oxford Apollo when one of Ian's tricks unwittingly went perfectly: 'Ian had a wind-up parrot and during one of Davey's solos he threw it into the crowd and it flew gracefully round the whole auditorium, right up to the gods. As he was walking back to his stand he put his arm up and plucked it out of the air. The solo ended just at that moment and he went on to the next bit of the song. It was magical. I could hardly play when he did those things, for watching.

'Later he got these walking sticks that were magician's walking sticks with invisible thread. He'd walk onstage with one, then in the middle of the solo he'd throw it away and it would come back to him. I caught him practising in the dressing room once. He had a Tommy Cooper bucket containing all sorts of things that he gave away to the audience. Sometimes we'd arrive in a town for a gig and Fred or Kozmo would be despatched to a joke shop to find interesting things. Most of his tricks were a bit Tommy Cooper in that they often went wrong, except for the parrot, which went perfectly.'

The long-awaited album was finally released on 18 May 1979 with Ian pronouncing it to be twice as good as *New Boots*. Some of The Blockheads were more sceptical. Mickey believes the album was 'too comfortable and clinical', adding, 'It's not decadent, but I think if we were hungrier it would have sounded better. This whole album lacks the hunger of *New Boots* and even, later on, *Mr Love Pants*.'

Norman shares this view, arguing that he 'missed the rawness of *New Boots*. *Do It Yourself* was over-produced because we had the time and money to do that, whereas *New Boots* was done on a shoestring and we had to get it done as quick as possible. To my mind we spent too long on it and it sounds over-produced.'

Laurie Latham concurs, but blames the musicians themselves for their insistence on endless tinkering with the sound: 'It got to the point where we'd be overdubbing snare drums on their own sometimes. Everything was done on click track except for "Sink My Boats". Ian would be saying "Oh, that beat's out there, let's change it." The band were getting too muso and the overall picture had been lost.'

Peter Jenner has another version of events, remarking simply that 'Ian had written all his best songs already and there just weren't as many good songs on *Do It Yourself*. Ian had mined his original seam and became more self-conscious in his lyrics. He would sit for yonks writing lyrics and then crossing them all out.'

In an interview with *NME* two years later Ian confessed that the songs on *Do It Yourself* were inferior to those on his debut album. He added, 'I'd recommend to all aspiring rock 'n' rollers that you write two LPs before you release the first one. Then you've got space, time to relax, a year to enjoy. Because the enjoyment goes right out when the pressure's on.' [17]

But any fears that a change from the rawness of *New Boots* to a new, more polished, style would backfire were quickly dispersed. Helped by a barrel-load of gushing reviews, *Do It Yourself* reached number two in the charts behind Abba's *Voulez-Vous*, selling 200,000 copies. Paul Morley wrote in the *NME*, 'The music from the extraordinary *Do It Yourself* collection is smooth. This doesn't signify passivity, but a dreaminess. And as well as being smooth it's tingly cool, subtle and throbs with toughness. It's something to adore.'

Despite impressive sales, the album only just broke even, with the three-month European tour losing a staggering £40,000. Ian's extravagant decision to put up the band and crew in top hotels, along with their families, was a costly error. In fact the band's entourage was so large that it required two lorry-sized coaches to accommodate everybody. Mickey joked, 'We drove across Europe like a big penis. It was so over the top.'

Fortunately, Ian, The Blockheads and indeed Blackhill were saved from financial meltdown when the singer was inspired by a terrifying incident on the tour to write one of his best-known songs, 'Reasons To Be Cheerful (Part 3)'.

As the band prepared for a show in Italy their soundman, Charlie, received a high-voltage electric shock onstage from a microphone. It was only the quick thinking of another brave member of the road crew that saved Charlie's life. Ignoring the threat to his own life the roadie managed to kick his convulsing colleague away from the mike and break the electric charge. Fortunately, Charlie was one of the fittest members of the crew, an amateur mountain climber, and survived the incident. He was left with a scar that ran up the whole of his arm and across his chest as a reminder of his brush with death.

Appalled by the dangerous facilities and mindful of the fact that Ian wore a metal calliper that was a potential magnet for electricity, the band called off the gig. But getting on the coach and on their way to the next show in Bologna was to prove difficult. The road crew were aware that Italian roadies took exception to their British counterparts calling their professionalism into question and would be seeking vengeance.

According to Mickey, members of the crew who had previously worked in the country said that the Italians would be expecting a fight. Furthermore, if the British showed themselves unwilling to scrap then the Italians would bizarrely turn upon each other and inform the police that the foreigners had caused their injuries. The visitors' equipment would then be impounded and the entire tour put in jeopardy.

With this in mind the band and their entourage quickly assembled their equipment into the trucks, with Fred 'Spider' Rowe standing guard. Mickey said, 'Fred was a burglar, who'd done time and was as hard as nails. He'd spent five years doing two years' National Service because he was so out of order and kept getting sent to military prison. He was a great character and had this technique where he stood flat on the ground focusing his weight into the ground so he was immovable. He stood there glaring at the Italians.

'When we'd packed up we got back on the coach, but the Italians then parked all their cars across the car park entrance so we couldn't get out. Our coach drivers went right across the grass verge and managed to get on to the road. The Italians realised we'd got away and were standing there chanting "Bologna, Bologna", which was where the next gig was, so we said, "Bologna? Fuck Bologna", and proceeded to Rome.'

With time to kill, the band decamped to a hotel in the Italian capital where Ian pulled together a new lyric. As Ian explained in 1996, 'We cancelled the Italian gigs and went to our hotel, where we quickly wrote 'Reasons To Be Cheerful'... The phrase came because Charlie was still alive – that was the reason for being cheerful. It's a bit like saying "count your blessings".'[10]

Ian had an Italian record deal with RCA, so suggested working on his new lyric with the band in the label's Eretcia Studios. With the band's equipment already on its way to the next gig they were forced to use hired instruments. Johnny was one who found the experience not entirely enjoyable: 'I remember Ian saying to me, "We don't have any pedals, just plug your Strat straight in the amp and go for it." With those heavy strings, it was really painful, but I managed to get the sound in one take. The groove was so infectious, and Chaz already had a rhythm, which we answered with organ, guitar and bass. It was much longer on the first recording and we had to edit it down for a single.'

Charley also suffered in the studio, according to Mickey, who claims that Ian and Chaz removed the hi-hat from his drum kit. 'The natural thing for a drummer to play on this would be a hi-hat. I thought it was a little heavy-handed to take it away.' Davey, on the other hand, was far happier, his outstanding sax solo earning him a rare writing credit.

The song began with The Blockheads repeating the line 'Why don't you get back into bed?' for four bars before Ian began a breathtaking list of 'reasons to be cheerful'. These included such quaint pleasures as 'Cheddar cheese and pickle', 'porridge oats', 'Health Service glasses' and 'Round or skinny bottoms' while the line 'Going on forty, no electric shocks' was a clear reference to Charlie's accident days earlier.

The song contained other oblique references to his band, including 'Balabalabala', taken from a story told to Ian with great zest by Mickey.

'When I was in the Chosen Few with Alan Hull we went out to Germany one Christmas. I was about 18 and it was the first time I'd played abroad. One of the songs we did was a three-chord bash in which the lyric was just "Balabalabalabalabala", over and over. It was a joke song, but all these Germans fucking loved it and used to jump up and down singing along. They requested this ridiculous song every night. Ian thought that was hilarious.'

Name-checking Buddy Holly, Elvis Presley, Steven Biko, the Marx Brothers, Woody Allen, Salvador Dali and John Coltrane among others, the song was derided by some critics, who for the first time had turned against Ian. In a withering put-down in the *NME* one reviewer wrote, 'This is another mouldy old shopping list in the mould of "What A Waste". People who release shopping lists as records must be very smug, or consider themselves to be awfully interesting. Or both…Dury's a little too precious for my taste, I'm afraid, although I realise for many of you he makes life worth living.'

Mickey is scathing of the criticism: 'By this time, as the press does, it builds you up and knocks you down, and one of the things that was said was, "This is just a shopping list." But what a shopping list. When people ever said that to me I'd say, "You make a fucking list and see how that sounds."'

Having recorded the single the band laid down 'Common As Muck' for the b-side, a track written some months earlier by Ian and Chaz. A witty lyric that wouldn't have been out of place in a Lionel Bart musical, the song saw Ian comparing himself and his 'girl' to a series of icons of the stage and screen: 'You're not Brigitte Bardot/I'm not Jack Palance/I'm not Shirley Temple/On any circumstance/Or Fred Astaire'.

On its release, 'Reasons To Be Cheerful' leapt straight to number three in the charts. A second successive number one beckoned, but fate intervened in the shape of a technicians' strike on the BBC's flagship music show *Top Of The Pops*. Denied the increased profile that a primetime television performance brought, the single slipped to number four the following week. The show's policy was never to feature a song that was on its way down the charts, resulting in the record's momentum being lost overnight.

Despite the disappointment of missing out on the top spot by such a cruel stroke of fate, Ian and The Blockheads had maintained their position as darlings of the record-buying public. The stage was set for the band to go on to even bigger and better things, and cement their place as one of the decade's leading artists. But unbeknown to almost everyone, a bombshell was waiting around the corner.

5 Laughter

In August 1979, as 'Reasons To Be Cheerful' began its descent down the charts, Chaz announced his decision to quit the band, this time permanently. Securing his own album deal with A&M, The Blockheads' musical director gave five months' notice to the band and in January 1980 said his goodbyes, leaving behind a huge void.

Chaz admits that his fight in Madrid with Davey, coming as it did towards the end of a 72-date tour, contributed to his decision to leave: 'It triggered a very interesting chain of events because it became a time to re-evaluate my life. The whole scene with the band had become so intense and small, it was all-consuming and very insular. That's why I needed a break, to breathe the air outside of this strong energy force.'

In an interview with the *NME*, almost two years after his departure, Chaz admitted that he had also found it increasingly difficult to play second fiddle to Ian. He said, 'I may have arranged the music to a great extent, composed the back-drops and all, but everything barring a few touches here and there was constructed around Ian, because Ian's insights, his perceptions – his whole personality really – was what gave everything around it a reason for being there... This new album of mine [entitled *Chaz Jankel*] is me finally creating something that was totally my own statement. Like okay, this is Chaz Jankel.'[11]

Peter Jenner claims that a mutual jealousy had developed between Ian and Chaz, a chasm not uncommon in successful rock 'n' roll writing duos. 'Ian was hung up with the fact that he should be the drummer while Chaz wanted to be a frontman,' said Jenner. 'Ian resented the need for Chaz and I think Chaz resented the fact that Ian got all the glory and he didn't. I kept telling Chaz, "You're lucky, you don't have to do all the interviews. You just get paid the production royalties and half the publishing royalties." Basically,

Chaz wanted to be a star and Ian wanted to be a musician, whereas Ian was the star and Chaz was the musician.'

Exhausted by two and a half years of writing, recording and touring, Ian decided to take a break to recharge his batteries. He invited the band and their partners on a busman's holiday to Barbados, although only Johnny and the demob-happy Chaz accepted. According to Norman, 'The plan was to live in two houses together, but we were all sick of being with one another, having been on the road for so long.'

Mickey was desperate to capitalise on the success of 'Reasons To Be Cheerful' and was appalled when Ian extended his break. Although mindful of the physical toll that touring took on the disabled singer, the financial implications of Ian's record deal meant the only way individual Blockheads could earn a living was from touring. At the time Blackhill had signed up The Clash, who were busy breaking America, and Mickey eagerly accepted the band's invitation to play on their US tour.

Meanwhile, rejuvenated by a short break, Davey, Johnny, Norman and Charley decamped to Milner Sound studios in Fulham to write some music of their own. By March 1980 his stateside Clash tour was over and Mickey returned home to weigh up his options. With the band in limbo, waiting for Ian to rediscover his enthusiasm for music, Mickey was asked to join The Clash full-time.

'It was a great experience touring with The Clash, and they were great fellas, but I didn't find it demanding enough musically. They never knew when they did good gigs. One night they played a fantastic gig in Santa Monica Boulevard and I came off and said, "Hey guys, you really played a stormer", and they said, "Did we?" They had no idea. So I decided to carry on with The Blockheads.

'I never regretted turning my back on The Clash because I don't think I'd ever have been totally integrated, I would always have been a sideman.'

Mickey immediately returned to the studio with the rest of The Blockheads to find the atmosphere far less tense without the imposing dual control of Ian and Chaz. With the exception of Davey, who without Ian winding him up was a much calmer proposition, the band had reverted to the Loving Awareness line-up and assembled a considerable amount of work in progress.

But any possibility of producing their own album ended when Ian reappeared on the scene. Arriving at Milner, having rediscovered the urge to record, Ian commandeered proceedings and began writing lyrics to tunes already composed by The Blockheads, a decision he would eventually regret.

Not content with appropriating their music, Ian proceeded unilaterally to appoint a replacement for Chaz, believing the band needed another songwriting input.

The recruitment of a sixth musician took place at a benefit concert for The Stranglers at the Rainbow Theatre in April. The Stranglers' lead singer and guitarist Hugh Cornwell had been jailed for five weeks for possession of a Class A drug, heroin. Cornwell's conviction, for what was his first offence, shook the rock world and when word got around that the band faced potential bankruptcy from the cancellation of a series of gigs, their friends rallied to the cause. A string of new wave stars, including Toyah Wilcox, Hugh's then girlfriend Hazel O'Connor, Wilko Johnson, The Cure's Robert Smith, and Jake Burns from Stiff Little Fingers were recruited for two nights.

Having provided vocals for 'Wrong Way Round', a song on Cornwell's 1979 solo album *Nosferatu*, Ian was pleased to help out, and took Johnny and Davey with him. Alongside the three remaining Stranglers, Ian belted out raucous versions of 'Peaches' and 'Bear Cage', having greeted the crowd in typically blunt fashion: 'We're here to remember our friend and comrade Hugh Cornwell. It's only six [*sic*] fucking weeks, innit!'

Backstage after the first show Davey came across a miserable-looking Wilko, the former Dr Feelgood guitarist and songwriter whose subsequent band The Solid Senders were on the verge of combusting. Wilko (real name John Wilkinson) was disillusioned with the music business and informed Davey of his decision to quit the profession.

Wilko recalled, 'The second night Ian came up to me and said, "The Blockheads are in the studio and we're getting into different projects. Would you like to make a single with The Blockheads backing you?" Naturally, I said yeah. I then had a meeting with Ian and he said, "I was watching you out onstage with The Stranglers and, man, you looked so lonely. I want you to record this old Don Gibson song called 'Oh Lonesome Me'." After we recorded that as a single Ian asked me to join The Blockheads full-time.'

The decision came as something of a surprise to the other Blockheads. Mickey explained, 'Ian threw a spanner in the works by announcing Wilko was joining, without consulting us. We didn't really know him at the time. It was a nice gesture on Ian's part to help Wilko when he was down, but we had to incorporate Wilko's style, which was great on some things, yet on others sounded strange.'

Having recovered from the shock, the band went back in to Milner to record a new single, 'I Want To Be Straight'. According to Norman, the new recruit earned his corn, 'giving us a whole injection of energy'. The song began with an introduction by each member of the band, an idea that Ian came up with in the studio: 'I'm Charley, you know. I'm Norman, pleased to meet ya. I'm Mickey, 'ello. Wilko. I'm Johnny, how ya doing? Alreet? Champion. My name is David. And I'm Ian and guess what…Oi. I want to be straight'.

The song was a clever riposte to the lyric of 'Sex And Drugs And Rock And Roll' released three years previously: 'I want to be straight, I want to be straight/I'm sick and tired of taking drugs and staying up late'. Mickey, who composed the music, said his brief from Ian was to produce a 'marching rhythm'. He added, 'It was difficult to do anything else considering the way Ian wanted the lyrics to sound. I stuck the chords in and made an arrangement. It didn't have a lot of melody. He liked getting the Geordie boys – me and Johnny – to do the backing vocals.'

The backing vocals were indeed a popular feature of the song, with Mickey and Johnny delivering the word 'straight' as 'street' in their best Newcastle dialect. The song was slower than most of Ian's previous work, with a funky bass and simple keyboard riff played at a blues tempo. A splendidly mad sax solo from Davey added another ingredient to the mix.

However, after the departure of Chaz, it was perhaps inevitable that the music press, scenting blood, would pull holes in the composition. The *NME* moaned, 'The plodding, unimaginative funk riff behind a thin lyric was just not up to Blockheads' standards attained with Chaz.'

The single was backed by 'That's Not All', a tribute to Dr Kitt, a female facilitator who gave Ian rigorous swimming lessons in her hydrotherapy pool in south-west London. The facility helped Ian build up the strength in his muscles and was credited with revolutionising his levels of fitness. Speaking in a 1984 documentary on his life, Ian revealed his sadness when his inspirational guru died before he was able to play her the song, which he had written with Davey.

'For about four months I used to come down here every day and it was the night before her birthday…and there was a party for her the next day. The b-side was for her and I usually played her the demos and I didn't play it to her because I wanted to save it for her birthday. She died the eve of her birthday party...I think she's probably the most totally beautiful person I've ever met.'[18]

'I Want To Be Straight' peaked at number 22 in the charts, a far cry from the band's previous single, but a position that gave Wilko the satisfaction of his first and only appearance on *Top Of The Pops*. Despite the criticism from the music press, composer Mickey said he was proud of the record, adding, 'Number 22 wasn't bad. Not as good as Skip Bifferty, though. We broke up because our first single only got to number 21!'

If Ian's diehard fans had been surprised by the softer, more polished sound of *Do It Yourself*, then they were left reeling by the opening bars to *Laughter*'s opening track, 'Sueperman's Big Sister'. The listener could have been forgiven for thinking they had mistakenly picked up a classical record when the sweeping orchestral strings of Ivor Raymonde radiated gently through their speakers.

Although the song started and finished with Raymonde's delicate orchestration, 'Sueperman' was a basic R&B composition, written by new boy Wilko. 'I conceived it pretty quickly and the next day the band bashed it out and it sounded like The Rolling Stones. Some of my R&B pals in Southend heard it and loved it. Then when I was out of the studio it got changed completely and all these fucking violins got put on. I didn't see the point at all.'

The lyric was inspired by a photograph of a female 'teddy boy' that Ian was particularly fond of, with the title's unusual spelling based on the girl's name Sue. 'The idea that Superman has a big sister has got to be pretty cool,' explained Ian.[10] The song was lighthearted, a far cry from much of what was to follow, with a throwaway fantasy chorus: 'You know, she's Sueperman's big sister/Her X-ray eyes see through my silly ways/Sueperman's big sister, superior skin and blister/It doesn't seem surprising nowadays'. In addition to Raymonde, Ian also invited famous percussionist Ray Cooper to play various tambourines and clackers.

Forsaking his policy of not issuing singles from albums, Ian agreed to release 'Sueperman's Big Sister' in October 1980, backed by 'You'll See Glimpses', and the band recorded a rare video at a petrol station in Camden. Ian sat in a Ford Anglia while his band made the transition from members of an orchestra dressed in penguin suits to petrol pump attendants. As Charley played his kit with petrol pumps his colleagues engaged in a spot of country and western line dancing. Despite the humorous video the single stalled at number 51, bringing to an abrupt end Ian's run of chart success.

The unorthodox decision to mix classical music and rock also created a minor misunderstanding when the band mimed to 'Sueperman' on a Dutch television show. On their arrival at the studio The Blockheads found that the station had hired a female string quartet from a local music college. Despite their orders to mime, the girls insisted on playing along to a score sheet containing the song's melody, as opposed to their violin parts.

According to Wilko, 'the girls were sawing away at this melody line and Mickey was shouting, "No. You're only supposed to play on the bits between the lines where you can hear the violins." One of them said, "We haven't got the music for it", and he said, "Can't you just bleedin' pretend?" It ended up with Mickey conducting them and saying, "Come in *now* and scrape the bows." That's what you get for putting bloody violins on songs.'

The mildly amusing 'Pardon' told the story of a nervous job hopeful panicking as he awaits his imminent interview: 'Breath and armpits feet/For Christ's sake please stay sweet/An ever present threat/Of hands that want to sweat/My head aches and I'm bursting for a piss/Why should I subject myself to this?'

The song's chorus consisted of the petrified interviewee giving fumbled answers to his interrogators: 'Pardon, sort of, oh/Pardon, y'know, oh/Pardon, urm, oh/Pardon, err, oh'.

Ian's lyric was originally added to a funky groove written in Milner by Norman before the singer commandeered The Blockheads' writing session. But Ian's refusal to accept a simple marriage between words and music left Norman frustrated: 'I had this funky tune that I wanted Ian to use. Two weeks later he came back with a lyric for "Pardon". The lyrics fitted the music but it meant me having to try and teach him the melody, to make him sing it a certain way and to come in at a certain time. He spent the whole morning saying "Let's change this little bit", so much so that by the end I'd written a completely new piece of music.'

Mickey, for one, believed that the subsequent composition was inferior: 'Ian wanted a "walking" sound, whereas Norman's music was much funkier. Ian didn't like us to get complacent and we had to accept this or leave the band basically.' Although irritated by Ian's intransigence, Norman resurrected part of the rejected piece to good effect more than 15 years later as the bridge in 'Jack Shit George'.

Ian's intervention on 'Pardon' was not the only time that he was to cause problems for his bandmates while recording *Laughter*. Norman claimed, 'Having asked Ian to stay at home to write the lyrics to our demos, we literally made the whole album on our own and it sounded great. But when Ian came down and listened to it he said he wanted to record it all again using click tracks. Ian had to be in control of everything and because he wasn't there when we'd done it, as good as it was, he refused to let it go.

'About four months later we were on tour in Bristol and Johnny had his beat box with him backstage and he was playing one of the tracks we'd recorded before. Ian said, "What's this version? I've never heard this before." Johnny replied, "This is what we recorded which you made us scrap." Ian said, "Blimey. It's much better." We were saying, "You cunt. That's what we told you at the time."'

Wilko found the whole recording experience on *Laughter* bizarre. Preferring to give his own records a live feel, Wilko would limit overdubs to a handful per album and found Ian's perpetual tinkering unfathomable: 'We'd record a song and then pull it to bits and start again. I couldn't understand why, but I never said anything because I hadn't had as many hit records as Ian, so it wasn't for me to question what he was doing. But he had a great band with really talented players who could slap down a terrific recording immediately. Maybe that was a product of Ian having lost Chaz, and him trying to get everything dead right.'

Members of The Blockheads are convinced that the lyrics to 'Delusions Of Grandeur' were autobiographical. Yet Ian insisted that the song, with lines such as 'I've got megalomania' and 'I'm up to the armpits in self-esteem', was in fact a critique of various other rock 'n' roll artists. The music was dominated by Wilko's chopping guitar licks and was notable for Norman's first ever bass overdub. Wilko's solo also heralded a new sound for The Blockheads. 'A lot of the tracks on this album have got that abrasive guitar of Wilko's,' explained Mickey. 'It's great in its place but I don't think it worked on everything Blockhead-wise.'

Fellow guitarist Johnny remains a great fan of Wilko and, in particular, his ability to incorporate effortlessly both lead and rhythm guitar into his playing: 'I love Wilko's playing and his attitude is great. I've toured with Pete

Townshend and people like that and seen how they mash it up, with blood flying off them, and it not bothering them. Wilko's the same.'

When given the lyric to work with, co-writer Mickey congratulated Ian on confessing to his increasingly high-handed behaviour: 'I said to him, "Ian, what an own-up. Fantastic." He said, "It's not about me. It's hypothetical, as is all my work. I'm just observing life." But it was obviously about him. He wanted to be Poet Laureate and do Shakespeare with Vanessa Redgrave. Because of his way with lyrics, directors and producers would say, "Ian, you should write a play, darling. Your lyrics are fabulous." He even brought Vanessa down to the studio.

'Ian changed very quickly. The rest of us hadn't changed because we couldn't afford to. We were jobbing musicians. Ian had always hung out with the Peter Blakes and the intelligentsia and we were used to that, but suddenly it was the theatre lot coming down. Ac-*tors*. The best thing Ian could have done when I challenged him was to agree with me, but when he denied it I lost a bit of respect for him.'

Both Johnny and Norman also believe the song was about their master and the line 'Stiff me, hype me up the charts' would seem to back that up, being a blatant reference to the record company with which he had enjoyed such success.

Those who worked with Ian at this time blame his rapid ascent to stardom for his increasingly unpleasant and dictatorial behaviour. Towards the end of his life Ian himself admitted that fame had not sat comfortably with him and that the period of 1979–80 saw him reach a low point in his life. Speaking in 1999 he said, 'As Andy Warhol said, everyone should be famous for 15 minutes. I reckon we had 20 minutes and that really was enough. I wouldn't go there again even if I had the choice, which I probably haven't, but if that was to occur again it's too strong… So many people tell you you're wonderful, so many people pat you on the back, so many people tell you you've achieved, that you begin to doubt it very quickly.' [5]

Ian explained that his disability made him 'doubly recognisable' and that when spotted in the street he became paranoid about falling over, something that happened to him frequently when his left leg gave way: 'I read somewhere that Paul McCartney said when he's walking through Soho he would get recognised and then he'd walk briskly away, but if I walk briskly away I'd be falling over.' [1]

To cope with the pressures of fame Ian began taking Mogadon tablets at the start of 1979 and quickly became addicted. When he realised that the sleeping pills were taking hold of him he cut them out overnight, resulting in extreme withdrawal symptoms. According to Mickey, Ian became convinced that his subsequent depression was caused by his success, not realising the effect of his withdrawal from the tablets.

Ian's management bore the brunt of his volatile moods, especially those fuelled by alcohol consumption. Peter Jenner claims that he had never seen anybody changed so much by fame. He said, 'Ian would be really unpleasant, especially when he drank. I had some horrible rows with him. He could be really charming, but he could also be an absolute arsehole. I was really shocked by how he changed from being a nice, entertaining companion to someone I dreaded speaking to on the phone. I guess he got scrambled by his fame.'

An incident at the beginning of the *Laughter* tour well illustrates Ian's attitude at the time. Having finished a gig in Dublin, the band retired to the prestigious Gresham Hotel, where Ian had booked himself into a suite. Realising that various members of the band felt aggrieved at this perceived slight while they were stuck in single bedrooms, Ian offered to host a party. The band invited some guests and sat in the foyer awaiting Ian's signal to come upstairs. As time dragged on, hotel staff informed the band that their guests had to leave the foyer.

Making a dash for the telephone at reception Mickey called Ian, only to find that the party was off. 'What had happened was that Ian was upstairs ensconced in one of his favourite pastimes, which was to have a girl who really fancied him up in his room with her boyfriend. He would then take great delight in making the boyfriend look a twat. I eventually persuaded him to let us up, but while I was on the phone I could see Davey looking at me from across the room. Davey could see I was having a hard time and was already pissed off because he'd had a bad gig.

'When we got up to the suite I was standing next to Davey but all the time I was talking to him his eyes were checking where Ian was. I said, "Davey, whatever it is, you've got to let it go, mate." The next thing I know he'd left me and was holding Ian under his arm like a battering ram. He then ran against the wall and smashed Ian's head into it.'

Wilko recalls a contrite Davey appearing at his side, informing him that he had knocked Ian out cold: 'We went back into the room and at that point

Ian's minder Raymond came in cradling Ian in his arms like a child, with his shades all askew. The management said, "Right, band meeting in half an hour", and we all had to leave the party. At the meeting there was a very disgruntled Ian sitting on the bed, forcing everyone to feel this huge lump on his head. Ian was threatening to sack Davey and I remember giving this speech saying, "Listen, guys, I've been in one really great band that blew itself apart through nonsense, and I'm fucked if I'm going to be in another one." It got smoothed out and Davey was fined. For the rest of the tour the road crew had a blackboard at the back of the stage on which they were running a book on who would be next to hit Ian.'

According to Mickey, this incident was another example of how people outside the band's inner circle became blinded to the truth, creating alternative explanations of events they'd witnessed. Realising that the guests had been left unattended, Mickey returned to the party to find the conversation dominated by how Ian had fallen over and Davey had picked him up. 'In their heads they couldn't comprehend what happened, so they interpreted it in a different way.'

'Yes And No (Paula)' was undoubtedly the throwaway song on *Laughter*, an off-the-wall, avant-garde composition constructed by the band's two artists, Ian and Davey. The lyric consists of Ian conducting a conversation with himself, with Davey singing 'yes and no' in an increasingly discordant tone. 'This song was bread and butter to Davey,' said Mickey. 'In the 60s he was in all these weird, expressionist bands who never rehearsed. They just went on and played in different keys.'

In among the freeform jazz was a staccato guitar rhythm by Wilko and some beautiful pocket trumpet playing by Don Cherry. A jazz legend long admired by the band, Cherry was yet another musician brought in by Ian as part of his over-compensation for losing his soulmate. Winning over the band with his eminent charm, Cherry was invited on to the *Laughter* tour and made a lasting musical impression on his new colleagues.

'As well as being a lovely geezer, Don was a beautiful player who taught us a lot and gave us a maturity,' said Mickey. 'He was a consummate musician who taught us not to panic. I've got some great versions of "Sex And Drugs" with Don Cherry on. On the songs where our playing was manic he was the complete antithesis.'

'Dance Of The Crackpots' saw more experimentation by The Blockheads and yet more additions to their cast, with Ray Cooper again guesting on percussion and black American 'hoofer' Will Gaines tap dancing throughout, having brought his tap board to the studio.

'Crackpots' was a rare example of Ian working speedily, writing the song with his guitarist in one afternoon. Johnny composed the music on an East German banjolele, a birthday present from a friend, having learned four rudimentary chords to take him through the song.

Being a more than competent singer himself, Johnny's melody failed to take into consideration Ian's difficulty in reaching high notes. With Ian forced to shout most of his delivery, Johnny's more tuneful vocal was included high in the mix to help retain the song's jovial mood. 'Crackpots' remains one of Johnny's favourite Blockheads songs. 'It's one of his great lyrics which really holds over time. All those crazy lines like "Invite the Germans home to tea", was Ian at his best. It's all up and positive.'

Johnny's own mood throughout the recording of *Laughter* was far from 'up and positive', the result of a freak accident suffered at Ian's flat near Baker Street. Having been offered a lift home from the studio by Johnny, Ian discovered he was locked out and asked his colleague to kick down his front door. 'I was wearing my DMs at the time and went for this door, which was quite thick. It took me three or four kicks and shoves to break in. Soon afterwards I felt very odd mentally.'

Bizarrely, the impact of one of the kicks had jarred the whole of Johnny's spine, moving the position of his skull. 'My skull was rubbing on a part of my brain and this had the effect of producing a change in the chemicals. I did go doolally and away with the fairies for a few weeks. People were saying, "Give me some of what you're on" and I'd say, "I'm not on anything." I was babbling like nanny goats on acid and Ian said, "You'd better go home to your mum." We took a break and I got the train to Newcastle to be with me mam and me dad. I was hearing voices and all sorts. It was a very strange experience, like having a breakdown 'cos one minute I'd be ecstatically happy and the next I'd be on the floor weeping and imagining strange things with the worst possible doom for my friends and family.'

After a few weeks Johnny eventually made the connection between his condition and kicking down Ian's door, and visited a cranial osteopath who, over time, manipulated his skull back to its original position.

Mickey said he barely recognised his friend of 15 years at this time and believes that Johnny's breakdown was not helped by Ian's attitude during the album: 'Johnny's a sensitive flower and he suffered working with Ian at this time. He also had to give Davey a lift home every night and had to put up with all his grumbling.'

According to Norman, Ian felt that Johnny played his best music when he was angry and would often antagonise the guitarist in the studio: 'In one sense I could see what Ian was getting at because in his eyes he thought he was helping the guy, but onlookers like us were saying, "Hang on, Ian, it's not doing him any good." Ian loved to play mind games, and coping with them depended on how strong you were as a person. Things like that don't affect me, whereas Johnny allowed it to get to him.'

The humorous 'Over The Points', another Dury/Turnbull composition, brought side one to an end on a high note. The song saw Ian immersing himself in the role of 'an actual train', accompanied by a wonderful abstract performance from The Blockheads.

During his journey 'backwards and forth south and north on down the line and up' Ian details matter-of-factly the daily minutiae of rail travel. For instance, 'Upon me at any given moment ten or twelve people might be taking craps'. The obvious target of the anorak-wearing trainspotter also receives a mention: 'All over the shop hundreds of people, invariably male, write our numbers down/We as trains are agreed that this is because we are extremely phallic'.

Many of the stories, which include such delightful vignettes as 'the track is lined with decapitated schoolboys' heads still wearing their caps', are believed to have been based on Davey's time working as a waiter for British Rail in the West Country.

'Over The Points' was the one unadulterated success of Ian's obsession with working to a click track. Instructing the band to 'try and sound like a train' Ian stood in the control room and fed a metronome in to Charley's headphones. As usual the band followed Charley's lead and when Ian gradually speeded up the click track halfway through, the drummer, and subsequently his colleagues, picked up the pace. Towards the end of the song Ian slowed the click down to give the impression of the train coming into a station.

For once Ian entrusted his musicians with the total freedom to play exactly what they wanted, to great effect. As the song developed into a free-for-all Davey used his whole repertoire of tricks, at one stage sounding uncannily like a train horn, while Ray Cooper played castanets and various bells, and Don Cherry ad libbed on his pocket trumpet. Only Wilko failed to shine, admitting that the vast pot-pourri of sounds relegated him to a bit-part player.

The recording of '(Take Your Elbow Out Of The Soup) You're Sitting On The Chicken' was not such an enjoyable experience, particularly for Charley. The drummer's natural rhythm was frustrated by his being forced to play to a click track and then finding his drum parts continuously dissected by Ian. 'Ian had Charley playing all sorts of things that weren't natural for him,' explained Johnny. 'He said, "I don't want the ordinary beat there, I want you to play fours on the snare drum, and your bass drum's got to be a reggae bass drum, and your hi-hat's got to be ska." There were real battles over the beat. We wanted a more funky feel on the chorus and Ian's rigid beat didn't sit right with Charley, or any of us for that matter.'

Charged with writing the music, Mickey also found himself disappointed by what he regarded as an inadequate lyric: 'I was thrilled to get a funky rock track to write instead of an oompah song but when I saw the rest of the lyric I thought, "What the fuck does this mean?" But you couldn't question Ian on his lyrics. It was like the emperor's new clothes. If you didn't see it, you weren't of the privileged few. The lyric was a load of bollocks, but he had this phrase, "Trust is a must", that he used whenever anyone doubted him. He thought he could do anything and get away with it.'

Considering the vast swathes of high-quality lyrics lying unused in Ian's flat, Mickey was entitled to be disappointed when handed a song with lines like 'The mouse runs up your leg, oh, it's one o'clock in China'. By the song's end the chorus had been changed to the even more nonsensical 'Take your elbow out of the soup, you're sitting on the kittens', repeated ad nauseam. One wonders what Chaz would have said if handed such an inferior lyric.

'Uncoolohol' saw Charley receive his first ever writing credit with Ian, creating a groove around a bass riff originally written by Norman for Loving Awareness. Don Cherry features heavily on the track, at one stage appearing to indulge in a friendly battle of the solos with Wilko. Fortunately Ian resisted the temptation to interfere too much with his colleagues' playing, making 'Uncoolohol' one of the highlights of *Laughter*'s second side.

Ian's lyric was undoubtedly close to home, chronicling the anti-social nature of heavy drinkers: 'The war cry of the drinker of the drink/Can send your senses reeling to the brink/What's your poison breath and outlook, puke and bile/Lose all sense of reason, humour, style'.

Johnny described the song as Ian 'looking at himself in the mirror' and claims the singer would often coax him into heavy rum drinking sessions. Mickey, on the other hand, remembers Ian's favourite tipple as Budweiser or Guinness, 'liquid speed', as he referred to it. What is not in dispute is the dramatic change that came over Ian once under the influence. According to Wilko, 'Ian could be very difficult, particularly if he'd had a couple of drinks. I don't think I've ever met anybody who could be quite so offensive, but I always liked him, even though he could sometimes be a terrible bastard.'

After gigs, Mickey, arguably the most reliable member of The Blockheads, often found himself lumbered with Ian while the singer embarked on a bender. 'We knew that once we came offstage the best thing to do was get as far away from Ian as possible. He'd go looking for trouble, especially if he'd had a good gig. If he knew the band were in the bar feeling good he'd seek us out and tell us we'd done something wrong. When Ian walked into a room you couldn't ignore him; he had a larger than life persona that demanded attention.

'When he was pissed Ian would spit at people, but people covered it up throughout his life. Before his mum died the one thing that scared him was that she would open a Sunday newspaper and find a picture of him drunk in a street. He was terrified that she would find out what a horrible sod he was.'

On one occasion in the early 1990s when Ian launched a vicious verbal assault on Mickey, the easy-going keyboard player could take no more, leaving him floundering on his back in the road. The occasion was the last knockings of a post-concert dinner in France, laid on by the show's promoter. Realising that his colleagues had abandoned him to what they dubbed 'Dury Duty' Mickey tried in vain to persuade a by now almost comatose Ian to go back to the hotel. Ignoring his pleas Ian invited the waiters to his table for a drink.

'They couldn't speak a word of English and when Ian sussed this he immediately started insulting the shit out of them, but with a smile on his face so they wouldn't realise, saying things like "You silly twat."' Having finally persuaded Ian to leave, Mickey faced the difficulty of getting him out of his seat. 'He could only get up if he had a chair that was secured at the back, so he could push himself against the wall, and when he'd get to his feet he could click his leg in. But he was so pissed he couldn't get up, and instead ordered another Guinness.

'It took another three-quarters of an hour to get him out and by this time I was really pissed off. As he grabbed my arm to support him he said, "Your missus is a fucking maggot." I said, "Excuse me, Ian, don't get personal. I know you don't get on, but let's not go there." He said, "What are you doing with her?" and then started insulting my kids. Usually he could never rile me, but this time he was really getting near the bone and as I was bringing him over the road he tripped and fell. When he carried on shouting at me I just said, "Fuck you", and walked off. He was on his back like a turtle with the traffic going past him. I went up to my room and I could hear him shouting for our soundman Ian Horne, who went out and picked him up.'

Perhaps the most celebrated of Ian's drunken escapades occurred while recording *Laughter*, during an incident that became known simply as the 'Omar Sharif fight'. Ian and Norman were appearing in Roger Daltrey's latest video at a Harrow boxing club and when the pair arrived shortly after 9am the booze was already flowing. Filming lasted all day and during regular lulls in activity the pair necked free bottles of champagne with gay abandon. At around 7pm they received permission from Daltrey to take a short break to attend an exhibition of work by one-time Kilburns member Humphrey Ocean. Having been whisked over to the National Portrait Gallery in a car laid on by Daltrey, Ian was invited by old friend Peter Blake to a late-night dinner at the exclusive Le Caprice restaurant in the West End.

After returning to Harrow to finish their scenes, Ian and an equally heavily refreshed Norman arrived at Le Caprice for dinner with Blake and his wife Chrissie. No sooner had they arrived than Ian spotted a girl whom he had taught at art college, sat with Hollywood star Omar Sharif, and two of the star's minders. Ignoring the advice of both Norman and Peter, Ian staggered over to their table to re-acquaint himself with his former pupil, a girl called Felicity.

Norman kept an eye on proceedings while a concerned Blake and his wife, who had their backs to the action, asked him for a running commentary. 'Ian was chatting away and it all looked OK. But then I saw Omar lean over, say something and sit back, and he didn't look very happy. Then I saw Ian lean over and say something and lean back, and it continued like that.

'I could see in his face that Omar was thinking, "Who is this fucking geezer?" The next minute Omar gets up, grabs Ian by the shirt and punches him three or four times. Ian's walking stick went flying and he was falling about like a rag doll. I leapt up and grabbed hold of Omar from behind and pushed him off, shouting, "He can't hit back, man, that's enough." He fell back on the settee and then his minders jumped up to have a go at me. I put my hands up and said, "Woah" and then picked Ian up and carried him back to our table.

'I sat Ian down and he was so pissed he was asking me what had happened. Peter went over and had a verbal with Omar about what a cunt he was for hitting him and then Omar stormed out of the restaurant with his minders.' Sharif's ire was allegedly stoked by Ian's statement that he had enjoyed the actor's first feature film, *Lawrence of Arabia*, but that every movie he had made since was 'shit'.

Having cleaned the blood from Ian's face, Norman wisely decided it was time to turn in for the night. On the taxi ride home Ian could speak of nothing but his beating. 'He said to the cab driver, "'ere, I just got punched in the teeth by Omar Sharif", and the driver said, "That's probably the most expensive fist you'll have in your mouth."'

For weeks afterwards Ian continued to make mileage from the story and was even caught applying make-up to his right eye when the bruising started to go down. Ironically, some years later, Ian and Sharif found themselves starring in the same film. Racked with remorse the actor invited Ian to his dressing room, poured him a drink and apologised for punching him. According to Mickey, 'From that day on Omar Sharif became "my mate Omar", as opposed to "that cunt Omar", which is how he'd been referred to before.'

'Hey, Hey, Take Me Away' was *Laughter*'s darkest moment, containing one of the most shocking lyrics Ian ever wrote. The song was autobiographical, relating to his three-and-a-half-year spell in Chailey Heritage Craft School for the disabled. Co-writer Mickey said, 'This is the song that shocked everybody and we were a little wary about putting it on the album, but Ian was determined to do it. All the stories on here are true because Ian told them to us long before this song was written. It's a great exposé of institutionalised life where, if there's something wrong with you, you're thrown in a corner and told to fend for yourself.'

Ian was not quite nine years old when he arrived as a boarder at the school in East Sussex. Chailey, which in many ways resembled a public boarding school, was divided into three parts: two residential centres for disabled children (one for the boys and one for the girls) and a hospital. Alongside Ian were other polio victims, tuberculosis sufferers and children with appalling deformities, some of whom never reached adulthood.

The school's philosophy was simple, that killing with kindness wouldn't get the pupils anywhere. If a child fell over they had to pick themselves up off the floor, no matter how disabled they were. In the morning the ritual of visiting the bathroom was equally rigid. First up would be the 'sliders', those who had to slide their way along on their fronts to the toilet. Then it was the turn of those in wheelchairs. Those with one good leg, like Ian, would go last. Anybody who had wet the bed in the night, or worse, would inevitably find themselves exposed to ridicule by the orderlies. In the early 21st century such a policy appears more than a little misguided, but in 1950s Britain those who ran the school genuinely believed they were helping to create strong, independent adults.

Indeed, for all Ian's harsh experiences in Chailey, his feelings for his stint there were decidedly mixed. In his 1974 *Penthouse* interview Ian said, 'The law of the jungle reigned in that place. There was a lot of behaviour that just don't happen in the outside world. Later you pretend to be arty about it but when I was there I was just there, it was real. Thinkin' about it now I realise it was fuckin' heavy. It was like a hospital in one way, like a school in another way. It was very uncomfortable. Guys would die there.'[7]

Ten years later in a Channel 4 documentary, Ian's view had softened: 'I'm really glad I went there, it sounds really heavy but in fact it was really good… It was a very equalised place. Disablement cut across barriers of class and creed quite effectively.'[18]

'Hey, Hey' begins with Ian in apparent conversation with another pupil before a teacher blows a whistle and utters the immortal line, 'What's all this spunk on the duckboards?' Ian then calls out to his friend Lawrence to abscond with him, 'Come on Lawrence…come on Lawrence/Let's go out and have a prayer meeting/Take a chance with our new shotgun'. As Ian told the Channel 4 documentary makers, he and Lawrence escaped from Chailey three times, each time being returned by locals who instantly knew where two youngsters wearing leg braces had come from.

There follows a piercing scream before Ian begins recounting the unorthodox nature of his institutional life: 'Hey, hey, take me away, I hate waking up in this place/There's nutters in here who whistle and cheer/When they're watching a one-legged race'. The verse continues with a graphic account of the sexual abuse among the pupils that such a coarse existence engendered: 'A one-legged prefect gets me in bed/Makes me play with his dick/One-legged orderly shouting the odds/Driving me bloody well sick'.

In a 1998 interview with *Time Out*, Ian was remarkably sanguine about the abuse that permeated life at Chailey: 'It wasn't all wanking off geezers. I never 'ad it up the 'Arris nor anything like that. I never had to gobble anybody. A little bit of sixteen-year-old boys touching up nine-year-old boys, but I don't know if there was any sodomy or fellatio. Bit like a good public school, bit of wanking, bit of bullying. I told my mum and she put a stop to it.' [19]

Ian's lyric goes on to reveal his confused feelings about the beatings that were handed out: 'They're making me well, if they're caring for me/Why do they boot me and punch me?/Why do they bash me and crunch me?' According to Ian, there was a considerable amount of fighting at Chailey, operating under fairly strict rules: 'If you fought a kid who wore two leg braces – I only have one – then you sat next to him on a bench and started beatin' fuck out of each other like that. I could use one leg and one hand so I usually won. I put the boot in.' [7]

The frequent change of pace in his lyric succeeded in making the listener understand the torrent of emotions Ian had experienced at Chailey, alternating between fear, paranoia and unbridled anger. It required sensitive handling by Mickey, who stylishly tailored an arrangement to fit a lyric that flitted between a quiet, semi-whispered delivery and an impassioned, 100-mile-an-hour rant.

Having released his anger mid-song, the narrator's mood changes, sobbing his way through the following verse: 'One-legged Peter who knows bloody well/He's got worse ever since he came in/This other poor cunt, he was born back-to-front/And he's always got stuff on his chin'.

Mickey claims that Ian had an innate ability to fool people into believing he was crying: 'This was his best acting voice, which he probably developed as a boy in those institutions, to get people on his side. He could turn it on, especially if he thought you believed it, and actual tears would come. The next minute he'd be laughing. Although it sounds like Ian was building himself up to deliver that lyric, he wasn't. He was always like that and he got a buzz from it.'

Ian frequently turned on the waterworks when encountering his *bêtes noires*, the Germans, on the road. Ian's burning hatred of the Nazis for sending disabled people to the gas chambers led to his tarring all Germans with the same brush. Woe betide any Teutonic men or women who crossed Ian's path after a few drinks, as Mickey explains: 'When Ian picked a fight with Germans they'd initially be amused. But then he'd be really insulting and get their hackles up and as soon as that happened he'd start to cry. They'd say "Vot's going on?" and he'd reply "You killed my parents in the camps." It was a huge lie, but he'd make these people feel awful and they'd be apologising profusely.'

When the band toured Australia in 1982 Ian even turned on two Swedish men in a bar, mistaking them for Germans. Dismissing the pair's protestations Ian began causing a scene, requiring the band, aided by their minder Raymond, to drag him to his room. According to Mickey, 'Raymond picked him up but Ian grabbed the counter at the bar. Ray had hold of his feet and was pulling him horizontally, but Ian was gripping the counter like mad. We all started hammering at his fingers with our fists. It was hilarious, the kind of thing you see in cartoons. We got him into the lift but he was pulling Ray's hair, leaving big clumps of dreadlocks on the floor. We got him in the room and nicked his calliper so he couldn't go anywhere. He was like a wild animal.'

Returning to the song, the most chilling lyric appeared towards the end: 'The linois brown/And the walls have been scraped/With blood where someone has hanged themselves/I hope so!' Despite this graphic description of a pupil taking their own life, Ian later denied that he had come across such a scene: 'There was no despair, there weren't any suicides as far as I recall.' [1]

With his wrath again dampened, Ian concluded his lyric with a brief discussion of the age-old 'nature/nurture debate', questioning whether the institutionalised should blame their upbringing for their behaviour in later life: 'I ain't done nothing wrong, but I'm unhappy/Question: Do you blame your life on life/And say it all began before the nappy?'

Certainly Ian's colleagues are united in their belief that both his ultra-defensive posture and the control-freakery he displayed over The Blockheads was a result of his five years in Black Notley Hospital and Chailey Heritage School. Steve Nugent summarised Ian as follows: 'Ian's whole posture towards the world was formed in those institutions. He had major chips on his shoulders, although he was aware of the fact that he did. One of the things he learned to do was to become adept in moving into different types of social circle. The accent he presented to the world was pretty far removed from the one he grew up with. All the "gor blimey" stuff was laid on with a trowel. A lot of it came from the fact that he felt he had to struggle out of being institutionalised and being physically marked as somebody who was different and not able to do what most people could do, like get up and move across a room without worrying about falling over.'

Underneath his gruff exterior Ian was racked with self-doubt during the making of *Laughter*, a fact illustrated by his endless tinkering with the record, fuelled by the devastating loss of Chaz. According to Wilko, at his initial meeting to discuss joining the band, Ian seemed oblivious to his immense popularity: 'When he was telling me what his plans were he was drawing a picture on a piece of paper. After a while I said, "You're really shitting yourself, aren't you?" and he said, "Yeah, I am." I said, "You've got to understand people really love you, Ian. You've got absolutely no need to worry."

'Sometimes I used to think he couldn't believe that people loved him. Once he'd had a few he'd want to find out how much they liked him by provoking them mercilessly. I can't say he wasn't vindictive, because he was, but that guy had a lot to put up with in his life, and if he sometimes got a bit boisterous I would try and remember that.'

Ian continued to pour his heart out on 'Manic Depression (Jimi)', the name in brackets a tribute to legendary guitarist Jimi Hendrix, who had written a song of the same title. The lyric again reflected Ian's unhappy state of mind: 'The mind is a very precious flower/That finds itself a strand amongst the weeds/The cause and effect is what you might expect/And going round the bend is where it leads'.

The depression caused by his withdrawal from Mogadon was a constant presence in the studio at this time. According to Mickey, 'He was terrible to be around at that time. He was nasty and very resentful, particularly about having to rely on the facilitators who helped him get around. They wouldn't last too long, because he was so horrible to them. If he was paying someone a retainer to drive his car he'd resent it, and it would come out in odd ways, especially if he was depressed.

'Ian lashed out at those who were closest to him, so we used to physically distance ourselves from him. He used to get Fred to put him on his back and run fast into the studio to catch people chopping up lines of coke. He sacked my roadie Chris for chopping one out on the piano. He did it because he could. When I asked why he'd sacked him he said, "He's getting too big for his boots, he can't afford to do that stuff." Ian was trying to be the Holy Roman Emperor of the band.'

Having gone through his 'cold turkey', Ian returned to a semblance of normality after the album's completion. 'When he realised it was the barbiturates then it wasn't his fault any more and he could free himself of all that guilt,' said Mickey.

The song's arrangement, by Mickey, successfully created an incongruous marriage between a hard-hitting lyric and a gentle melody with a Hawaiian flavour. The contributions of Johnny and Davey in particular stood out, the former using Davey's Echo-plex machine to get an arpeggio sound, while the saxophonist impersonated a butterfly with a bewitching performance on flute. The pair certainly helped Mickey achieve the 'light and flowery arrangement' he was seeking. Norman added a bass line from his Loving Awareness days, one the band had used for Dick Fontayne's film of NASA's alternative 'Views From Space'.

Ian's vocal delivery did not reflect the unhappiness of his lyrics, and a non-English speaker would be surprised to discover that they were hearing not a love song, but a tale of despair. As Johnny pointed out, 'The content and the music don't really add up, but the way it trips off the tongue does. I could imagine someone walking down the street singing "Manic depression, manic depression/Is not a pleasant fucker, pheasant plucker" and getting some very weird looks.'

The line in question was one of Ian's rare forays into the world of spoonerisms, the substitution of the first letters of alternate words to create a completely different phrase. It was an example of the lengths Ian would go to while honing a lyric. According to Mickey, 'When Ian wrote a lyric it wasn't just out of his head, he'd consult a dictionary or thesaurus. On his desk he'd have notes everywhere. Some of those lyrics would take weeks to get right.'

'Oh Mr Peanut' saw Ian's sense of humour return with a vengeance. Backed initially by some flatulent sax from Davey, Ian shouts 'Oi, rotten hat/Where'd you get that haircut?/Brent Cross Shopping Centre?/I bet your muvva fed you with a catapult'. Based in north-west London, Brent Cross was then the capital's largest shopping mall, and was often Ian's point of reference when mocking someone's attire.

As Chaz recalled, 'I arrived late to the studio one day wearing a brand new white bomber jacket and Ian said, "'ere mate, where did you get that jacket? Brent Cross Shopping Centre." Everyone cracked up. The funny thing was that I *had* bought it from Brent Cross, but I kept my mouth shut.'

The song features a string of politicians who had irked the singer, including of course, Mr Peanut: 'Oh Mr Peanut/I don't like you at all/Not only are they poisonous/But your eyes are much too small'. According to Johnny, this was a reference to the then US President Jimmy Carter, who had made his money from a highly successful peanut business. Johnny says that among the politicians included were the new West German Chancellor Helmut Kohl: 'Oh yeah, Mein Herr, you must be up the creek'.

Wilko found himself thrust into the co-writer's chair, with 'Oh Mr Peanut' replacing a song written with Mickey, called 'Duff 'em Up And Do 'em Over (Boogie Woogie)'. On Kozmo's advice, Ian had scrapped its recording, concerned that the song would become an anthem to football hooligans. Mickey confessed to being 'a bit peeved' by the scrapping of a song that he had spent considerable time on, but understood the decision: 'We did have a certain responsibility and Ian recognised that this song could have rallied the "Oi oi" brigade that followed him.'

Wilko believes that Ian overreacted and that the lyric in no way advocated violence, but was happy to help write the new song, despite having to use a 'fucking click track'. He explained, 'My attitude was if you've got a fucking drummer like Charley Charles and a bass player like Norman Watt-Roy you don't need a bleedin' click track. There was sometimes a bit of argy-bargy about this and eventually I refused to use it and told Ian I'd listen to Charley instead. When we were recording "Oh Mr Peanut" Davey was standing in the control room while the rhythm section were putting their track down and got hold of the click track and turned the knob up, so it got faster and faster. You can hear this on the record.'

But the person who suffered most on this recording was Johnny, who was forced to sing at full throttle a whole octave above Ian. He said, 'This was very painful to do, and I ended up being mixed down to virtually nothing. It was hardly worth fucking doing.'

'Oh Mr Peanut' was a vehicle for one of Davey's magnificent off-the-wall sax solos as the music sped up into a wild thrash. Charley ends proceedings with a spot of sustained cymbal abuse before the song segues into the grand finale, 'Fucking Ada'.

The first minute contains no warning of the sustained Anglo-Saxon assault to be inflicted on the listener's ears, with Ivor Raymonde's measured string arrangement accompanying Ian's twee, 'olde Englishe' lyric: 'Lost in the limelight, baked in the blaze/Did it for nine pence, those were the days/Give me my acre and give me my plough/Tell me tomorrow, don't bother me now'.

Any misconceptions are immediately shattered by Ian and The Breezeblocks screeching 'Fucking Ada' four times at the top of their voices. In his subsequent genteel verses Ian appears to give voice to various internal demons, such as 'Greed forms the habit of asking too much', 'Failure enfolds me with clammy green arms', 'Bodily, mentally doubtful and dread' and 'Too late for regret or chemical change'.

The final three and a half minutes of the song are taken up with the band screeching the popular Cockney phrase 'Fucking Ada' as Raymonde soldiers on gamely. 'Ivor's string arrangement was glorious,' says Mickey, 'but the look on his face when he saw he had to work to this lyric was priceless.'

Johnny suffered the acute embarrassment of being chastised by his family when 'Fucking Ada' appeared on the b-side of the 'Sueperman's Big Sister' 12-inch, mistakenly credited solely to him: 'I remember me mam buying it for me aunties, two Catholic spinsters, Cissy and Katie. They said, "Eeh, Lillie, how could you let him write a song like that, with all those F words in it?" I made her point out that I didn't write the lyrics, I only wrote the music and the chords underneath. One of them said, "Eeh, I don't care, he can't say that." It freaked them right out.'

The band all confess to getting immense satisfaction from their vocal performance, helping to rid them of the tension that recording with a depressed and spiteful Ian Dury had engendered. 'The song was the perfect sentiment to sum up the album,' says Mickey. 'It was an absolute joy to sing that chorus and get out all that frustration. The fact that it has those lush strings, like it's going to be a cinematic epic, and then goes into that chorus made most people laugh. You'd have to be a real prude not to laugh.'

Wilko also has fond memories of the song: 'It was very enjoyable to sing a song like that, coming from Essex, as I do, and people always say they can hear me shouting "Fucking Ada" on the chorus. In many ways it epitomised that whole period, because it's vulgar and amusing, and yet there's lots of dark things being said. We would close the show with it sometimes and Ian would say, "This is not a miserable song, it's a happy song." After the album came out we were in France after a gig and for some reason we were pissed off with the French and as we drove through the middle of town we played "Fucking Ada" at full volume with the doors open, so it was quite useful then.'

The downside of screaming 'Fucking Ada' at the top of their voices was that the band had recorded yet another song that could never get radio play.

Mickey believes that Ian's vindictive mood may have led him to deliberately destroy all hope of the album being a success: 'Nothing on this album could get radio play. It was OK for him because he'd already made lots of money, but this was *our* album and it seemed like he sabotaged it on nearly every track.' Certainly *Laughter* was a relative disaster commercially, peaking at a dismal number 48 in the album chart, in which it appeared for a mere three weeks.

Mickey also believes that Ian had already negotiated a new deal for himself with Polydor and simply wanted to get the final of his three albums for Stiff out of the way before ditching the band. The subsequent announcement of the deal came as a hammer blow to Mickey, who recalled a promise made in 1978 by Ian to include the band in his next contract: 'We went out to the garden at Rolvendon and he said, "I realise we're successful now and I'm getting all the dairy because it's my record deal, but if you lads stay with me for my next two albums with Stiff we'll then do a deal involving everyone."

'When I questioned him about it later, Ian said, "The goalposts have moved. It's down to my accountants." From then on if any of us tried to talk to Ian about the band he'd say, "You have to talk to Ronnie Harris [Ian's accountant]." It all started during the recording of *Laughter*. I got the impression that decisions had already been made, I just wasn't sure whether or not they would include The Blockheads. As time went on it became clear that they wouldn't.'

Mickey blames Blackhill, whose management deal only involved Ian, for encouraging him to abandon them: 'They thought Ian was the goose that laid the golden egg, whereas we felt we had helped make him a success. The only good thing was that instead of getting £100 a week each we got £350 a week on the *Laughter* tour, so they didn't completely trash us.'

Peter Jenner, understandably, has a very different perspective on events, and states that Ian's insistence on paying salaries to The Blockheads was draining Blackhill's finances. He states bluntly that Ian and the band were living almost entirely off the royalties for *New Boots And Panties*, an album that was in effect a solo record. Indeed, within a year Blackhill had gone to the wall, brought down, Jenner believes, by the commercial failure of *Laughter* and the company being dumped by The Clash, who owed it large sums of money.

'Ian wasn't earning money and the tax bills were catching up with us. As long as your income is going up you can put off your tax but when it starts going down seriously then it's a problem. We didn't have a contract with The Clash, it was all verbal, and they didn't pay us any commission for gigs. In the end The Clash told us we had to choose between working with them and Ian Dury and we said, "We have to stay with Ian because he was here first." So we got blown out by The Clash and we never got any money from them, which was scandalous.

'I knew if we went to litigation it would get nasty, and we probably wouldn't get paid. I felt bitter because we did a fantastic job for The Clash and I think they treated us like shit. I didn't feel bitterness towards Ian, I was just angry that he didn't grab the opportunities he had. He just wanked around and didn't fulfil his promise.'

Jenner does, however, have sympathy for the band over their predicament during the post-*Laughter* hiatus: 'They were always willing to work, but Ian didn't like them working for anyone else. I feel very sympathetic to them because at the end of the day they didn't make much money. It all went while they were sitting around waiting for Ian, who kept them on a dangle.' He also confesses that the financial arrangements made at the outset by Blackhill were 'fudged', adding 'It wasn't a well-worked arrangement, which to an extent was our fault, but there were never clear instructions from Ian. It was impossible not to fudge it because Ian would never give them straight points on record sales.'

As 1980 came to an end The Blockheads, hardened by the experience of recording *Laughter*, retired to their various homes to recuperate. As Big Ben rang in the New Year they awaited Ian's call to reassemble The Blockheads for a third album. It would be another 16 years before it came.

6 Place Your Hard-earned Peanuts In My Tin

'You don't mind if I turn my back, do you? I want to look at this band. I think you're great, Blockheads, you know that?' Ian uttered those appreciative words to a Düsseldorf crowd in 1979. Less than two years later Ian turned his back not on the crowd, but on The Blockheads.

Armed with his three-album deal with Polydor Ian decided not to re-employ the services of The Blockheads, instead rekindling his partnership with Chaz, whose absence from *Laughter* had so pained him. Chaz was on a creative high, having struck gold with a song on his eponymous debut LP, 'Ai No Corrida', being pounced on by Quincy Jones and turned into a worldwide hit.

On the suggestion of Polydor the pair jetted out to the Bahamas for two weeks' intensive recording with legendary rhythm duo Sly Dunbar and Robbie Shakespeare. A fortnight would barely have been enough time to record an album of established songs, yet Chaz and Ian were so unprepared that many of the tracks on *Lord Upminster* were not written until they arrived at Compass Point.

The record was a resounding failure, stalling at number 53 in the UK charts. A review in *Record Collector* magazine summed it up as follows: 'Ian Dury's schizophrenic fourth album finds him not only without The Blockheads but also, half the time, without his own identity. Side two is basically mediocre, mid-paced disco funk, with none of Dury's usual Henry Fielding-style ribald vivaciousness.'

The one saving grace was the extraordinary 'Spasticus Autisticus', one of Ian's finest ever lyrics and a song that would become a mainstay of his live set until his death. The inspiration for the song came from Ian's feelings of disgust at the patronising attitude of governments and 'well-meaning' organisations towards the disabled. Speaking in 1999 Ian explained, '1981 was the [International] Year of the Disabled, which meant that in 1982 everybody was going to be all right. I thought that's a load of bollo, so...I thought I'll make a band called Spastic And The Autistics, and my friend [Ed] Speight goes, "No, no, Spasticus Autisticus, the freed slave", based on the Kubrick epic. So it started from there.'[1]

Ian's lyric pulled no punches in describing the life of disabled people. In the first verse he sang, 'I'm Spasticus, 'I'm Spasticus, 'I'm Spasticus Autisticus/I widdle when I piddle 'cos my middle is a riddle'. By the next verse the second line had been changed to 'I dribble when I nibble and I quibble when I scribble'.

Ian also included some clever wordplay, altering the black dance chant 'get down', his Jamaican backing vocalists singing, 'Get up, get up, get up, get down, fall over. Woooh'.

Although critics accused him of deliberately courting controversy, Ian refused to back down, and released 'Spasticus Autisticus' as a single in August 1981. Predictably, the record was banned by the BBC, who failed to understand that as a disabled person himself, Ian could hardly be said to be mocking the afflicted. The UN also rejected Ian's offer of making 'Spasticus' its theme tune for the International Year of the Disabled.

Ian believed that as a prominent disabled artist it was his duty to attack the ignorance surrounding the issue, and described the song as 'a war cry'. He added, 'My awareness within the record of "Spasticus" wasn't a shared awareness amongst "walkie-talkies", so I obviously knew there was a risk that I was going to alienate a lot of people and they were going to get the hump with me, [and say] "What's this fucking spazzer doing squeaking?" Well, I wasn't moaning, I was actually doing the opposite of moaning. I was yelling.'[1]

Ian was amused to discover that the BBC's ban only covered the period before six o'clock and that it was deemed an acceptable song to play after that hour. According to Chaz, 'Ian said, "What does that mean? After six o'clock are the disabled off the streets or something? Can't they be seen then?"'

Chaz, who wrote the music, agrees that 'Spasticus' was the standout track on *Lord Upminster*, although he insists that 'Lonely Town' was a vastly underrated track: '"Spasticus" was a very clever song and full of frustration; for instance, "Place your hard-earned peanuts in my tin and thank the creator you're not in the state I'm in". Nobody else was writing songs for the disabled.

Most people didn't know what it was like to live like that, but Ian had the nerve to write about being disabled and what it was really like.'

As the song draws to a conclusion Ian and his assorted backing vocalists indulge in a pastiche of the classic scene from Stanley Kubrick's masterpiece, in which dozens of slaves stand up and claim to be Spartacus in an act of solidarity with their leader. Instead of saying, 'I'm Spartacus', various voices cried out 'I'm Spasticus' at varying intervals while Chaz's disco groove continued.

While in the Bahamas, Ian was surprised to find himself mobbed by Jamaican band Smokey, who told the singer he was their hero and asked him to listen to their new album. Having been placed in front of an enormous set of speakers with a glass of rum Ian was horrified to see Chaz sneak out of the room grinning. As his enforced stint as a record reviewer unfolded Ian realised why Smokey were being so friendly. Chaz explained, 'In "Reasons To Be Cheerful" one of the lines says "Singalong with Smokey", which related to Smokey Robinson. The band thought Ian was singing about them and that he was a big fan. It was hilarious.'

Having seen *Lord Upminster* fail spectacularly, The Blockheads believed Ian had seen the error of his ways when he reassembled them for a five-week tour of Australia and New Zealand, beginning in November. The band were initially offered just £200 a week each for the trip, but this was to change after Johnny discovered that Ian was netting a £60,000 fee. To make matters worse, a large slice of the money was being spent on an over-sized entourage that included Ian's cousin, both his managers, his agent and two secretaries. Mickey, now ensconced as The Blockheads' 'union leader', waited for his moment before delivering a stunning coup of which Arthur Scargill would have been justly proud.

Having called a meeting with Ian and Peter Jenner, the singer played into Mickey's hands by arriving drunk. 'I told Ian the band wanted £5,000 each and he said, "Who do you think you are? Where's your portfolio?" I said, "I'm representing The Blockheads and what I'm saying is coming from the whole band." He said, "You can fuck off then." I said, "All right" and walked out. I knew Ian had spent £20,000 on non-returnable airfares, and as I was walking down the stairs I could hear Jenner saying, "Ian, you've fucking blown it. You've just lost 20 grand."

'After a while we were told we'd get our five grand each, so I said, "No, we want seven now", and we got it. We all had a great Christmas that year.

It was the only time we ever got anything like that amount and if Ian hadn't been pissed it probably wouldn't have happened. It was never easy because Jenner would say, "No one's indispensable, you're all replaceable."'

The Australian tour is also remembered for another volcanic outburst from Davey. The sax player was indulging in a theatrical trick in which he threw talcum powder into the air to give the impression that he was playing in a haze of dust. Standing nearest to him was Johnny, who found the powder catching in his throat and forming a large pink blob around a cut on his finger. While Davey was distracted by his solo the guitarist sneaked up from behind and threw the talc into the crowd. Davey immediately stopped playing and laid into Johnny with his fists and head, dislocating his colleague's thumb. Again, members of the audience congratulated The Blockheads on their fabulously realistic 'stage fight'.

On their return to the UK the band played one night at London's Lyceum Ballroom but, within weeks, Ian had developed hepatitis and, on his recovery, decided to take one, possibly two, years off. The Blockheads were in limbo. According to Norman, 'As a musician you need to play in order to earn money, so it was frightening when Ian said he was coming off the road. We were all tired and felt we could do with a break but players only want a holiday and then they get back to work. It was fine for Ian to take a couple of years off because he'd had a number one hit and had royalties coming in. He was also getting offers for films and voiceovers, so he didn't need to work.'

Ian's financial position was strengthened even further by the bankruptcy of Blackhill, allowing him to buy all his master recordings cheaply and negotiate new publishing deals for his back catalogue.

Norman, by contrast, faced the ignominy of life at the DHSS: 'I went and signed on the dole in 1982 for nine months. I'd stand at the queue and people would come up and go 'Here, you're Norman from The Blockheads? Can I have your autograph? What ya doing here?' It's bizarre when you think about it. We'd made Ian a big star and now we were being dropped, and no one gave a shit. It left us all thinking, "Well, fuck you, Ian."'

The Blockhead who took most offence was Charley who, at various times over the remainder of his life, instructed lawyers to pursue money from Ian. Norman backed his rhythm partner 100 per cent: 'The Blockheads felt ripped off. We were promised points on various records, but it never amounted to anything because we were told that our wages were an advance on the points.

So we had been paying ourselves to do all these tours, and that pissed everyone off. Charley took it very badly and said he wouldn't work for Ian again and I stuck with Charley.'

What galled the band members even more was their unshakeable belief that Polydor had handed Ian a lucrative contract thinking they were getting The Blockheads into the bargain. Norman claims that on one occasion Ian clumsily tried to hoodwink his own management into believing he had used The Blockheads' rhythm section on a demo: 'Jenny Cotton [Ian's co-manager] rang me up one night and asked if Charley and I had done a session for Ian the week before and I said no. She said, "I thought it wasn't you." He was trying to tell his management it was me and Charley on the demo because he was being told, "You need Norman and Charley", and the stuff he was doing with other people wasn't as good.'

As Ian began preparing for his second album on Polydor, his management asked The Blockheads to back him on the record. Having initially agreed, the band were stunned to discover that they wouldn't receive any money for their input, being informed that Ian had spent most of his initial advance making *Lord Upminster*. When Norman asked what the band's incentive to record the album was, he was informed that, if the album was a success, some money would float their way. 'Me and Charley thought, "Bollocks to that."'

Johnny and Mickey also passed on the opportunity, resulting in Ian hiring a group of young, unproven musicians, whom he named The Music Students. The idea came from a meeting with gifted 20-year-old American keyboard player and bassist Mike McEvoy, who, ironically, had been introduced to Ian by Davey, one of The Blockheads left behind. In early 1983 Ian began writing songs with both Mike and ex-Kilburns collaborator Russell Hardy.

Completing the line-up were German drummer Tag Lamche, Jamie Talbot on sax and Merlin Rhys-Jones on rhythm guitar. Merlin became a close friend of Ian's until the singer's death, deputising regularly for Chaz when The Blockheads re-formed, and co-writing four songs on Ian's final two albums with the band.

Merlin was in his early 20s when he met with Ian and jumped at the chance of working with him. 'I was working at Matrix Studios as a tea boy and, when Mike got me involved me with Ian, it vindicated my decision to leave university and take up music. For me it was a big break.'

Not feeling entirely confident about the album's sound, Ian delved into his past to recruit *New Boots* veterans Ed Speight and Geoff Castle, as well as re-calling Chaz for a spot of lead guitar and Charley on backing vocals. But despite this desperate attempt to paper over the inadequacies of the songs, *4000 Weeks Holiday* was another embarrassing flop. Lacking the inventive spark of The Blockheads, the album sounded as flat as a pancake, with cheesy tracks such as 'You're My Inspiration' and 'Friends' leaving Ian's legions of fans shaking their heads in disbelief. When 'Very Personal' was released as a single in February 1984 Ian found himself, for the first time, mocked by reviewers. The *NME* wrote, 'This monotonous heavy-breathing vocal and polite piped music doesn't sound dirty, sparkling or offensive – it just sounds dull... "Very Personal" is Benny Hill without the laughs.'

Having completed their album, Ian Dury And The Music Students embarked on a difficult UK tour, not helped by the behaviour of the highly strung Mike. According to Merlin, 'Mike was all right in the studio, but on the road he found the pressure a bit too much and would go bonkers and start smashing up hotel rooms. One night in Manchester he came onstage playing bass and wearing a big coat and scarf as if he was cold, and then stuck his head in the bass drum for about three numbers. He decided it was all a bit too much for him so we had to replace him.'

Towards the end of the tour Mickey came on board, playing seven nights in Israel, as well as a handful of UK dates. In his review of a gig at Hammersmith Odeon in April 1984, David Quantick claimed Mickey's presence only succeeded in showing the paucity of The Music Students' abilities. He sneered, 'While the Students plunked away like musical stickmen, Gallagher's keyboards spilled beautifully over everything.' Concluding his review, Quantick quoted a lyric from 'Sweet Gene Vincent' to damn the entire Music Students project: 'I see in Ian Dury no decline to mourn with Thunderbird wine and black hankie, just an annoying tendency to surround himself with the wrong kind of blockhead.'

4000 Weeks Holiday, a reference to the approximate life span of the average human, was released in November 1983, months behind schedule. The reason for the delay was Ian's initial refusal to remove the song 'Fuck Off Noddy', despite the threat of legal action from Enid Blyton's estate. The song contained lines such as 'Winnie the Pooh's having a wank' and spawned a popular range of 'Fuck Off Noddy' T-shirts. Having removed the offending track, the album reached a paltry number 54 in the charts, leading to a disenchanted Polydor axing Ian from the label.

The Blockheads had already realised they were destined to be a mere side project for Ian to dust down whenever he received a suitably tempting offer to play live. But any hopes of continuing as The Blockheads without their inspirational frontman were crudely dashed. The band had already recorded an unreleased album of cover versions around the time of *Laughter*, from which they had released a version of The Beatles' 'Twist And Shout' as a single. But when 'union leader' Mickey visited Stiff to negotiate a deal for the band he was given short shrift.

'I went in and said I was from The Blockheads and they said, "Really? Who are you then?" I said, "I'm Mick Gallagher and I play keyboards." They replied, "Chaz Jankel plays keyboards for The Blockheads", and I was more or less escorted out of the building. It was terrible.'

During the 1980s the various band members went their own way, as they tried to earn a crust. Mickey joined The Eurythmics on tour in 1984, followed by a stint in The Topper Headon Band, with Topper, The Clash's manic drummer. He also went with Norman to the States to help write and record The Clash's *Sandinista!* LP. Despite co-writing a number of tracks, the pair found it almost impossible to receive writing credits once The Clash's lawyers had intervened. Mickey and Norman also played with old friend Eric Goulden (Wreckless Eric) on his 1984 LP *Captains Of Industry*. Towards the end of the decade Mickey embarked on a fruitful seven-year collaboration with Ian on various theatre projects, both with the Royal Court Theatre and the Royal Shakespeare Company.

Norman returned to session work with Charley, an existence that he found far from satisfactory: 'What happened was that people would ring me up for sessions thinking I might end up "doing a 'Rhythm Stick'" on their record. But some of the sessions I did were on really terrible songs. I'll come up with great bass lines if I'm given something great to work on. I can't come up with a great bass line if the song is rubbish, so sessions could be a nightmare.'

Among the musicians Norman played sessions for were Pauline Black of The Selecter, Jona Lewie and Nick Lowe. But the session he is most remembered for was one he and Charley undertook with Frankie Goes To Hollywood. By chance, Norman had met Frankie's lead singer, Holly Johnson, days before the session, having been introduced by a mutual friend.

Johnson and his writing partner Paul Rutherford were in something of a dilemma, with hit-making producer Trevor Horn expressing an interest in recording their material, but using session musicians as opposed to their regular band. Norman advised the fresh-faced Liverpudlian to take the opportunity, telling him that once the record was made he would be able to re-install his back-up band. After his wife Patti had fed Johnson and given him the money for a train ride home, Norman waved the singer goodbye, thinking he'd probably seen the last of him.

The following Saturday, Horn phoned Norman and offered both him and Charley a generous £400 each to play on a session that afternoon. Arriving at the studio Norman discovered he was working with Johnson on the recording of 'Relax'. The experienced Horn was very much in control of the session and instructed a bemused Norman to simplify his bass riff: 'Trevor said, "It's great but can you take out some notes?", which I did. Trevor still wasn't happy and said, "Bear in mind, Norm, less is more." I said, "I'm only playing two notes, if I take any more out there'll just be one." He said, "Well, what'll that sound like?" I played the one note and he loved it.' Horn later transferred his bass part through a Fairlight sampler.

Later in the day Johnny arrived to lay down a guitar part, while Mickey was called in to play keyboards. The single, with its controversial lyric blatantly depicting homosexual acts, was a smash hit, staying at number one for five weeks and making Holly Johnson a star.

With the recent formation of PAMRA, an organisation dedicated to securing royalty payments for session musicians, Norman and Johnny have both enquired about their work on 'Relax', only to find that the grey area of 'sampling' may preclude them from any rights. To add insult to injury, Norman remains convinced that another bass line he was jamming on that day ended up on Frankie's follow-up single 'Two Tribes', which topped the charts for a staggering nine weeks.

Mickey had better luck, receiving an unexpected bonus from Paul McCartney, who has often been unjustly portrayed in the press as being mean with money: 'I did some sessions on a rock 'n' roll album with Paul. I'd received a healthy session rate, but years later I got a cheque from Paul for five grand, as an ex gratia payment. It saved my bacon, as I was really on the edge at the time and I'm very grateful to Paul because he didn't have to do it.'

In 1985 Norman received an offer to play five gigs with former Blockhead Wilko. The pair have played together ever since, touring Japan annually for the past 18 years, as well as undertaking a gruelling schedule across Britain. When Ian first realised that Norman was playing regularly with Wilko he tried to put a stop to it, but the bassist soon killed the argument. 'I told Ian that when I was playing for him I gave him 100 per cent, and I would do the same with Wilko. He said, "Wilko is just your grocery stall", and I said, "Damn right he is."'

Johnny was also busy during the 80s, touring the world with Dave Stewart's Spiritual Cowboys and Paul Young, and making albums with London Beat. In the early 1990s he met up with Karl Wallinger and joined World Party, and also began a long-standing touring and recording relationship with Bob Geldof.

Davey Payne and Charley Charles embarked on brief solo careers, although neither achieved the success that Chaz was enjoying across the Atlantic. Chaz's second album, *Questionnaire*, spawned the number one US club hit 'Glad To Know You', and by the middle of the decade the offers from Hollywood to write film scores had come flooding in. Between 1985 and 1990 Chaz penned seven scores, on films such as *Killing Dad* and *The Rachel Papers*.

Occasionally the band would get together with Ian for a one-off show, but for most of the 1980s The Blockheads simply did not exist. One exception was a brief tour of Japan, instigated by the Japanese singer Kiyoshiro Imawano, a fan of The Blockheads. In September 1986 he invited the band to play as his backing band, providing them with an unexpected windfall. The tour was a great success and the band persuaded Ian to tour with them the following June.

The subsequent tour saw yet another clash between Ian and Davey, who harboured major grievances about his boss's treatment of his charges. One night the band was invited to Imawano's home to watch a video of their performances the previous autumn. Flirting with a selection of Oriental beauties, Ian began mocking Davey's performance. According to Mickey, 'I could feel this terrible vibe and the next thing Davey picked up a bottle and went for Ian with it. I grabbed his arm, inches away from Ian's face. There was glass all over the floor and because we were in Japan nobody had shoes on, so it was a nightmare to clear up. I was mortified, but Kiyoshiro was chuffed to bits and saying "Ah, lock 'n' loll, man. Lock 'n' loll."'

Having returned to Britain, Ian disbanded The Blockheads again and returned to what had become his main career: acting. After making his debut in 1981 in a charity production of *Hamlet* (backed on piano by Mickey), Ian appeared in 16 films, four stage plays, various TV shows and numerous commercials, from Toshiba to *The Sunday Times*. Ian was enchanted with acting and his high profile meant that his services did not come cheap. At one stage he was paid a reported £40,000 to spend barely a week in Los Angeles filming *The Crow*.

In the late 1980s Ian's assimilation into the world of acting was completed when he began dating a young Jane Horrocks, having starred alongside her in Jim Cartwright's play *Road*. The affair, which lasted around a year, was another in a long line of Ian's fiery relationships with women. According to Merlin Rhys-Jones, 'Ian told me they had a row one night and Jane walked off and went up to her flat. Ian ran up to the front window and head-butted it so hard that it smashed. That was one of the times the police were called out.'

In 1989, the musical impresario Max Stafford-Clark asked Ian to write a show for the Royal Court. Ian had already begun writing songs in his Hammersmith flat with Mickey. The keyboard player had hoped that their compositions would be used on a Blockheads reunion album, but when the lure of the theatre came along, Ian could not resist. Mickey explained, 'Ian said we could use the songs we'd written for this musical, which he called "Apples", but what he did was to write a story around the songs, which was completely the wrong way round. The story was as shallow as fuck.'

In addition to his new songs, Ian delved into his past, finally finding a use for the majestic 'England's Glory' and also 'Apples', both written in the mid-1970s with Rod Melvin. But Mickey believes the project was doomed from the moment Stafford-Clark handed over the reins to young director Simon Curtis: 'Simon was very good but he didn't have the authority Max had and wouldn't confront Ian with the inadequacies of the play. He just went with it, hoping that Ian's magic would come off.'

Charley, still in dispute with Ian over money, turned down the opportunity to play on 'Apples' and, out of loyalty to his friend, Norman also declined. Johnny and Davey did take part, though, alongside Mickey, Merlin Rhys-Jones, bassist Dean Garcia and young drummer Steve Monti. Ian played the part of the lead character, tabloid reporter Byline Browne.

For ten weeks 'Apples' was played out in front of largely unenthusiastic audiences and was an immensely frustrating experience for all involved. Even Ian admitted the project had been a mistake. In a 1998 interview with the *Guardian* he confessed, '[It was] a bit of a disaster... I read somewhere that most writers write seventeen books before they get one published, and I've just steamed in and wrote a play...a bit naughty really.' [20]

In a salvage operation, Ian secured a record deal with WEA to lay down 'Apples' on vinyl. It was Ian's first album for five years and led to a tour of Japan under the name The Apple Blossom Orchestra. The LP was recorded under the guidance of Mickey, who found himself dismayed by Ian's profligacy: 'We were given £70,000 to complete the album and I'd completed all the backing tracks with overdubs and backing vocals for about 25 grand. Ian then spent £30,000 putting his vocal on it. I could see the money disappearing in the studio. I remember one day at 4am Ian saying, "Any more alcohol?" and I said, "Ian, I think you've peaked", which only made him worse. He made me stay until eight in the morning.'

In June 1990 Ian and the disparate Blockheads received the devastating news that Charley had been diagnosed with stomach cancer. It was Norman who persuaded his sick friend to visit hospital, after Charley's GP had failed to recognise his symptoms. Charley and Norman had remained great friends after the disbanding of The Blockheads and saw each other regularly, either at Norman's house in Fulham or Charley's home in Willesden, where he lived with his common-law wife Suzy.

Concerned at having neither seen nor heard from Charley for more than a week, Norman made numerous phone calls to the drummer's home, but received no answer. Eventually he got through to Suzy, who told him Charley was ill and had back pains. When Norman arrived at their home he was shocked by the sight that greeted him: 'I couldn't believe how he looked. I said, "Charley, you've lost so much weight, man", and immediately took him to hospital. When we arrived I said to the guy at reception, "We're not leaving here until someone has checked him out thoroughly." We sat there for nearly four hours, with Charley in a wheelchair. Finally he was seen by a doctor, who diagnosed cancer.'

In addition to this devastating news, the doctors uncovered an old fracture to Charley's back that they believed had been caused around 12 years earlier. Charley immediately traced it back to an incident in the West Country in 1978 when he and Ian had been arrested. According to Norman, 'The cops took them in and beat Charley up in the cell, and one of them kicked him in the back. They wouldn't touch Ian 'cos he was a cripple. For years Charley was complaining about his back, but never did anything about it. He just carried on playing.'

Having taken Suzy back home, Norman called the various Blockheads and gave them the shocking news. Wilko suggested a series of benefit concerts to raise money for Charley's treatment and, having secured the agreement of Ian, the band arranged three gigs at the Town & Country Club in Kilburn for the nights of 25–27 September. An added bonus was to be the appearance of Chaz, who had recently returned to live in Britain. At one stage the band took replacement drummer Steve Monti to see Charley in the White City clinic where he was being treated. Mickey recalls, 'Monti asked Charley what advice he had and Charley just said, "Smile." That was Charley all over.'

Tragically, Charley died on 5 September of an embolism, just two and a half months after being diagnosed. The night before his death Norman and Wilko had popped into Charley's home on their way to a gig, and found the drummer in fine form. 'When we got there Suzy told us he'd felt well enough to eat some soup and when I saw him he did look a bit better. The last thing he said was, "I'm going to beat this." I remember saying, "You look great. We'll see you soon." The next day Suzy phoned to say he'd died on the way to hospital. It was horrible.'

Ironically, the last gig Charley ever played was during the encore of a performance by Wilko and Norman at a pub in Harrow after their regular drummer Salvatore Ramundo had been taken ill.

Still mourning their drummer, who had died at the tender age of 45, Ian Dury And The Blockheads played the three arranged gigs to sell-out crowds, but faced the problem of who to give the money to. According to Norman, 'Charley had a Malaysian wife, Patsy, who he still wasn't divorced from, and a boy, Hughie. It was chaos when he died because he didn't leave a will.' Eventually the money was divided between Suzy, Patsy, Hughie and various other family members.

Knocked out by the success of the gigs the band decided to stage a further show at the Brixton Academy in December, with Steve Monti on drums, Merlin Rhys-Jones on rhythm guitar and Will Parnell on percussion completing the line-up. A live recording of the show was released as the *Warts And Audience* album the following year.

The death of his musical soulmate hit Norman harder than anyone in the band: 'I used to see him nearly every day. We were really close, both as mates and as players. We'd played together almost 19 years and there were certain looks and winks he'd give me where I knew exactly what he was going to do next. He was a great guy.'

Mickey is equally fulsome in his tribute: 'From the minute he put his head through the door at our first session he gelled with us. Charley always had a lovely smile. He was a beautiful person.'

At the Brixton gig Ian announced to the audience plans to record a new album with The Blockheads the following year. In 1991 he began writing songs with Mickey and Chaz, but within months took the advice of his management and accountant and recorded a solo album instead. Mickey and Merlin were involved throughout the recording of *Bus Driver's Prayer And Other Stories*, while a variety of musicians, including Chaz, Johnny and Davey, made guest appearances.

The resulting album contained some of the best material Ian had recorded for more than a decade, but was let down by the strange decision to use a lifeless drum machine rather than a drummer. The absence of Norman only added to the feeling that Ian had missed yet another opportunity to make a hit record.

Four songs in particular stood out, the first being 'Poor Joey', a hilarious tale of life as a budgerigar, starring Chaz with his best budgie impression. 'O Donegal', an Irish folk song, was written by Ian and Mickey after discovering that both their families had connections with the region. Mickey had traced the history of the Catholic Gallagher family back to the 14th century, when one of his ancestors was the Black Abbot of nearby Raphoe. Ian's mother's family, the Walkers, were Protestants, having settled in Donegal with their Huguenot tribe. Mickey joked, 'When we wrote "O Donegal" I reminded Ian that his ancestors took all my ancestors' possessions in 1630.' The song, which the pair had already used in a play at the RSC called *The Jovial Crew*, later featured in the film *After Midnight*, starring Saeed Jaffrey and Hayley Mills. Ian also appeared, playing a disabled hotel porter.

'Two Old Dogs Without A Name' concerned the life of roadies, the people Ian regarded as the true rock 'n' rollers. According to Mickey, 'These people had Ian's ultimate respect. Near the end of his life Ian was asked to present the prizes at the annual roadies' convention in Lancaster Gate and the reception he got was fantastic.'

Undoubtedly the cream of the crop was 'Poo Poo In The Prawn', the best song Ian had recorded since 'Spasticus Autisticus'. In a similar music-hall vein to 'Billericay Dickie', 'Poo Poo' concerned the issue of pollution, although Mickey refutes any claim that the lyric was influenced by Ian's first-hand experience of the subject, having contracted polio at a Southend swimming pool aged seven: 'He wasn't trying to pass on any message about his condition. I love this song. We laughed the whole way through recording it. His sense of rhythm was superb, particularly on that wonderful line "They failed to send the technicians in to check the air conditioning, which was unfortunately transmissioning a case of Legionnaire's". No one else can write lyrics like that.'

One incident served as a reminder that Ian's propensity for alcohol-fuelled aggression remained intact. The trio of Ian, Mickey and Merlin had arrived at Jamestown Studio on the Mile End Road in London's East End to record 'Quick Quick Slow', a song inspired by tango dancing. The studio was owned by Merlin's friend Ben Barson, brother of Madness keyboard player Mike Barson. On their arrival Ian took immediate umbrage at having to negotiate a tricky flight of stairs to reach the entrance. When an engineer called Fraser wiped one of Mickey's keyboard parts, earning himself the moniker Fraser the Eraser, Ian's mood worsened further. Merlin had been handed the producer's reins for the track, but his excitement evaporated as Ian's temper spiralled out of control.

According to Mickey, Ian became increasingly unpleasant after each can of Budweiser disappeared down his neck: 'It affected his vocal. The first verse was great but by the second verse he was warbling like Dean Martin. After the long instrumental he had to do the coda of "Give me the quick quick slow" and he was slumped on the chair and gradually falling off.'

Merlin recalls what followed with horror: 'Ian was slagging off Fraser, who couldn't handle it at all. At one stage Ian asked me to go up the road and get some beers, which I thought might help the situation. By the time I got back Ian was threatening to torch the studio. I said, "We'd better go home, it's not working out", but unbeknown to me Fraser had called the police.'

When the police arrived they immediately recognised Ian, but having initially charmed the officers, he turned his hostility on to them. 'Ian was regaling anecdotes, but also being cheeky,' explained Merlin. 'He looked at one of them and said, "Are you homosexual?" After a while he was politely asked to leave the studio and told that if he didn't he would be forcibly removed. Ian ignored them, as he was wont to do, and so they grabbed him and dropped him on the pavement outside.

'I was pissed off because he'd endangered my relationship with the studio, so I said, "Ian, you've fucked up the session. I'm leaving you here. Give us a fiver to get home." He was a bit startled, but reached into his pocket and handed me a fiver and I went. I found out later he'd had a bit of dope on him and had eaten it so the police couldn't find it.'

After Merlin's departure events deteriorated further. Mickey recalls Ian shouting at the officers and spitting on the ground in front of them: 'He had no shame at all. One of them said, "I used to be a fan of yours but I've seen you in a different light." He was drunk and disorderly and causing a spectacle. They cautioned him but he still wouldn't calm down.

'I was saying to the police, "He's a bit pissed. I'll sort him out." But at this stage he'd really upset them and they were waiting for an excuse to arrest him. He was lurching about and his balance wasn't great, so he fell on to one of the policemen who said, "He's assaulting me", which was bollocks. I touched the policeman's arm and said, "You can see the guy's not all together, and he's got polio", and he said, "Take your hands off me or you'll be arrested too."'

Ian was bundled into a police van and taken to Limehouse police station, followed by Mickey in his car. At 3am, having been informed that Ian would be held overnight, Mickey returned home and, after ringing Ian's son Baxter, went to bed. 'The next day after Baxter had picked him up Ian accused me of deserting him in his hour of need. Looking back it was hilarious but at the time, with all the pressure of being in the middle of an album, I was mortified. Every time I hear this track I have a vision of Ian being thrown into the back of a police van.'

When the album was eventually completed Demon expressed its unhappiness at the end product and barely promoted it, despite the LP receiving generally favourable reviews. Mickey says that despite the reliance on drum machines, which 'took away all the record's urgency', *Bus Driver's Prayer* remains one of his favourite albums: 'When Ian died this was the album I mourned to. It seemed to me that his lyric writing on it was very apposite to his life, his slant on things. Where the album failed was Ian's refusal to use The Blockheads. If he'd used The Blockheads I really believe it would have been a monster hit.'

Having worked with Chaz, Davey and Johnny for the first time in years Ian was edging ever closer to recording with The Blockheads again. But it would take a piece of earth-shattering news to finally prompt him into action.

7 Mr Love Pants

The mid-1990s saw Ian's life change dramatically. In January 1995 he became a father again, his girlfriend Sophy Tilson giving birth to a boy, Billy. But great sadness struck Ian during the same month when his beloved mother Peggy passed away after many years of ill health. Three months earlier Ian's ex-wife Betty, to whom he had remained close, had died of cancer aged 52. The loss of two of the most important women in his life left Ian devastated.

According to Merlin, 'There was a genuinely emotional side to Ian. He was deeply compassionate and if the subject of someone's death came up you'd see his face crumple and he'd shed a brief tear, and then suddenly he'd be as right as rain again. He did get very attached to people. Even Charley's death hit him really hard, but his mum's certainly did.' In the months before her death Ian moved into his mother's Hampstead flat to be near where she was being treated. He was to stay there for the rest of his life, while retaining his former home in Hammersmith.

Mickey had spent the best part of a decade trying to persuade Ian to record a new Blockheads album. Employed for some years as his facilitator, Mickey would drive from his home in Harlow, Essex, to London and take his old comrade for walks. The pair would occasionally write songs together, but every time Mickey felt a reunion was in the offing Ian would take up another offer elsewhere.

He explained, 'The reason I stuck around Ian was to do another Blockheads album. I was like a dog with a bone. He kept coming up with projects that were nothing to do with The Blockheads, but he knew that as long as he had me then at the drop of a hat he could have The Blockheads, because I could round everybody up. He took complete advantage of that.'

Key to any Blockheads re-formation was Chaz, who had spent four months in 1993 writing songs with Ian in the singer's rented home in Charvil, near

Reading. After a series of arguments Chaz had cut short their reunion, with Ian calling in Merlin to fill the void. Despite having written some formidable songs in Charvil, neither Ian nor Chaz seemed willing to reignite one of the most potent writing partnerships in rock history. But in 1995 a larger-than-life character by the name of Derek Hussey persuaded the 'Richard Burton and Liz Taylor of rock' to rekindle their relationship.

Derek, known affectionately as Derek the Draw for his knowledge and interest in certain recreational substances, met Ian in 1991 through mutual friends. Within a year he had become the star's minder, albeit one with a different style to Spider and The Sulphate Strangler. 'Up 'til then Ian always liked slightly heavy sorts of minders, geezers who were potential psychopaths, but I wasn't one of them sort of blokes. I'm not seven foot tall and I'm not gonna go out and start whacking people, so Ian said, "We'll change the brief. From now on we'll cuddle them to death."'

Derek quickly became one of Ian's closest friends, being employed as a facilitator, at first unpaid, and accompanying him on numerous overseas visits. A down-to-earth Cockney with a similar sense of humour to Ian, Derek had set up a successful special effects company and was in a position to devote much of his time to his new friend.

According to Chaz, it was Derek who persuaded him to work with Ian again in 1995: 'Derek started to come round and see me in my old studio off the Holloway Road. He described my partnership with Ian as like a nice car that wasn't taken out of the garage enough. The band were all hanging around waiting for Ian to get his act together and Derek thought that if he came round and geed me up a bit, then I could gee Ian up.'

But the Chaz/Ian reunion was to be short-lived. Their relationship, which had become rockier than the Himalayas, soured again as a result of Ian's control-freakery. According to Chaz, 'Ian called me and said, "Wouldn't it be a good idea to do a tour of the States? But we'll have to share rooms and, another thing, I don't want you sloping off to see your uncle", and then he put the phone down.

'I had a friend with me who said, "I don't believe that conversation, you didn't get a word in edgeways." I said, "I don't believe it either. I don't even have an uncle there and if I did I'm not having Ian telling me who I can see or can't see." I was feeling very sensitive about being controlled, so two weeks later I called my solicitor and told him to write to Ian and Mickey, saying I would never perform with the band again, which he did. It was the only way to show Ian that I wouldn't be walked over. Then a couple of days later Mickey came to my studio and said, "Ian's just been diagnosed with cancer." I realised immediately that my timing was wrong and relented.'

Ian had returned from Hollywood where he had been filming *The Crow: City of Angels*, complaining of stomach pains. Convinced he was suffering from irritable bowel syndrome, Ian phoned Mickey to talk through his ailments. Having driven over to Hampstead, Mickey persuaded Ian to see a doctor immediately. 'He looked green, a really weird colour. I said, "You look really bad, man. I'll take you down to the doctors", so we jumped in his car and went to Harley Street where he had some tests. He was diagnosed with stomach cancer and booked himself straight in for the operation, which he had almost immediately. It was the same operation as Charley had undergone, and they took out his intestine.'

After treatment Ian went into remission, but his brush with death made him re-evaluate life and he decided that it was now time to re-form The Blockheads. Talking in 1999 he recalled, 'Four years ago I suddenly said I'm not going to do anything else except a Blockheads album. I'm not going to get waylaid or distracted. My ambition has always been to do a great album with The Blockheads and with Chaz.' 5

'Jack Shit George' opened the album, with Ian in the role of social commentator pointing out the failures of the country's education and welfare systems over a piece of classic Blockheads funk. The band had decamped to the expensive Air Studios to record it, and made full use of the best technology available to lay down a song that was multi-layered but never crowded.

Ian explained the meaning behind what he called his 'protest song' on a Channel 5 documentary: 'In the punk era everyone was shouting and screaming, waving their arms about and saying "This is all rubbish" and a lot of the time they were right to protest and scream and shout. Twenty years before that it was the Protest Movement, all moaning and grumbling, and I thought there are all these people moaning and grumbling and they're not actually replacing it with anything at all. Then I suddenly started moaning and grumbling myself a couple of years ago... The only way really to protest is to make it funny.' 5

The song showed how sorely Chaz's arrangement abilities had been missed. Ian had worked with a host of talented musicians with their own flair for arranging songs, but the singer visibly relaxed with his favoured musical director present. Chaz confessed, 'Music was a mystery to Ian and he used me as a conduit between himself and other musicians. He felt confident when he left musical decisions to me, and used to say "Chaz is usually right", which was amazing. He would champion me in front of others to the point where I'd feel embarrassed.'

A stunning performance by debutant drummer Steve Monti underlined the folly of Ian's decision to use a drum machine on his last album. Known simply as Monti, the drummer forged a formidable partnership with Norman, although both Ian and Laurie Latham, who mixed the tracks, were not convinced of his abilities. Norman, who still plays alongside Monti in Wilko Johnson's three-piece, provided a moment of magic in the song, laying down a backward reverb on his solo, which to his horror he subsequently had to learn to play live.

Originally entitled 'Jack Shit', the song was written by Ian and Merlin during their 1993 sessions in Charvil shortly before a row between the pair broke out. Merlin explains that, having been offered his own £5,000 publishing deal by Ian's manager Andrew King, Ian demanded that he pay the money towards the rent of Strawberry Acre Farm, where they were working. 'I'd been putting a lot of time in at Charvil and putting off a lot of work, so I really needed the five grand. He phoned me up in London and became quite abusive, so I put the phone down. Two minutes later he called and with a tone of pride in his voice said, "You cut me off, didn't you?" I just laughed. He knew he was wrong, but I think that was part of his way. He liked to push you into giving a reaction.'

Despite its great potential, the song's title meant 'Jack Shit George' could never be considered as a single. According to Merlin, 'For a long time the only title on my PRS statements was 'Jack Shit George' and a sum for about 67p. I used to think "I *am* Jack Shit George."'

'The Passing Show' saw Ian in reflective mood but, although many thought the lyrics were a reference to his serious illness, Ian claimed they related instead to the various friends and family members who had died over recent years. He told the *Guardian*, 'That song is not about me. I wrote it before I knew I was ill. It's about friends. Ronnie Lane that would include, and my late wife – and Charley. All kinds of people who died too young.'[20]

Lane, who had been working with Mickey, had recently died after a long battle with multiple sclerosis, and ironically had a band called The Passing Show, although Ian's song title was a mere coincidence. His catchy chorus was one of hope, but also of regret at the missed opportunities of life: 'Although we've got to go/With the passing show/It doesn't ever mean/We haven't made the scene/And what we think we know/To what is really so/Is but a smithereen/Of what it might have been'.

Although the lyric was ostensibly about others, Mickey believed Ian had become more spiritual as he ruminated on the possibilities of his own death. Citing the lyric, 'But when we're torn from mortal coil/We leave behind a counterfoil', he claimed, 'Even Ian, who didn't believe in reincarnation, believed people's lives continued in what they leave behind, that if you'd affected others then you'd live on.'

Chaz's brief was to write around Ian's lyrical rhythm, not dissimilar to that delivered by a US army sergeant jogging in front of his troops and, as requested, played 'a Bo Diddley-type riff' on guitar. Every band member revelled in the freedom that a newly mellow Ian allowed them. Mickey excelled on his trusty Hammond, Norman and Chaz played a counter-melody on bass and piano, while Davey waited his turn before delivering a sax solo with noticeably less menace than usual. Latham helped bring a touch of drama to the mix by keeping Monti's drums very low at the outset before turning him up to full volume as the second verse began.

Mickey believes that Ian's illness had a dramatic effect on his personality in the studio, making him far easier to work with: 'The illness humbled him somewhat. Everything we'd recorded after *New Boots And Panties* had this angst and difficulty about it, but he seemed to have a new angle on life now he might be losing it.'

Norman agrees, claiming, 'It took Ian a long while to realise what he had with The Blockheads. For the last couple of years all he wanted to do was work with us, and he became that humble old Ian again and wrote some great songs.'

'You're My Baby' was a rare Ian love song, written for his son Billy, and was notable for being one of the few occasions he used the word 'baby' in a lyric. Co-writer Chaz says Ian was amused by the idea that this would confuse the listener: 'Ian said, "Everyone thinks they know what to expect from me, but not this time." Generally you expect to hear someone like

Barry White singing "You're my baby", but Ian did it in a very clever way, because he meant it literally.'

Ian grabbed his second chance at fatherhood with relish, having been rather more preoccupied with making a name for himself the first time around. After the birth of Ian and Sophy's second son, Albert, in August 1997 he told Chaz, 'One thing I've learned is you should spoil your kids rotten.'

The song was arguably the most tender ever written by Ian, offering his son 'blankets of security', while being 'proudly at your beck and call'. His lyric captures perfectly the joys of watching one's children develop in front of one's eyes: 'Every day I look at you/And every day there's something new about you…Every time I hold your hand/I'm learning how to understand about you'.

Although popular with Ian's fans, he declined to sing the track live, believing it to be too intimate and personal to share with an audience. Chaz explained, 'He felt it was fine for a record, but not the kind of song he wanted to sing to 2,000 lagered-up punters on a Saturday night.'

Following the low-key 'You're My Baby' was 'Honeysuckle Highway', a hearty tale of unadulterated love. The opening lines sum up the narrator's feeling of gay abandon: 'Exploring every avenue of love on the honeysuckle highway/Eschewing every vestige of regret, we gaily slip along'. The song also contains a piece of magnificent alliteration: 'Cruising down carnality canal in my canoe, can I canoodle?' alone being worth the cost of the record.

With such a suggestive title it is hardly surprising that innuendo lurks close to the song's surface throughout before rising majestically in the final verse: 'Across the Savannah and down to the beach/You munched a banana/I nibbled a peach/You played a small solo/I muffled my drum/You offered a polo/I stuck with my gum'.

The Blockheads believe Ian's new relaxed attitude in the studio helped to improve his vocal delivery beyond recognition. Mickey explained, 'He stopped playing his little mind games because he saw the irrelevance of them. Suddenly he was crooning and singing with so much confidence.'

Chaz believes Ian never felt confidence in himself as a singer: 'It was a psychological thing. He felt insecure about his voice, but every now and again he let it go and just sang. That's what you're hearing on this track and probably on "Geraldine". He was really enjoying himself.'

The Breezeblocks excelled on backing vocals, delivering the line 'Come with me' in a suitably discordant tone in their own sound booths containing individual monitors. 'We had difficulty doing the out-of-tune backing vocals live,' admitted Mickey. 'They sounded in tune when they weren't supposed to. We played this a couple of times, but not for long.'

'Honeysuckle Highway' is Mickey's favourite track on the album, some compliment when one looks at the competition. 'It's so evocative of Paris, with 60s girls in mini-skirts. Chaz's melodica makes him sound like a little Frenchman playing accordion outside a café.'

Chaz, who wrote the music, says part of the lyric reminds him of a very different singer: 'The line "You want magic, I'll provide it", and the way he delivers it, is almost a parody of Michael Jackson.' Ironically, Jackson had been working at Air weeks before Laurie Latham mixed the album there with Ian. According to engineers at the studio, the star had fully lived up to his nickname 'Wacko Jacko'.

Latham says, 'I mixed the album in what Ian fondly referred to as "the Michael Jackson suite". He had a bit of inside information about Air because he only lived over the road and found out that Michael Jackson had been in there with Bubbles, his monkey. After I'd investigated further the engineers told me they were trying to recapture a rough mix that Bubbles had produced at Michael's studio!'

The rip-roaring 'Itinerant Child' saw Ian at his very best, delivering a story sympathising with new age travellers, yet another marginalised group whom Ian had taken to heart. The first verse describes the narrator's 'right old banger' with a humour not dissimilar to that displayed by Madness on their 1982 hit 'Driving In My Car': 'The windshield's cracked, it's a bugger to drive/It starts making smoke over 35/It's a psychedelic nightmare with a million leaks/It's home sweet home to some sweet arse freaks'.

The song showed Ian had lost none of his story-telling ability, with perceptive descriptions of the travelling culture, right down to 'my long-haired children and my one-eyed dog', allowing the listener easy access to his imagination. By the end of the story a fully fledged riot is in progress between the travellers and 'four hundred cozzers holding riot shields'. The result is messy: 'They terrorised our babies and they broke our heads/It's a stone fucking miracle there's no one dead/They turned my ramshackle home into a burning wreck/My one-eyed dog got a broken neck'.

Chaz, who wrote the song with Ian at Charvil, had similar sympathies with the travelling community, although he admits 'Ian articulated it a lot better than I could.' He added, 'Once again it's about people who don't really have any political punch, who don't pay taxes and are therefore unaccounted for. Ian recognised their plight, although there's also a lot of his own self in there. Ian loved to be on the road with the band, and I think that's why he could relate to the new age lifestyle.'

Musically straightforward 'Itinerant Child' was carried by Ian's rhythm, Norman's driving bass riff and Monti's tight drumming. A brief but exquisite piano solo by Chaz intervenes before the outbreak of the riot. At the end Davey's horns reflect the feeling of danger. Chaz remains fond of the track: 'I remember demoing this at Charvil with Ian's drum kit and a little eight-track machine. I liked the chorus and always thought it sounded a bit like The Rolling Stones. Davey's horns towards the end sound like the police arriving. There was often a potential riot in Ian's songs and in this one there actually was a riot, which was his way of showing his frustration and rage at the system.'

The track was mooted as the first Ian Dury And The Blockheads single for 18 years, but after the band recorded a video the plan was abandoned by their record company, East Central One. Mickey dismisses the video as 'abominable' and claims the band's original idea was better. He said, 'We wanted to get the road protester Swampy and his crew on an old battered bus on Hampstead Heath, with ourselves playing our instruments on board. But then Ian asked one of his artist acquaintances, Storm Thorgerson, to do the video. The only band members you saw on his video were me and Davey and we could only be seen either from the back or wearing dog masks. Ian was on a bike wearing a flying jacket, with his head squeezed into a leather helmet. He looked like a potato. It was pathetic and the record company refused to pay for it.'

Although the recording of *Mr Love Pants* was a generally trouble-free period, Ian still maintained the ability to surprise. Midway through recording he informed his shell-shocked band that he wanted Monti off the team, to be replaced by famous African-American drummer Bernard 'Pretty' Purdie. The drummer, whose technique inspired the so-called 'Purdie Shuffle', had a huge reputation across the Atlantic. But according to Mickey and Norman, he also had an ego to match.

Norman warned Ian about the dangers of hiring a musician who may not toe the company line and pleaded with him to stick with Monti. He said, 'Ian was friendly with Purdie and set up a jam with him, Chaz, Merlin and myself, which was great. After we'd jammed for a while Purdie said, "I've got a new name for you, boy. I'm gonna call you Norman 'Fingers' Watt-Roy", which made me laugh.

'But then Ian said Purdie wanted to join The Blockheads. I said, "Ian, he won't join The Blockheads." My mate Alan from The Average White Band knew Purdie well and he said Purdie was known as "Mr Bullshit" because he was always promising to join bands. I asked Purdie if he'd seen Chuck Rainey recently and he said he was doing a jazz session in Munich with him in two weeks' time. So he was the type of guy who goes where the money is and there was no way he'd join The Blockheads.'

Aware of the strong feelings against sacking Monti within the Blockhead camp, Ian tried a different tack. 'Ian was really devious,' says Norman. 'He'd say, "Who would you rather play with, Monti or Bernard Purdie?" I said, "Don't be silly. Monti's great, the album sounds great, and at least he's in the band. Purdie won't join the band, he'll be off doing other stuff and we'll never see him."'

Mickey held similar feelings and told Ian he couldn't stomach life on the road with 'Pretty' Purdie. Ian relented and stuck with Monti, although according to his colleagues, the pair never gelled. After the recording had been completed Ian made one final attempt to bring in Purdie. Mickey explained, 'We were playing the album back at Ian's flat and he said, "I want to do it all again and use Purdie." I said, "What? We've just spent all this money and time and energy." Monti had been our drummer for seven years and had played superbly on this record. Ian turned to me and said, "Ain't I horrible? Ain't I evil?"' When every other member of the band backed Mickey's stance Ian realised he had been defeated and Monti had earned himself a reprieve.

This incident was the latest in a long history of battles between Ian and drummers, reflecting Ian's frustration at never having made it on the sticks himself. Norman recalls that even the consummate musician Charley came in for criticism, from both Ian and Chaz: 'Ian and Chaz would try and get into the drummer's pattern and it would piss them off. Charley managed to fight back and say things like, "I'm the fucking drummer. Stick to what you're doing." I'm the same. If someone tries to tell me what to play I say, "I've been playing bass for 35 years. What do you know?" Ian fancied himself so much as a drummer that he would make Chaz do it as well, and both of them would end up getting to the drummer, Monti especially.'

'Geraldine' was a witty tale of unrequited love, and as Ian had managed so successfully on songs like 'Plaistow Patricia' and 'Clevor Trever', concerned a character whom few would think of writing about. In this case it was Geraldine from the sandwich shop: 'I'm in love with the person in the sandwich centre/If she didn't exist I'd have to invent her'.

The song was inspired by a fresh-faced girl working in a delicatessen in Henley-on-Thames, which Ian and Mickey visited regularly while working in Charvil. According to Mickey, the girl's name was not Geraldine: 'We decided to change the name and I remember rolling my eyes when he came up with the name Geraldine, but it worked in the end. Me and Ian used to go to the deli and, as two old geezers, were enamoured by this youthful girl, and Ian thought it would be funny to write a song about her.'

Ian's lyric contains some top-drawer double entendre, in particular the magnificent couplet 'But when she's buttering my baguette/I think I'm going to burst'. Although not technically complicated, the song did create problems for Chaz. 'I had a real problem remembering how many times Ian said "G-G-G-G-G-G-G-G-G." The band originally thought the "G-G-G-G-G-G-G-G-G" in the chorus was a cop-out but then we realised it was apt because the guy in the song was so besotted that he couldn't even say the girl's name.' The narrator is indeed so lost for words that the only thing he can think of as a conversational gambit is the embarrassing 'That's the nicest badge I've ever seen', a reference to the large name badge worn by the girl in Henley.

Mickey suffered similar difficulties to Chaz while playing the song: 'I played piano on this and Chaz was on the organ and the arrangement with the "G-G-G-G-G-G-G-G-G" was driving everybody crazy. They're not regular and we all had to work out how many times he was saying G.' Having written the music for 'Geraldine', Mickey is quick to praise Davey's solo, recorded after the rest of the band had completed their parts: 'It's a brilliant solo. Davey was such a good player. He painted with the saxophone. There's no unnecessary licks on this. It was the second take of his solo and it was perfect.'

'Cacka Boom' was one of the first songs Ian and Merlin wrote at Charvil, along with 'It Ain't Cool'. Merlin wrote the music with the rhythm of 'Hit Me With Your Rhythm Stick' in mind, but claims the energy of the pair's demo was lost on the version that ended up on *Mr Love Pants*.

Ian's rapping lyric demonstrated his growing maturity as a writer, using his 50 years of life experience to offer advice, without ever preaching. The song begins with a less than serious instruction: 'If you're cold, well here's a plan. Pull the plug out of your fan/If you're hot, now here's a scheme. Park your botty in the stream'.

As the track develops, Ian's advice occasionally ventures into the serious, with the occasional pearl of wisdom: 'No one said you must be good as gold/It's what you *haven't* done that matters when you're old'. He also sings, 'You'll have to come to terms with it, get on the firm with it/If you don't get to grips with it, you've had your chips with it'. As with his lyric to 'The Passing Show', critics later speculated that the song might have been about Ian 'coming to terms' with his cancer. Yet the fact that it was written two years before his initial diagnosis proves otherwise.

Ian's wide vocabulary had already sent listeners scuttling to their dictionaries, using 'necromancy' on 'Jack Shit George', 'encumbrance' on 'The Passing Show', 'sybaritic' on 'Honeysuckle Highway' and 'inamorata' on 'Geraldine'. 'Cacka Boom' was to be no exception, providing the couplet 'If you're dozy, here's a tactic: Tell 'em all they're too didactic'. The final word in the sentence summed up Ian's detestation of singers who preached to their fans. According to Chaz, 'One of the things Ian said to me was, "If you're writing a lyric don't be didactic, don't be preachy", and he was very careful never to do that. His lyrics were never like the Ten Commandments, even though you could pick up a code of living by listening to him.'

Chaz believes that 'Cacka Boom' contained many utterances that related directly to Ian's life: 'The line "You won't have much to talk about if you don't go on walkabout" summed him up. Ian felt that when he was out and about that he would see things around him, and collect information and knowledge for his art.'

The music was dominated by a wonderfully tight piece of drumming by Monti and, in Mickey's opinion, fully justified the decision to retain Ian's current *bête noire*. He said, 'Ian wanted to go down in history as having done an album with the great Bernard Purdie but that would have been a huge mistake. This song in particular shows why the *Bus Driver's Prayer* album doesn't smack you about the head. The drumming was so soulless on that but on "Cacka Boom" you could take everything else off and just listen to the drums.'

'Bed O' Roses No 9' got its unusual name after Ian instructed his manager to search through the records and find how many songs in history had been called 'Bed of Roses'. When Andrew King came back with the answer 'eight' Ian changed the song's name accordingly.

The track was a serious composition, reflecting the tension surrounding Chaz when he wrote the music. 'We were at Charvil and Ian was having a huge row with Ian Horne, our soundman. It was really ugly, the sort of row where neither cared who was listening. I thought, "Why has it always got to dissolve into this tension?" I went into the house and started playing the piano. It was like a lament, as if my soul was talking to me, responding to this atmosphere, but it had a rhythm and I wrote the melody to it and Ian later honed a lyric to it.'

Certainly Ian's lyric was suitably sombre, beginning: 'I've done a lot of things I wish I hadn't/There's other things I never hope to do/But sliding off the map in both directions/Is the sorry mess I made of knowing you'.

Chaz feels that as Ian had done on 'Don't Ask Me' almost two decades earlier, the singer had penned much of the lyric about him: 'Some of the song is having a pop at me. We had a relationship in which I had to be close to him but where I always retained some self-belief and would back off. You can see this in the line "Sliding off the scale of least remembrance is the way you chose to tell me where to go".

'Another example is when he says, "You robbed me of my natural sense of humour and nailed my poor cojones to the door". I gave him the word *cojones*, which I'd picked up from working in LA. It means "eggs" in Spanish and the Latinos say, "Hey man, put your cojones on the table", meaning "your balls". When I used that word in front of Ian he loved it and, needless to say, it came up in this lyric about me. He never actually said, "Chaz Jankel nailed my bollocks to the floor." I just got that feeling and Ian did draw on people for inspiration if he was spending a lot of time with them.'

The musical arrangement was not without its problems. Chaz says that the band tried playing it in 'every single key and we ended up using the first one. Ian couldn't find himself on it as well. It's practically off the scale, even in its final mix.'

'Roses' became a popular addition to the band's live set when they toured the album in 1998 but, as with many of the songs on *Mr Love Pants*, The Blockheads now refuse to play it live. As Mickey explained, 'There's a lot of songs on here that we've thought about doing live that are musically valid. If Ian was alive we'd be playing lots of them, but we find it hard playing them on our own because they're so much about Ian's life and his experience. It just doesn't feel right.'

Despite Ian's claim in an interview with the *Guardian* that 'You're My Baby' was the only autobiographical song on *Mr Love Pants*, his colleagues swear that 'Heavy Living' related to his battle with cancer. The first verse would certainly seem to back this assessment: 'Heavy living is the life that I've led/See the daylight through a curtain of red/Stands to reason why I'm staying in bed'.

Chaz describes the song as 'a portrait of what happens when you live Ian's kind of lifestyle, staying up late and bingeing. I don't think Ian regretted one day of his life but he was aware of the price to be paid for it. He knew he had to clean up his act because he was taking medication and had to be more careful. "Heavy living is the way I'll stay, as if I don't know" was Ian's way, I think, of saying that although he knew the consequences of his lifestyle, he still hankered after it.'

The phrase 'Heavy shitters' is believed to relate to the band's nickname for money. 'We'd say to each other "You got any shitters?",' said Mickey, 'so when he says, "Heavy shitters is the price you pay when you're on a corroder", Ian is pointing out that it takes a lot of money to destroy yourself.'

On his diagnosis, Ian cut back on alcohol dramatically, but Mickey says he found altering his diet more difficult: 'His eating habits were always dreadful. When he was drinking he wouldn't eat because it would make him fall asleep, so he'd drink and drink and drink, and then the last thing he'd say was, "I fancy a kebab." He'd get the kebab, by which time he was absolutely blotto, and stand there and ram it into his mouth. He'd eat the whole thing, including the paper.'

While recuperating from his first operation in 1995 Ian had hired a cottage with Sophy and Billy in Pevensey, Sussex. Mickey had come down for the day and during a coastal drive Ian suggested the pair stop for lunch. 'He had stitches, a bloody great zip in his stomach, and staples holding it together, so I thought I'd get him a nice salad. He said, "No, I want a fried egg sandwich on white bread and I want the yolk runny." I said, "You've just had an operation", but he said, "My doctor said I can eat what I like." Once he'd finished it he demanded an ice cream.'

The song's heavy beat, which fitted the lyric perfectly, was programmed by Ian on the digital drum machine at his flat. Chaz claims Ian gave poor Monti hell trying to recreate the various rhythms he had created at home. He joked, 'If Monti was an octopus he might have had enough hands to hold the number of sticks required.'

'Heavy Living' was notable for two other reasons. The first was Davey's sax solo, which, incredibly, was played without him even hearing the track. Ian simply told Davey the song was in the key of E and to play totally free for four minutes. His part was then slotted into various sections of the song. 'That was an art teacher's approach,' laughed Mickey.

The album ends with the glorious singalong 'Mash It Up Harry', a song that surely would have been released as a single had East Central One had the desire. Yet again Ian had created a character so rich in detail that, by the end of the first listen, the punter felt he had known Harry for years. The first verse describes Harry in a manner similar, yet unquestionably superior, to the character in Ray Davies's 1960s 'Plastic Man': 'He's got his little Y-fronts and he's got his little vest/He's got his little parting in his hair/He's got his little trousers and he's got his little shoes/And he wants a bit of Wembley up his you-know-where'.

Ian exhausts as many types of potato dish as he can get into one lyric, warning the listener not to use them to describe his beleaguered hero: 'Don't call Harry a human potato, don't call Harry a spud/Don't call Harry a walking King Edward/Harry's made of flesh and blood'. Later he sings, 'Don't call Harry a human potato, don't fry Harry tonight/Don't give Harry a chip on his shoulder/Harry's doing alright'. Even the chorus – 'Mash it up, mash it up, mash it up Harry' – sounds like an instruction to a canteen chef.

Ian admitted that when he first wrote the song he was mocking Harry, but eventually found himself warming to his character. He said, 'I think Harry's doing all right. I respect him for getting a house and a car and a garden and a mower…It's almost a wistful song from someone living the bohemian lifestyle, possibly like myself, who would love a bit of that routine. I do like him a lot, even though he's a spud, even though he's a walking King Edward. It's the bloke in Hancock's film *The Rebel*, with the bowler hat on, going off on his routine.'[5]

By the end Harry's salvation is revealed as the nation's favourite pastime: football. As the song plays out, The Breezeblocks engage in the terrace-style chant 'We're on our way to Wembley/We're on the Wembley Way'. As Ian explained, 'The only light that comes into his [Harry's] life is that Shearer moment when the ball goes in the net at Wembley.' [5]

Chaz makes the point that Ian's sudden empathy towards Harry at the death was similar to his change of heart in the last verse of 'Blockheads': 'It was the same as when he said, "You're all blockheads too". Sometimes Ian felt uncomfortable with his lyrics until he found that empathy.'

'Mash It Up Harry' saw Ian and Monti clashing yet again. The drummer was struggling with the rhythm dictated by Ian and, according to Chaz, asked the singer to allow him to 'play it the way I feel it'. Having tried out his own style at Chaz's rehearsal studio, Monti's suggestion was rejected by Ian. Chaz explained, 'Ian felt his rhythms were rooted in his reality. There was a struggle, a pain, an anger, and in a way he wanted to feel that spirit in all the musicians he played with. He wanted to feel that they weren't just there to play jazz funk with him, he wanted to feel commitment come through in their playing. That's why he used to wind up Johnny before a guitar solo because he thought it made him play better.'

More than 30 seconds after 'Mash It Up Harry' has apparently brought proceedings to a close we hear Ian holding court with his mother's dog, Lucky. 'It's Ian sitting in his flat late at night doing a bit of writing and interacting with the dog,' explains Mickey. 'He starts saying "woof" to the dog and it sounds like they're doing a duet and then you can hear him saying "Down, boy" because if the dog knocked him over there was nothing he could do. It was a nice touch, especially with the pictures of the dog on the album cover and on all the artwork.'

Mickey remembers Lucky, whom he regularly took for walks with Ian, with a mixture of affection and alarm: 'Ian looked after Lucky when his mum died, but he couldn't look after himself, let alone a dog. The dog was a cross between an Alsatian and a Dachshund. It had six-inch legs, one of which was disabled, so the two of them would limp round Richmond Park together. It was a hilarious sight. This dog was totally uncontrollable and was from Battersea Dog's Home. Ian couldn't walk it, so I had to do it, and it would tear around chasing everything, even the deer.'

The finished product was regarded by band members and critics alike as Ian's best album since *New Boots and Panties*. Ian even told interviewers that his new record was the only one worth listening to after *New Boots*, and claimed that spending more time on the writing process had been the key to

The Blockheads prepare to go onstage in 1978. Standing are Johnny, Charley, Ian, Norman and Davey. Seated is Mickey

'Oi Oi!' Ian prepares for a photo shoot, circa 1980

Ian wearing his prisoner's stage outfit, circa 1979

'You talking to me?' Mickey does his best Robert De Niro impression, flanked by Johnny and Davey, circa 1980

Life after Chaz – Mickey, Norman, Ian, Johnny, Davey, Wilko, and Charley at the Hope and Anchor, circa 1980

Norman, Ian, and Johnny alongside
a female violinist during the TV
recording of 'Sueperman's Big Sister'
in Holland, 1981

Clowning around – Norman and Ian prepare for their unofficial Royal
Wedding gig at Crystal Palace in July 1981

Pass the Durex – Ian holding a Greek
toilet roll in Athens, 1982

The Pearly King – Ian holds court
backstage in 1978. Fred 'Spider'
Rowe sports an Ian Dury T-shirt
behind

Charley, Ian, Mickey, Norman and Johnny milk the applause in Sittard,
Holland, March 1978

Ian (with a heavily made-up black eye on display weeks after his bust up with Omar Sharif), Davey, Mickey, Mike McEvoy, Norman, Charley and Johnny (seated), 1982

Norman, Mickey and Johnny plotting in Dingwalls, November 1984

Captain Dury and his men – Ian (wearing cap) with Chaz, Mickey, Norman, Johnny, Gilad (obscured) and Dylan, Croydon 1998

Ian with the beginnings of his trademark impish grin in Japan, 1996

Ian flanked by Mickey, Chaz, Steve Monti, Norman and Johnny, 1996

A gaunt Ian listens to Johnny after one of his final shows at Warwick in
December 1999

I'm a Blockhead, get me out of here – Mickey pleads to be let off the fire
escape in 2002 as Norman, Johnny, Dylan, Chaz and Gilad look on

Photograph courtesy of Robin Watson

Two heads are better than one – Chaz and Mickey playing keyboards at a 2001 show

Photograph courtesy of Jim Drury

The author sitting alongside Chaz in 2003, with Derek, Johnny, Norman and Mickey behind

its success. He said, 'If you've got time you can always get some quality. If you haven't got time you end up making not very good records, which is what I've been doing for a long time.'[1]

Ian's colleagues confess to being bowled over by the quality of Ian's lyrics on *Mr Love Pants* but fear that some songs may have too much depth for the listener to appreciate fully. Chaz explained, 'It's hard for people to feel the full measure of this record because there's so much good material on it. It will take years and years to unravel. Lyrically it's so rich, so well researched, and so witty. Most records have a lot less dimensions to them.'

It was perhaps ironic, considering the comparisons with *New Boots*, that Ian found it as difficult to muster the interest of record companies in *Mr Love Pants* as he had with his debut LP two decades earlier. By March 1997 the album had been mixed by Laurie Latham but, incredibly, it was not released until June the following year. Eventually it was the relatively small company, East Central One, that took on the album in Britain, Ian negotiating a separate deal for mainland Europe with another company. The record sold a respectable 20,000 copies in the UK, although nowhere near what the quality of the songs deserved.

The album's title came about during a conversation between Ian and Monti about a friend of the drummer who had written a song called 'Mr Love Pants'. Ian found the title highly amusing and decided it was ideal for his comeback album. Monti's friend, a lad named Dean, was not amused, as Norman recalled: 'Dean was this speed freak who used to come and watch Wilko. He'd be up the front pogoing all night, shouting, "Faster, faster." We got friendly with him and eventually he started roadying for Wilko. He had written his own electronic music, which wasn't very good, and had this song 'Mr Love Pants', which Monti helped him record.

'When Dean found out we were using his title he went berserk because he thought we'd nicked his song. I explained to him on the phone that we didn't even have a song called *Mr Love Pants*, that it was just the title of the album, and that titles couldn't be copyrighted. Dean wasn't having any of it and said his lawyer was going to sue us, which was ridiculous. When Ian heard he offered to take him on tour with us as a support act, but Dean didn't want to know. I was saying to Dean, "You can launch yourself with this." He could have cashed in on it, but he was silly and went to his lawyer. Of course, it all came to nothing in the end.'

In January 1998 Ian received the devastating news that he had secondary cancer after an ultrasound scan revealed nine malignant nodules on his liver. Doctors warned him that he could be dead within eight months. In his determination to survive, Ian began paying for various expensive treatments, at one stage admitting that he had spent £60,000 fighting the disease.[21]

That year Ian began taking an experimental form of self-administered chemotherapy in which he would receive bursts of chemo drugs for one 60-hour period per week. He explained to *Time Out* that every week he would be 'plugged into a machine from ten o'clock Tuesday morning until ten o'clock Thursday night'.[19] The treatment worked and Ian went back into remission.

Realising that the disease could strike again at any time and that he was probably living on borrowed time, Ian made further changes to his life. In April 1998 he married long-term girlfriend Sophy, the mother of his two young children, and a woman who had brought great stability to his life. In Mickey's words, 'Sophy was a very sweet girl who was great for him, especially in the years when he was having such difficulties. He was a very lucky boy and she was completely besotted with him and hung on his every word like a pearl of wisdom. She totally believed in him.'

A month after his wedding day Ian was confronted at home by two tabloid reporters who had got wind of his illness. Forced into a corner Ian decided that rather than giving the 'red tops' the satisfaction of announcing his illness, he would do a 'spoiler' interview with a broadsheet rival. Thus it was the liberal-leaning Sunday newspaper the *Observer* that exclusively revealed to the world that one of the country's most loveable stars had liver cancer. A media frenzy followed and at one stage that year Bob Geldof, relying on an erroneous newswire story handed to him in his radio studio, announced live on air that Ian had died. Having realised that the information was false Geldof was mortified and apologised profusely.

With rumours of his demise greatly exaggerated, Ian was eager to get back on the road with The Blockheads and booked some UK dates to coincide with the release of *Mr Love Pants*. Little was the band to know that by the end of the year two of its members would be sacked.

First to go was Monti, who was fired over a mix-up concerning a gig in Nottingham. Having only recently been given the responsibility of booking gigs, Mickey told all The Blockheads to be available on a particular date. He informed them that, although the gig in Nottingham was in effect a firm booking, ultimately Ian's doctors would have to give the all-clear nearer the time.

Two weeks before the gig Ian was given his doctors' blessing to perform and Mickey excitedly rang round his colleagues with the news. He was horrified to discover that Monti was unavailable because he was going to America to play with Curve. A dumbfounded Mickey recalled to Monti their earlier conversation: 'I said, "Hang on Monti, you've known about this gig for months." He said, "Yeah, but you never confirmed it."'

When Mickey informed Ian of the problem the singer sacked Monti on the spot. Although critical of the way Ian had treated his drummer during the recording of *Mr Love Pants*, Monti's colleagues had little sympathy with him over his dismissal, particularly Mickey: 'I was really upset at Monti. He put me in a very difficult position.'

Norman also backed Ian's decision, saying, 'Monti's loyalty should have been to us because he was a full-time Blockhead and we were promoting a record whereas he had already left Curve once before and he was only on a wage. Monti kind of sees it himself now.'

Ian asked Mickey to contact Bernard Purdie as a replacement, only to find that the drummer had committed himself the day before to another show on the same night. Ian decided to cancel the gig but, when Mickey called the band's agent to pass on this news, he was issued with a dire warning: 'The guy said to me that we should just do the gig with anybody. He said the shit that would hit the fan if we didn't turn up, with all the speculation about Ian's health, would be worse and we'd never get over it. His view was that even if it was a bad gig, it didn't matter.'

Ian was still not convinced, believing that the band's material was too difficult for a drummer to learn quickly. But a threat by Norman to quit The Blockheads helped change his mind. The bassist explained, 'I said to Ian, "Listen man, I need the money. I'm the bass player and if I say it's going to be cool you should have enough respect for me to go with it. If you blow out this gig then I don't want to fucking work with you any more because I'm fed up with this."' Ian relented, though not before phoning Monti to blame him for Norman's threatened walkout.

Chaz and Davey had a replacement in mind by the name of Dylan Howe, and gave his telephone number to Norman, who found the drummer keen to play with The Blockheads. Norman explains, 'I said to Dylan, "We've got three days' rehearsals booked in. How long will it take you to learn our set?" He said he could do it in one afternoon, which he did. I sent him all our songs and he listened to Charley and scored all his parts out exactly the same.

'At the rehearsal Ian sat in the corner and never said a word, which was unheard of. Dylan sounded exactly like Charley because he'd learnt Charley's drum parts note for note and Ian thought it was incredible.' Dylan has remained with the band ever since.

Although disappointed at his dismissal, Monti held no bitterness towards either Ian or Dylan and, indeed, turned up to watch his replacement play with The Blockheads at a gig that summer in Victoria Park, where they were supporting Paul Weller. According to Norman, 'I was walking offstage with Dylan, who'd had a blinding gig, and I heard Monti shouting out, "Oi. You stole my gig." Dylan didn't know who Monti was at first, but when he found out they had a good laugh about it.'

It was at the same eventful gig at East London's Victoria Park where Davey was finally to receive his marching orders after 21 years with The Blockheads. The sax player had been in a volatile mood all day, having been informed by Mickey that there was not enough room on the band's coach to accommodate all his family.

According to Mickey, 'I arranged enough transport for everyone to take wives and kids, but Davey had something like eight kids coming and there wasn't enough room. I said to him, "You'll have to arrange some transport 'cos ours doesn't stretch to ten people for one member of the band." I got his wife and two youngest kids in, then queued myself in the searing heat to get tickets left at the gate for the rest of his family. He had the raging hump and didn't enjoy the gig.'

After the show Davey, who rarely drank, downed a large whisky before storming into Ian's changing room to complain about not getting enough money. Mickey recalls that Ian's response was to say, "Davey, I'm dying. I don't give a shit." Unable to counter such a remark Davey walked out, seeking a way to vent his angst.

Catching sight of his wife chatting to Mickey's eldest son Ben, Davey steamed over and punched him in the face. 'Ben's a big lad who could have knocked the shit out of Davey, but because it was Davey he didn't want to hit back,' claims Mickey. 'Davey was really going for him. We all jumped on him and said, "What's going on?" Davey's shouting, "Ask Ben. He knows."

I took Ben aside and asked what had been happening. He said, "Absolutely nothing, I'm just talking to her."' Having convinced those restraining him that he had calmed down, Davey broke free and launched himself at Ben again, kicking him repeatedly.

After the pair had again been separated Mickey sought out Ian with the demand, 'It's either him or me.'

'The fact that he'd gone for my son said to me he really wanted to go for me, and that given enough time he would have. Davey was the type of person who'd smile at you, then you'd turn your back and he'd smack a frying pan round the back of your head.' With Mickey being the 'bagman' responsible for getting gigs and handling the money there was no contest for Ian, who immediately sacked Davey. The sax player's apologies for once fell on deaf ears and his 26 year relationship with Ian Dury was over.

Strangely, Mickey still claims to be 'good friends' with Davey, and attributes much of his former colleague's violent temperament to the strained relationship he had with Ian. He says, 'I don't think Ian was good for him at all. Without saying a word Ian could wind Davey up, just by his attitude. In retrospect some of the mad incidents with Davey were amusing, but at the time they were scary.'

Norman also keeps in touch with Davey, confessing, 'I love him to bits. He's an amazing guy, not technically the greatest player or musically proficient, but he played in such an eccentric way. The stuff he came out with was so off the wall that he'd blow you away every time. Davey was, and still is, a total original. He'd never repeat himself when he was playing, which isn't easy to do. He was an important factor in The Blockheads musically and visually but, unfortunately, he didn't get on with anyone except me and Wilko.'

Whenever Davey comes up from his Cornwall home to visit London he stays with Norman, whom he believes shares the same sense of humour. The bassist explains, 'Davey often used to say to me, "The others don't get it, Norm. Ian thinks I'm a dangerous person, but he sits there and watches *Goodfellas* and when Joe Pesci shoots the guy in the foot he said it's great. All I'm doing is fisticuffs, like at school." Now I can understand that. But the fact is he was hard work for the others.'

Davey's replacement was Gilad Atzmon, a six-foot-plus Israeli who had recently moved to Britain. An accomplished, award-winning jazz musician with his own record deal, Gilad had taken the British music scene by storm. He had a remarkable background, one that his fellow band members were in awe of. In Norman's words, 'Gilad's such a learned guy. He's got a degree in philosophy, he's been in the Israeli army and written a book all about his experiences there. Some of the stories he tells are amazing. He's only 40 and I think, "Shit, he's done so much in that time, more than I ever have. I've just been playing bass all these years."'

Norman claims that it is too simplistic to say that Gilad replaced Davey because both their styles are so different: 'I miss Davey, but I love Gilad's playing so much. Davey couldn't do what Gilad does, just as Gilad doesn't do what Davey did. Gilad has to be the best sax player musically I've ever seen. He's a genius, the Charlie Parker of today. He's so musical and his playing is so exciting. Everything he plays sends a shiver down my spine.'

Having completed a stunning comeback album with The Blockheads Ian was eager to return to the studio and start writing again and, by the end of 1999, had recorded four songs for a new album. This was despite yet another relapse earlier in the year, one that many thought would prove fatal.

The band had booked two weekend gigs in Belfast and Dublin but, after the first night, Ian called Mickey at 4am complaining that his legs had swollen up. A doctor was called out to see Ian but after a quick examination advised Mickey to take him to hospital immediately. 'I took him to Belfast Hospital and, 'cos it was a Saturday a night, it was chaotic and full of pissed people screaming at the police. We waited for ages and Ian kept trying to let other people go before him because he thought they looked worse. I said, "No fucking way, we'll take our turn."

'When he was eventually seen he was told he'd be kept in overnight, and he went chalk white. He'd always been a private patient and now faced the prospect of staying in an NHS hospital in Belfast. So he turned to me in front of the doctor and said, "We've got a gig to do. I'll be back in London on Monday morning." We got him out of the hospital at about 8am, got a bit of a kip, took the train to Dublin and he did the gig. He raised his game and was superb.'

But the two gigs had taken their toll on Ian and when the band arrived at the airport Mickey thought the worst: 'He looked yellow and I thought, "That's his liver packing in." I took him to Harley Street the next day and he was told that the cancer had clamped over one of his liver ducts in such a way that they couldn't bypass. They said, "There's nothing more we can do." By this time he was so yellow he looked like the King of Siam.'

There was one remaining hope. One of Ian's doctors advised Ian of a controversial new treatment called gene therapy, illegal in the UK, but available in Egypt. With nothing to lose Ian decided to become a human guinea pig and travelled to Cairo, accompanied by his loyal lieutenant Derek.

'Ian's doctors had said the doctor in Egypt wasn't cutting edge, he was just behind the cutting edge,' explained Derek. 'It was a considered stance, so Ian decided to give it a whirl. When we got to Cairo Ian had to go into a clinic and have a jab every day for three or four days. It was a very simple, non-invasive treatment and we'd chill out the rest of the time.'

Mickey had convinced himself that Ian's death was imminent and was astounded to see the singer return from Egypt looking fit and well: 'When he went to Egypt we all thought we'd never see him again. Then two weeks later he came back looking fantastic. His hair had even started growing back. He thought it was a miracle cure and his doctors in Harley Street couldn't believe it.'

Ian's colleagues are full of admiration for the courage he showed throughout his five-year battle with cancer. According to Chaz, 'Ian was incredibly stoic. I never once heard him complain about the pain he was in. He was such a fighter.'

Derek believes Ian's disability helped Ian to come to terms with cancer: 'Ian's disability paved the way for dealing with this problem. In a way Ian's whole attitude to life was that he was invincible. He had polio but he acted like an ordinary person, even more so, and never let it get in the way of what he wanted. When he got cancer he kept the same positive attitude.

'When CancerBACUP approached him for help for their charity, which looked after the relatives of people who have got cancer, he never let anyone get despondent. He never sat back and felt sorry for himself. From the day he first knew he had cancer until the day he died I only ever saw him show his worries once. We had a hug one day and he said, "This is really getting me down", and then two seconds later he was back to normal and saying, "Spin up a joint, Del."'

When interviewed in the late 1990s Ian always insisted that he would not let his illness affect him mentally. He told BP Fallon, 'I try not to let it change anything. I haven't shaken my fist at the sky. I had a couple of cries early on and I cry when people write me amazing letters. I got one from this hard nut saying, "No way are you going to roll over on this one."' [21]

In the same year Ian admitted to the BBC that he was in all probability dying, but that the financial cushion he would leave his family helped soften the blow. He said, 'It probably will be terminal, but whatever the time span I've got I've no idea. I don't really spend a great deal of time thinking about it. I only get upset when I look at my kids and I think I might not be there to see them grow up. That does me right up but as regards looking after my family, luckily I can do that as well.

'I'm not anywhere near a millionaire or anything like that, but I've got enough [so that] they can survive. Anyway, Sophy's a brilliant sculptress so she'll make a living anyway, but knowing there is that cushion there is very good for my spirit. Having seen my other two kids grow up I've had a good crack anyway. Plus the fact I've had a major crack at life, more than most people get, so I won't feel hard done by.' [1]

In addition to providing his services to CancerBACUP, Ian also found the time to perform charity work for UNICEF. In the role of a goodwill ambassador Ian was joined by Robbie Williams for a mass inoculation programme against polio in Zambia in 1997 and Sri Lanka in 1998, eventually being named a UNICEF Special Representative. On both visits he was accompanied by Derek, who recalls how moved Ian was by the experience.

'In Zambia Ian spotted straight away the patronising way that people in charge of the vaccine programme spoke to the kids. It was like a 1950s children's home and I think it brought back a lot of memories about his childhood. Ian would report back to the UNICEF offices and tell them what he had seen and how the money was being spent, and he got quite a lot out of that. He was chuffed to be asked because he knew he was regarded as a potential loose cannon. Ian did a lot of stuff for other people but he never blew his own trumpet. He always tried to arrive unheralded and leave by the back door.'

Towards the end of 1999 Ian's cancer had taken hold again and a second trip to Egypt was unsuccessful. In November he was honoured, along with Chaz, at the Q awards, winning the Classic Songwriter Award, but was too ill to walk to the stage to collect his trophy. Speaking from his seat at the band's table he paid tribute to The Blockheads. He said, 'There's only one thing for me better than writing songs and that's playing with them Blockheads and they're all sitting here.'

Chaz, whose idea it had been to thank The Blockheads, added, 'It's really down to the band as much as anything. They give the songs the character they wouldn't have if we'd just done them as a duo.'

Ian was by now desperately ill and some in the audience believed it might be the last time he would be seen in public. But this was clearly not a man to roll over and accept his fate. In any case, Ian still had one long-held aspiration that lay unfulfilled. As the world moved into a new millennium the singer would finally achieve a life-long ambition.

8 When We're Torn From Mortal Coil

In the 1950s Ian's mother had regularly taken her son to London's West End to attend *Sunday Night At The Palladium*, then a staple of British entertainment. It was here that Ian watched his music-hall heroes Max Miller and Max Wall and, on one occasion, he sat open-mouthed as American crooner Johnnie Ray was showered with bouquets from adoring female fans. For the rest of his life Ian had dreamed of playing at the Palladium but the opportunity had never arisen. It was therefore a fitting finale to Ian's career when he was invited to perform there with The Blockheads. It was to be his last ever concert.

On 6 February 2000 Ian Dury And The Blockheads took to the stage in a show billed as 'New Boots and Panto'. Ian arrived at the theatre in a wheelchair, looking frail and gaunt, and many of his friends and fans found themselves visibly shocked by his appearance.

Laurie Latham had been working with Ian towards the end of 1999 on four songs that would provide the basis for *Ten More Turnips From The Tip*, but Ian's relapse had halted proceedings. When Laurie arrived backstage at the Palladium he hadn't seen his old friend for months and left the gig in little doubt that the end was near: 'I saw Andrew King at the bar after the show and he said, "Laurie, you've got to go and say hello to Ian because he'd be really upset if he knew you were here and didn't speak to him." Reading between the lines I thought this might be the last time I saw Ian. It wasn't what Andrew said, but the tone of his voice.

'So I got backstage with my kids and there was Ian sitting in a wheelchair. He'd looked so good onstage but I was quite taken aback. He'd obviously deteriorated a lot since I'd last seen him. He was so charming and had a chat with the kids. He said, "Laurie, we're gonna get back in the studio really soon", and I was thinking, "I can't really see it." He looked so gaunt. Sure enough we didn't go back in.'

According to Merlin Rhys-Jones, Ian's former manager Jenny Cotton was left distraught and Chaz recalls various other people backstage appearing momentarily stunned on their first glimpse of Ian.

The gig itself was a roaring success with Ian, unable to stand, sitting onstage on a flight case, singing his heart out. Chaz claimed it was the most in tune he had ever heard the singer. He said, 'I wondered if it was because he'd always needed to be "earthed" because he had something to sit on. When he was standing up he was always very unsteady on his feet, but this time he didn't have that to worry about.'

Despite his frailty Ian still performed some of his old stage tricks, waving handkerchiefs in the air and pulling various items from his bag to amuse the crowd. He even mustered the strength to sing the high-energy 'Spasticus Autisticus' in a set based largely on his first and last albums. The band played in the following order: 'Wake Up And Make Love With Me', 'Clevor Trever', 'Passing Show', 'What A Waste', 'Billericay Dickie', 'Itinerant Child', 'Mash It Up Harry', 'Spasticus Autisticus', 'Bed O' Roses No 9', 'Reasons To Be Cheerful', 'Sweet Gene Vincent', 'Hit Me With Your Rhythm Stick' and a blistering encore of 'Sex And Drugs And Rock And Roll'.

At the end Ian received rapturous applause from his devoted fans and the show received rave reviews in the press. The *Daily Mail* opined, 'His East London humour and music hall charm is best witnessed onstage... With the crowd accompanying him loudly on older songs, the warmth of Dury's reception transcended the usual enthusiasm of a pop audience.'

Having seen Ian regularly over the previous six months, members of The Blockheads had witnessed his decline in gradual stages, so it was perhaps inevitable that the looming certainty of Ian's death passed them by. According to Chaz, 'To be honest, at that point we all knew he was ill but I didn't know how ill. None of us knew it was going to be our last gig. Maybe I was a little bit more naïve than the others.'

But Chaz was, in fact, no more naïve than his comrades, who refused to believe that it was the end. Indeed, The Blockheads continued booking a series of gigs for the rest of the year.

Norman said, 'The Palladium was a brilliant gig, but I didn't think it was going to be the last one. I dropped him off that night with Derek. He was very frail, but I never thought I wouldn't play with him again.' Only Johnny admits to thinking 'at the back of my mind' that Ian would never appear with The Blockheads again: 'I didn't want to give that thought the light of day because I always try not to focus on the negative.'

Ian never gave up hope of a recovery and the week before he died bought a brand new computer on which he planned to write his autobiography. Tragically the world was to be denied what would no doubt have been a hugely entertaining read.

On 27 March 2000 Ian passed away at his Hampstead home, surrounded by his family. Mickey was the first Blockhead to hear the news, having received a call from Sophy. The grief-stricken keyboard player then phoned his fellow band members and various other mutual friends to inform them of Ian's death. The Blockheads were stunned.

According to Chaz, 'It was a shock because although I'd been used to seeing Ian unwell, he was such a fighter and I just thought he'd hold it at bay. I saw him about ten days before he passed away and he was finding it more difficult to walk. He was a one-way ticket at that point but I didn't realise it would be the very last time I saw him.'

Norman was equally distressed: 'I was gutted when I heard Ian had died. I loved the guy. When I met him I was only 25 and he was about 35 and I'd never come across anyone like him. He changed my life. The only person who was comparable was Bob Dylan, who influenced a generation by using lyrics that everyone could relate to. Ian did that in this country using his own accent. He died far too early. I wish he was still around because he had so much more to give.'

Two of his former colleagues both admit to feelings of guilt at Ian's death, an understandable but entirely illogical reaction common to those grieving for a loved one. Johnny had driven over to Hampstead to see Ian a few days before his death only to find the singer sleeping. 'I was talking with Sophy and Baxter and, knowing I was outside on a yellow line, I went and put some money in the meter. As I came back in he woke up, so I went in to see him, but he was struggling to breathe and was coughing. I said, "I'll come back another time" and, stupidly, I left because I thought I was going to get a parking ticket. I didn't realise he was dying, so I never got to sit with him and have a final chat. I feel sad that my last vision was of Ian trying to sit up and coughing.'

Merlin had last seen Ian two weeks earlier but received a phone call a few days before he died. 'I didn't realise it, but he was saying goodbye. I said "I'll see you Monday" and he replied, "Yeah, right, see you Monday", and there was a tone in his voice that suggested it wasn't going to happen. It was only after he died that I realised this and I felt awful. I'd love to have seen him one more time.'

The next day the newspapers were packed with fulsome tributes to one of Britain's greatest entertainers of the past quarter-century. In an obituary in the *Guardian* Robin Denselow wrote, 'Ian Dury, who has died of cancer aged 57, was one of the few true originals of the English music scene, the only man to successfully combine the energy and excitement of rock 'n' roll and funk with the bawdy humour, wit and home-spun philosophy of music hall and of his native Essex. The fact that he had been crippled since childhood, and was severely ill during his final years as a performer, merely added to his stature. He was truly brave – both physically and in the way he approached his music.' [22]

It wasn't just the press that paid tribute to Ian. Within hours of his death, CancerBACUP, for whom Ian had worked tirelessly, issued a moving statement on its website. It read, 'The work Ian did with CancerBACUP made an enormous impact and his character and enthusiasm made a lasting impression. He was our hero.'

Speaking more than three years after Ian's death, the remaining Blockheads still get misty-eyed when asked about his passing.

Norman echoed the thoughts of the band when he said, 'Everything brings a smile to my face about Ian, even the bad times. Nothing makes me angry. You had to go though the bad things and we all learned from them. He was a very caring guy and there was a side to Ian where if he could do things for you he would. He would help people financially if they were going through hard times. And I think he cared about The Blockheads because he knew we were special as well.

'If we hadn't met Ian we would have been just another muso band, a bunch of shoe-starers. By that I mean musicians who just stare at their shoes while they're playing. We never fell into that category because although we could be boring old farts musically, we had this guy in the middle that was taking all the attention.'

Derek also remembers with great affection the friend with whom he had spent so much of the past nine years: 'Ian could be a bit of a so-and-so at times but, during his last few years, he had a deep sense of love towards everybody. When we were out and about Ian would always keep me in the conversation and tell people what I did. He made me feel very much part of the family. In our downtime we'd go to art galleries and it was educational. I always felt I knew a little more about Ian than I did when I went in.'

Chaz believes that Ian's spirit remains 'in the blood' of The Blockheads. He explained, 'Ian and I always had a very spiritual relationship and, in the light of that, I don't believe his death was the end. It might be the end in terms of him printing out lyrics on a page and me writing music to them, but Ian's death didn't end our thoughts about each other. I believe that Ian's spirit endures in The Blockheads and is still driving us on.'

On 5 April Ian's funeral took place at Golders Green Crematorium, bringing north-west London to a standstill. Ian's coffin was carried in a horse-drawn hearse, the police having blocked off several roads to cope with the crowds. On the hearse's arrival at the cemetery Chaz, Johnny, Norman and Mickey carried Ian's coffin, alongside Lee Thompson and Chris Foreman from Madness. A black cloth embossed with the Blockhead logo had been laid on his casket.

Some 250 mourners from all walks of life attended the humanist service, including former government minister Mo Mowlam, various painters, and singers Robbie Williams, Neneh Cherry and Nick Lowe. There was barely a dry eye in the house when The Blockheads assembled at the front of the crematorium to play an acoustic version of the beautiful 'You're The Why', one of the last songs Ian had written.

It was a day of high emotion for all present and it took some serious effort from The Blockheads to concentrate on their performance. Johnny recalls, 'I just felt like my heart was ripped out and put back together with Blu-Tack. I was a shambles emotionally, but I managed to get through the day and we then had a wake for him that night.'

The wake took place at the Forum in the form of a mass drinking session, accompanied by plates of jellied eels and pie and mash. It was the kind of evening Ian would have loved. As the booze flowed through the day a variety of performers got up to sing, including Wreckless Eric, Wilko Johnson, Humphrey Ocean, Carl Smyth from Madness and Ronnie Carroll. In a wonderful tribute, Ian's son Baxter was led on to the stage by Derek, just as his father had been for the past nine years, and sang 'My Old Man', accompanied by The Blockheads.

A few months later Derek and his wife joined Sophy and all four of Ian's children at the singer's old home in Digby Mansions, Hammersmith, to conduct a final farewell. Derek explained, 'We went outside with Ian's ashes and I'd written a passage by Kahlil Gibran, from *The Prophet*, about friendship. I made it into a little paper boat, on to which we sprinkled some of his ashes. Me and Jemima and Baxter climbed over the fence and on to the jetty and sent him down the river towards Southend. They used to throw his old legs off Hammersmith Bridge, so Baxter threw one of his sticks off the bridge, and we watched the boat sail off. We had a cuddle and a little cry and a couple of glasses of port and that was it. It wasn't sad at all.'

9 Ten More Turnips From The Tip

In the months before Ian died, East Central One had expressed its desire to release a new version of *New Boots And Panties* for the 21st century. The plan was to ask ten leading artists known to be admirers of Ian to record a song each from the record. Ian informed his label that he wanted no involvement himself in the album, but gave the project his blessing.

The brains behind *Brand New Boots And Panties*, East Central One's Jamie Spencer, found that it wasn't difficult to persuade artists to take part, but that coaxing them into the studio was another matter. In the months immediately after Ian's death just two songs were recorded, 'My Old Man' by Madness, and 'Billericay Dickie' by Billy Bragg And The Blokes. Spencer sensed that the project was losing momentum and asked The Blockheads to record the music for the eight remaining songs themselves. This would leave eight artists with the simple task of sending a recording of their vocal by post.

Robbie Williams appeared briefly at the studio to sing 'Sweet Gene Vincent', beating a disappointed Paul McCartney to the punch. McCartney, who also visited the studio, chose instead to deliver a mighty version of 'I'm Partial To Your Abracadabra'. Wreckless Eric found himself singing 'Clevor Trever', the track originally written for him 23 years earlier, while Sinead O'Connor selected 'Wake Up And Make Love With Me'. The remaining songs were divided up as follows: 'If I Was With A Woman' – Cerys Matthews; 'Blockheads' – Grant Nicholas; 'Plaistow Patricia' – Shane MacGowan; 'Blackmail Man' – Keith Allen.

Released in April 2001, *Brand New Boots And Panties* featured a painting of Ian by Peter Blake on the front, while the 1977 cover of Ian and Baxter appeared on the reverse. Fifty per cent of the album's net profits were donated to CancerBACUP, the organisation for whom Ian had done such sterling work.

The album had brought The Blockheads back together in the studio for the first time since Ian's death. Each band member found the experience enjoyable, and in some ways cathartic, but was still unsure of what lay in store for The Blockheads.

Although grief-stricken by the loss of their mentor, there remained a feeling of unfinished business in the camp. Four new songs recorded with Ian six months before his death lay on the shelf, while a handful of others had been abandoned once the singer's illness entered its final stages. Remaining sensitive to the ongoing mourning process within the Dury family, The Blockheads felt it unseemly to ask permission to finish the follow-up album to *Mr Love Pants* that Ian had so wanted to complete.

The six musicians went their separate ways and, according to Mickey, it looked like the end of the road for the band. Their only planned engagement for the remainder of 2000 was a tribute gig for Ian at Brixton Academy. A variety of artists joined The Blockheads onstage that night, including Mick Jones, Robbie Williams, Wreckless Eric, Tom Robinson and Kirsty MacColl. Other guests included former Kilburns member Humphrey Ocean, comedians Keith Allen and Phil Jupitus, actress Kathy Burke, and Ian's former girlfriend Denise Roudette. Davey Payne also rejoined The Blockheads for the night.

After the Brixton gig the band were apart for three months, before Ian's widow Sophy made a chance discovery among Ian's papers. Mickey recalls, 'Sophy found a list, which was almost like a will. It was a list of song titles, including the four we had already recorded, underneath the title 'Ten More Turnips From The Tip'. Sophy then spoke to Chaz and gave us her blessing to finish the album.

'Ian had kept the writing and formation of the album very close to his chest. He probably had songs under way when he died but we didn't have access to them. His estate said we could have only limited access to archive material, so we dug out our demos from the previous ten years in order to find six songs to make up the record.'

The band decided to bring in Laurie Latham to help produce the album, in a bid to maintain continuity of sound. Latham was initially sceptical about the project, but soon found himself won round: 'I hate it when somebody dies and shabby records are thrown together with out-takes and demos and you know it's just to cash in. So I was a bit reluctant and suspicious about doing it but when I heard the quality of the material I thought it would be great. The songs were really strong and I think Ian would have endorsed it and been happy with it. Sophy was very concerned as well, but I reassured her that I wouldn't have worked on it if I thought it was inferior.'

'Dance Little Rude Boy' was one of the initial quartet of tracks recorded with Ian at RAK Studios, and supervised by Latham. The song originated from a piece of music written by Chaz, to which Ian added a lyric. Chaz remembers, 'I came up with the idea for the skanking rhythm guitar pattern that Johnny plays after sitting and imagining I was onstage rocking with The Blockheads. I came up with a funky groove, went into my studio and built up a whole piece of music based around it.

'I mapped the verses and choruses out and gave them to Ian. After he'd finished his lyric he said that it was the one of the easiest songs he'd ever written. Ian had written so many songs that he sometimes wanted someone just to give him a brief rather than having to conjure something from nothing.'

The music allied off-beat reggae to funk, with Norman adding some typically stylish bass lines. Ian's lyric had a lighthearted feel, representing another colourful vignette of British life, this time concerning the dance floor: 'With your sweet cologne and your mobile phone/And the moves of a desperado/You will cut a swathe on your gangster's lathe/With an overdose of bravado'.

Shortly before mixing the song with Ian and Laurie, Chaz spotted two unusual out-takes on a demo while listening at home with wife Elaine: 'Just before Ian comes in at the beginning he says, "Hey", and the timing was so off the cuff that when he tried to record it again it didn't come out right. So I suggested to him that we keep the original "Hey". Elaine then noticed that just before he got to the first chorus he said, "You've got to know somethiiiiing" in a really eccentric manner, which he never did on his final vocal.' Having made the suggestion to Ian, Chaz persuaded Latham to add it to the mix.

According to Mickey, 'I Believe' is a prime example of Ian producing his best vocal delivery in his first take: 'Many of Ian's first guide vocals were the best but for some reason he wanted to slave away and lash himself to death trying to get a better vocal out.' Mickey held the only known recording of the song, having demoed it with Ian at Sonnet Studios in 1991. Ian's performance contained one minor slip in which he stifled a laugh, but his colleagues believed the error added character.

Mickey explained, 'A lot of the time with Ian you'd never get the whole lyric. He'd give you a chorus, a verse and the middle eight and develop from that. Often he wouldn't finish writing it until the morning of recording. I'd written "I Believe" with him but had only been given part of the lyric. I was in the control room that day and when he got to the line "I believe in good advice and not too much to drink" everybody cracked up because Ian could drink for England. Ian saw our reactions and in the next line he laughed. He would never have used that himself, but we thought it was so endearing that we felt he would have forgiven us our trespasses.'

The song had been written at Ian's Hammersmith flat, where Mickey had brought his Hammond organ. It was originally intended for submission on *The Bus Driver's Prayer And Other Stories*, but Ian had surprisingly rejected it. 'I don't know what his reasoning for scrapping the song was,' admits Mickey. 'Sometimes if you liked a track then he would say he didn't like it and scrap it, which was a bit demeaning. He'd ask your advice, you'd give it, and then he'd do the opposite.'

The omnipresent drum machine that had so hampered the tracks on *Bus Driver's Prayer* was present on this original demo, accompanied by Mickey on organ and a synthesised bass. Convening at Helicon Mountain Studios with Laurie in early 2001 the band transformed the song with a series of overdubs. Norman and Johnny were added on bass and guitar, while Chaz played both keyboards and guitar, on the latter creating a driving riff that dominated the song. Dylan and Gilad, both making their debuts on a Blockheads record, were also included, the Israeli playing the flute. 'I Believe' has since become a mainstay of The Blockheads' live set, with Johnny successfully adapting his Geordie tones to sound like a fully fledged Cockney.

'It Ain't Cool' was written by Ian and Merlin at Charvil in 1993 but, according to the latter, was vetoed from the batch of contenders for *Mr Love Pants* by Chaz, who believed the vitriolic lyric was aimed at him. According to Chaz, 'I remember when he first played it to me he walked out of the room and left me listening at full volume. We had been battling at this time and the atmosphere was very tetchy. He never actually said it was about me, but there are lots of references that I can see.

'For instance, the line "You think it's cool to brush aside the little people you despise". I think Ian sometimes thought I could be a little cold when he asked me about people. He'd say, "What do you think about so-and-so?" and I might say something witty about them and it would sometimes backfire. I could tell he didn't think I was compassionate about certain issues or people.'

Merlin has some sympathy for Chaz's claim, explaining that the singer had 'ways of talking in riddles and parables when he wanted to make a point. During one rehearsal I was showing Ian some chords and he went into a parable about a man sitting on his veranda. It was a long, shaggy dog story, the moral being "Don't build your veranda on somebody else's back lawn." We were all sitting hushed in the studio, thinking, "Which one of us is building a veranda on Ian's lawn?"'

Yet Chaz insists that his primary objection to the song was on musical grounds: 'To be honest I didn't particularly like the song because I find the melody a little mundane. It's "Last Train To Clarksville" by The Monkees revisited.'

When Ian and The Blockheads reconvened in late 1999 Chaz was persuaded to rearrange the song: 'I changed a few chords and made it a bit more Blockheads friendly.' Laurie Latham is given credit for the song's intro, switching the jam that The Blockheads had originally chosen to end the track to its beginning.

Mickey remembers the song fondly because of the interaction between himself and Chaz on keyboards: 'We'd started getting more into playing two keyboards. Chaz played the original electric piano on the track and then I overdubbed some piano and organ parts. The first piano solo is mine and the electric piano solo is Chaz. We'd been playing together for 20 years and were starting to blend and complement each other. Sometimes I listen to the later songs and think, "Is that me or is it Chaz?"'

Written by Ian and Chaz, 'Cowboys' was another song taken from the 1991 Sonnet sessions. Ian's original vocal from the demo was enhanced, along with the backing vocals of Chaz and Mickey, the latter describing their performance as 'sounding like a couple of old geezers from Kentucky'. Again the various Blockheads added overdubs, with Dylan and Norman replacing the original synthesised rhythm section and Johnny playing banjo.

The track reflected Ian's love of country music, the singer being a particular fan of Patsy Kline, Willie Nelson and Jim Reeves. Chaz says Ian had great respect for the ability of country lyricists to convey vivid stories: 'Ian thought the most interesting lyrics were tales of everyday events, which you find in country music. He also liked the whole image of country music singers.'

Ian's lyric in 'Cowboys' acts as a detailed critique of fame, the singer dismissing the predictable warnings that rising stars are issued with by so-called experts: 'They quote the many stars who died so young/From the firmament you seek to walk among/They tell you who went mad, who went from good to bad/And they warn you of the dangers that await the highly strung'.

Ian attacks the negativity of the critic, in particular the peculiarly British habit of building up and then knocking down the country's heroes: 'Who the hell are they?/And who cares what they say? Who only seek to worry and alarm/Don't give those dogs their day/Don't let them get their way/Cos I can see that fame's done you no harm'.

Although the song was written many years before Ian met Robbie Williams, some critics falsely believed 'Cowboys' related to the former Take That star. It was not an unreasonable assumption to make, and indeed Ian, who offered Robbie his wisdom on their trips with UNICEF, made the comparison between the two singers during a Channel 5 documentary: 'I work with Robbie Williams, who's experiencing that very thing [fame] now, probably four times as much as I ever had and it's extremely hard work and extremely important that you hang on to whatever it is that keeps you thinking you're OK, whatever that little nugget of something is, self-belief.' [5]

Mickey cites the lyrics to 'Cowboys' as proof of Ian's writing becoming more masterful with age. He said, 'The song has one marvellous couplet: "They tell you cherish every minute that you're hot, so at least you'll have some memories when you're not". It's a killer line. People don't know what they missed if they haven't read Ian's lyrics. Ian saw them as a way of passing on knowledge indirectly. He would intrigue with his lyric and there was nearly always a killer punchline. That line is the killer for me on this whole album.'

The tour de force that was 'Ballad Of The Sulphate Strangler' followed, a fulsome tribute to Ian's former minder, the larger than life Pete Rush, who died in the early 1990s. A former roadie with Yes and Led Zeppelin, Rush had met Ian in 1976 after a Kilburns gig. Impressed by his imposing physical presence Ian befriended Rush, dubbing him 'The Bournemouth Buckaroo'.

As Ian's lyric stated, Rush was 'born to Jack and Marge in 1951'. Ian wrote the song in around 1993, but decided to omit it from *Mr Love Pants* to spare the feelings of Marge, who at the time was still alive. Mickey explained, 'Ian was very sensitive to that but Marge, bless her, must have known what Pete was like, because he lived with her for most of his life. He was addicted to vodka and all imaginable pills. Marge was a fitness fanatic, one of these old dears who went swimming in the sea every day.' With Marge's death in the late 1990s The Blockheads felt able to resurrect the song for *Turnips*.

An occasional presence on the Stiff tour, Rush initially found himself in Spider's shadow. Yet by the time the band toured the States in 1978 his behaviour had become the major talking point backstage, earning himself the rather more apt moniker 'The Sulphate Strangler'. According to Norman, 'He was absolutely mad and used to drink a bottle of vodka neat in one go. Mickey and I came back to the hotel in Cleveland after a night out and the Strangler was sitting there out of his head.

'We went up to him and said, "How's it going, Pete?" and he said, "I'm gonna strangle that geezer over there", while pointing at this tiny little guy sitting across the bar. Then he lunged at the guy, grabbing him by the throat with his massive hands. Me and Mickey jumped on him and pulled him off, but he then caught hold of my throat and I could feel him squeezing. I thought, "He's trying to strangle me", but Mickey got him off me on to the floor and I kicked him in the balls. Luckily our tour driver was there, an ex-Vietnam paratrooper, and he got hold of the Strangler. Fred [Spider] came down from his room and calmed everything down, so that the hotel wouldn't call the police.'

At the beginning of the song the listener can hear Ian sipping a mug of tea and saying 'Are we rolling?' before counting in the rest of the band. The band added this unscripted studio moment as 'a tribute, a little reminder of what Ian was like in the studio,' explained Mickey. Chaz's musical arrangement recalled the start of 'Sweet Gene Vincent', with Ian's introduction being sung melodically over a 3/4 waltz rhythm before the song's sudden transformation into heavy rock. The chords for the song's introduction had been written years earlier by Norman, earning himself a rare writing credit.

Ian's lyrics describe Rush's physical appearance in great detail, with lines such as 'He wore a thousand earrings and a diamond on his tooth' and 'The Strangler on his roller skates was over six foot ten'. As a roadie for stadium bands, Rush often used roller skates to get around venues.

According to Chaz, 'Ian described Pete very well. He was all high energy, speeding everywhere, with black curly hair, pockmarked skin, and earrings. He looked a bit like Brian May and wandered around in boxer shorts and a vest. He always wore very bright clothes.'

Norman remembers Rush turning heads as the pair strolled around San Francisco: 'He said "'ere, Norm. All these people are staring at me." I looked at him and said, "You're six foot seven, you've got a tiny pinhead, and 12 earrings in each ear. You don't exactly look normal." He was a bizarre guy, but a lovely geezer.'

Mickey also recalls the Strangler with affection: 'He was a fearsome sight but soft as anything really, although very volatile. Ian dubbed him the Sulphate Strangler early on because of his love of drugs and his speciality of grabbing people by the throat, lifting them off the ground, and biting the end of their nose hard. He used to have an asthma inhaler, which contributed to his drug intake 'cos he got a bit of a high off it.'

As the Strangler's behaviour in the States degenerated further, Ian was eventually forced to sack his minder: 'When we got to New York City we had to let him go/Cos the dramas going on backstage were better than the show'.

There are two versions of Rush's dismissal. Mickey recalls one of the band finding a firearm stored by the Strangler in the drum kit. Norman remembers Rush at one stage pulling out the gun, but says the final straw for Ian was when Spider caught him attacking a girl backstage.

Having been sacked, Rush lost touch with Ian but was persuaded to contact his old friend by Chaz in the mid-80s, after watching the then former Blockhead perform with his Johnny Funk Band. After their reconciliation Rush left the Bournemouth council flat he shared with his mother and moved in with Ian and Baxter in Hammersmith. He eventually returned to Bournemouth before suffering a fatal heart attack while in police custody.

'I Could Lie' was the last Ian Dury And The Blockheads song ever written and is believed to have been one of six titles on the list found by Sophy Dury. It was also the first time anyone other than Ian had sung a lead vocal on one of the band's records. Ian had never been well enough to lay down a vocal, so Chaz had sung on the demo and on recording the song in 2001 manfully stepped into the breach again.

Chaz continues to perform the track with The Blockheads and says he has to 'method act' to deliver his vocal. He joked, 'Ian's lyric was autobiographical, so when I sing the lyric it sounds like that's the sort of character I am.' The song is brutally honest, with lines such as 'I could sneer before I could sigh' and 'I was awful in thought, word, and deed'.

The chorus was more simplistic, consisting of Chaz singing 'La-la-la-la-la-la, La-la-la-la-la-la-la': 'When I recorded the demo I thought Ian needed to put a chorus in so I just put "Lalalalalala" in there temporarily, but Ian thought it was great and kept it in. It was almost as if he'd written all he had to say on the subject and couldn't think of anything else.'

A harpsichord skips through the track's beginning, recalling Ian's work writing Elizabethan plays with Mickey. 'I did stuff with Ian for the RSC, plays written in the 1640s, but that Elizabethan beginning was suggested by John or Chaz,' explained Mickey. 'It was an indulgence that had nothing to do with the song, but it nodded in the direction of the Shakespearean work we'd done.'

The original track included Chaz on a Wurlitzer piano, to which Mickey overdubbed his organ. Gilad's weighty sax solo added further colour to the spectrum. In addition to helping the band reach the number of tracks required, it also acted as a marker for what The Blockheads could do without Ian. As Mickey said, 'It was important because it represented being on our own. If people wanted to know what we sounded like without Ian this was a step in that direction, even though the song had been written by Ian.'

'One Love' was another from the Sonnet archives, written by Ian and Chaz after the latter had returned from living in America. The song contained one of Ian's rare romantic lyrics and, according to Chaz, reflected his feelings of contentment at the time: 'If Ian had been off the road for a while and left to his own devices he would write very warm, philosophical pieces. When he was calm that came across in his lyrics, but when his life wasn't happy he would use lyrics as a form of attack.

'During one of the periods when he was in a happy disposition we wrote a lovely song called "I Want To Get Lost In The Country", which I hope one day we can do something with. Unfortunately we don't actually own the tapes.'

In fact, there are numerous demos of Ian's songs that the band does not have access to, and that sadly may never see the light of day. Songs written with various members of The Blockheads include 'It's Down To You', 'Come And Find Me', 'Christopher True', 'The Ghost Of Rock 'n' Roll', 'Dick The Dancing Duet' and 'Plastic'. He even hooked up with Steve Nugent in the late 1990s to write a fabulous track called 'The Actor', in which Ian adopted the air of the luvvies that he had so enjoyed working alongside during his screen and stage career.

'One Love' has a strong Latin American feel, containing steel drums and Johnny on maracas. Chaz, who revealed that Billy Ocean plans to record the track one day, says it reminds him of Bob Marley's song of the same name:

'It's got a universal endorsement of love, in the same way Bob Marley had in his song.' 'One Love' now has a permanent place in The Blockheads' live set, with Johnny on vocals, and the band playing a slightly different musical arrangement.

In the lyric Ian writes fondly of the idea of there being 'one love' for everyone, and Mickey believes the song may have been written as a riposte to the AIDS epidemic forecast at that time. The chorus is idealistic, almost naïve: 'One love, and only one/One love to last forever/One love, only one love/One love, it's now or never'.

'Happy Hippy' was a relic of the *Mr Love Pants* recordings, narrowly missing the album's final cut. The Blockheads chose not to re-record the drum or flute parts, so the contributions of Davey Payne and Steve Monti were retained, as they had been on 'Ballad Of The Sulphate Strangler'.

The humorous lyric saw Ian playing the role of a spaced-out hippy who has 'disavowed' the 'rat race' in order to reach a higher spiritual plane. Wearing 'beads and Roman sandals from now on', and eschewing chairs and tables for a 'purple cushion on the floor', Ian sings of his character's ability to 'keep my head above the clouds'.

As Johnny's sitar conjures up images of the narrator meditating on the floor Ian's hippy expresses his joy at having dropped out of society: 'Immune from all achievement since I threw away my telly and my phone/In my pastel pyjamas spending every waking moment getting stoned'.

Merlin, who lectures at the London Centre of Contemporary Music, as well as playing with various bands, wrote the music to 'Happy Hippy' at Charvil. The guitarist claims he never fully understood the brief given to him by Ian and, as a result, is unhappy with his composition.

He said, 'I had problems with this because Ian wanted us to do it at quite a high-tempo pace and I thought it should be a bit more laid back. It wasn't until quite recently that I realised the irony of the song, that the character wasn't really a hippy, but an uptight person, hence the fast tempo. Ian would never explain things, he'd just let you get on with it. I think if I'd properly perceived what the song was about I would have made a better job of it.'

The story behind the composition of 'Books And Water' is remarkable, and worth telling in depth. In late 1998 Ian and Chaz were walking around Primrose Hill when the former uttered the phrase 'books and water' out of the blue. Six months later Chaz was working in his studio and constructed a complicated piece of music, which he thought would be perfect for The Blockheads. Without thinking he called it 'Books And Water'.

After demoing the music Chaz called Ian to say he had an unusual piece of music that he thought his writing partner should hear. Chaz recalled, 'I went over to Ian's home the next afternoon and he looked at the cassette which said, "Books And Water" on it and smiled. As he was listening to it he said, "No no no, I didn't have this in mind at all. I was expecting something much more vulgar."

'He stopped the cassette and rummaged through his lyrics and eventually found a piece of paper and read a cappella his verses for a song called "Books And Water". He had in front of him three 16-bar verses and as he was reading it to me my bubble had burst because I thought I had something very exciting and he was telling me what I'd done was of no use to him. As I was listening I had a sudden bit of lateral thinking and said, "Hang on a minute. In the piece I've written there's two 16-bar verses." I restarted the cassette and when it got to a certain point I said, "Start your verse here", and when he did it fitted like a glove.

'He and I looked at each other and my hair stood on end. I said to him, "There is a God", and he replied, "Yeah, there is." It was the only time he wasn't agnostic. It was like telepathy. I believe that's what happens when you have a very close bond with somebody. We'd known each other for so long and we knew and liked each other's styles, and that's why this must have happened.'

Chaz and Mickey both insist that the lyrics relate specifically to Ian's impending fate. According to Chaz, '"Under every slab there's even more kebab" is referring to bodies under gravestones; "And with your arse in hock" relates to him knowing that he was in trouble, and didn't know how much good his chemotherapy was doing. In the first verse he sings, "It's the sea green snot that really hits the spot". That was part of the chemo, all this stuff inside his body that was an uninvited guest that he couldn't get rid of. The title summed up what Ian thought was important in life. Ian loved reading and had a thirst for knowledge, and swimming was a great therapy for him.'

Chaz's complicated arrangement reflected his desire to allow his colleagues complete freedom to show their abilities: 'I did things like put a bass solo slap in the middle of the piece. It was almost like I was saying to Ian, "Look, these guys you've got are something else. Let's not just give them solos in unimportant places, let's give them solos where they matter." Johnny got a guitar solo as well.'

The marriage between lyrics and music successfully expressed the emotion of what Ian was going through with his illness, and his widow Sophy is said by Chaz to regard the song as 'extraordinary'. The sarcastic, atonal laughter of The Breezeblocks added to its poignancy.

'Books And Water' was played live by The Blockheads, both with and without Ian, who dubbed the song 'the hard one'. As Mickey explained, 'The song is quite intricate in the way it is built, and everybody's part is integral to what happens next. It's not a straightforward song at all. It has a strict arrangement that Chaz wrote and everyone adhered to.'

Performing the song since Ian's death has involved sharing the three verses between Johnny, Chaz and Mickey, adding to the stage drama, but the band have now removed it from their set. They believe, in the same way as with the majority of *Mr Love Pants*, that the lyric is too personal to Ian. Mickey said, 'We don't do it any more, even though Dylan and Norman really like playing it. I was wary about us singing about Ian's condition. It never sat well with me, but I'm glad we recorded it for this album.'

Between 'Books And Water' and the album's final track, a poem written and read by Ian's old drinking partner Jock Scot was included, at the request of Sophy. Their friendship went back to the Stiff tour of 1977 when the band played Green's Playhouse in Glasgow. Scot came backstage in full Black Watch regalia, with kilt and sporran, and began spouting Scottish poetry. Having told Kozmo Vinyl that he had never been outside of Glasgow, Scot was cajoled on to the bus and stayed for the rest of the tour. He is now a successful poet.

Mickey recalls, 'Jock was very funny and everybody loved him. He was always a sounding board for Ian. Jock wrote that poem after Ian died and it's very much in the spirit of their relationship because they were both interested in words.' Scot still follows The Blockheads and can be seen pogoing in front of the stage whenever they play in London.

Having sung 'You're The Why' at Ian's funeral, Chaz might have been expected to repeat the trick when it came to recording *Ten More Turnips From The Tip*. But a chance conversation between Johnny and Robbie Williams at the service changed events.

Johnny revealed, 'Robbie heard us play "You're The Why" at the funeral and said, "That's a really gorgeous song. If you ever want anybody to record it, I'll do it." I told Robbie that was really odd because I'd actually dreamt the night before that he'd done exactly that.'

'You're The Why' was the penultimate song that Ian and Chaz wrote together, but the singer had been too ill to perform on the demo with The Blockheads. According to Chaz, 'I'd had Ian's lyric for a while and now and again I'd look at it in my studio to see if anything came naturally to me. Eventually I got the basic idea together and recorded it with my acoustic guitar.

'I got very excited when I came up with the guitar line at the point where the lyric goes "I want you 'til the seasons lose their mystery". When it appeared in my mind I felt it was a gift from above. I put a guide vocal on and gave it to Ian and he smiled and said "ker-ching", making a sign with his hands indicating a cash register.

'The lyrics were incredibly succinct. In fact, I could have done with an extra verse, although I wouldn't say it was actually incomplete because Ian had said everything he wanted. When we first started to write together Ian was a lot more wordy and I'd often have the unenviable task of editing his lyrics. When we came to record this song we repeated the last two verses. But it's so economical, and beautiful to look at on paper.'

Chaz is justifiably proud of the song, believing it to be as good as anything he ever wrote with Ian: 'For me it was symbolically the climax of our writing and shows a man at peace with himself. The lyrics sound passionate without being syrupy. It's a very special song and I feel very lucky to have written the music to it.'

Former Northern Ireland Secretary Mo Mowlam invited The Blockheads to her house after Ian's death, and when they played her their recording of the song the politician was overwhelmed by its power. During a subsequent television interview she quoted the entire lyric, leaving The Blockheads open-mouthed.

Mowlam had become friendly with Ian in the final years of his life, having fought cancer herself with courage and dignity. Derek recalls with fondness a trip he made with Ian to the MP's house in Islington when she was Northern Ireland Secretary.

'I pulled up outside her house with Sophy and Ian, and a copper walked down the drive and said, "I'll park your car, sir." It was full of marijuana fumes, but he turned a blind eye. When we got to the house Mo was at the door and said "fuck" six times before we'd even hit her front room. We had dinner with Mo, her husband, Michael Cashman and Lord Falconer. We had roast beef and got well lashed up. It was a very relaxed evening and I went out and had a spliff in her garden, which was probably caught on CCTV.'

Ten More Turnips From The Tip is both lyrically and musically accomplished, its quality perhaps only fractionally below that of *Mr Love Pants*, a remarkable achievement considering the circumstances in which it was made. A fitting epitaph to Ian's career, the album also persuaded The Blockheads that they still had much to offer, and ended any suggestion of the band splitting up.

Chaz echoes the feelings of the four original Blockheads still remaining, by stating that 'everybody played fantastically' on *Ten More Turnips*. He is also full of praise for Laurie Latham, an ally whose long history of working with the band helped them get the best from each track. There is no doubt that, together, Latham and The Blockheads had constructed a genuine Ian Dury studio record, as opposed to what many feared would be a hotch-potch of studio out-takes. As Chaz summarised, 'The balance between production and music is spot on. I have a few minor gripes, but it's a fitting tribute. We should all be proud that we did Ian justice.'

10 Where's The Party?

Nobody within the Blockhead camp was under the illusion that life after Ian would be easy. Despite its obvious commercial value as the last ever album by Ian Dury And The Blockheads, the band initially struggled to interest their record company in *Ten More Turnips From The Tip*. According to Mickey, the band also felt hurt by a series of thoughtless remarks by those working for the label.

'When we went into East Central One we were told that the reason we'd had reasonable sales for *Mr Love Pants* was because we "had the pity vote going for us". How could anybody say we had Ian's illness "going for us", as if it was a positive? It was horrible and uncalled for, but that's the way people are in this business. Another person at the record company said, "What you need is a little bloke with a Cockney accent and a walking stick", and we said, "That's exactly what we don't need."'

Nine months after Ian's death The Blockheads played a one-off show at Dingwalls. The band acknowledge that they were terrified before the gig, not knowing whether they could carry off a good enough performance without their talismanic leader. Originally The Blockheads had asked TV comic Phill Jupitus, a long-standing friend and fan, to compère the show, but as the evening of 4 December neared, his role was to change dramatically.

Mickey explained, 'We were shitting ourselves. We'd had 20-odd years of doing gigs but none of us knew the lyrics. We then realised what a wordy bastard Ian had been and decided to lay "cheat sheets" all over the stage. Phill then said, "If you've got any problems, lads, I know all the words", so we said, "You're on", and he came on and sang six or seven numbers. People loved it. Then we got some gigs for March 2001. Phill told us which dates he could do and said we could put any money due to him towards the next album. He also got Mark Lamarr and Keith Allen to come down.

'Phill took us around in his massive van and we stayed in hotels on the Jupitus shilling. He was lovely. At the end he left us to do the last gig on our own in Wrexham on a Sunday night.'

Although Jupitus still occasionally joins The Blockheads onstage to sing classics like 'Billericay Dickie', 'Hit Me With Your Rhythm Stick' and 'Sweet Gene Vincent', the band knew that the comic was not a viable long-term option. The possibility of hiring another singer was in fact never discussed, with the band united in its belief that Ian Dury was simply irreplaceable. The one addition to The Blockheads' line-up was Derek, who had previously played guitar in a two-piece pub band in Wimbledon, and was already a cult figure with Blockheads fans because of his regular appearances onstage.

He explained, 'I used to watch from the wings every night and then help Ian off after 'Hit Me', and that's when I started joining in a bit on backing vocals. He said, "Help me out with the 'Hit Mes' and, when we've finished, we'll just turn around and walk off and let the boys finish it off." We developed a theatrical bit where I'd walk out with two brandies, we'd both have a drink, then shake hands, and I'd walk off.

'I'd walk on with a spliff in "Reasons To Be Cheerful". While the boys were jazzing it up in the middle I'd stand in front of Ian and he'd take the spliff. The audience would see streams of smoke coming up from behind my shoulders while Ian was puffing away. Then he'd give it back to me, and I'd help him up and walk off. The spliff was a reason to be cheerful.'

As the band returned to the road in 2001 Johnny and Chaz learned the words to much of the band's back catalogue, but asked Derek to learn a handful himself. Among his repertoire are 'Inbetweenies', 'Itinerant Child', 'Ballad Of The Sulphate Strangler' and 'Dance Little Rude Boy', Derek's Cockney persona, strikingly similar to Ian's, helping to add continuity to the band's sound.

Seemingly endless negotiations with both lawyers and Ian's accountant Ronnie Harris delayed the release of *Turnips* by six months. Having released the record in March 2002, Mickey says The Blockheads are only now catching up with their planned schedule: 'It was crucial time wasted by shenanigans with lawyers. But over the past two years we saved enough money from all our gigs to make an album and have formed our own publishing company. There's no middlemen any more, which is a good feeling, but it hasn't been easy.'

Crucial to the band's continuity over the past three years has been Lee Harris. The enthusiastic 31-year-old, a fan of The Blockheads since the age of seven, has helped Mickey steer the ship as the band's 'personal manager'.

A mean guitarist who occasionally joins the band onstage, Lee was introduced to the band by Norman, having met via a mutual friend. Lee explained, 'Shortly before Ian's death I had a jam with Norman, who was one of my idols, and we kept in touch over the next few months. One day I was looking at The Blockheads' website and thought it was very negative. I didn't think enough effort was being made to sell tickets for my favourite band, so I contacted the site and told them of my concerns.

'I received a reply telling me to call Mick. During the subsequent conversation I asked this guy, "What do you do for the band?", and he said, "I play keyboards", and then it dawned on me I was speaking to Mickey Gallagher. I was well chuffed.'

Lee has been working for the band ever since that initial phone call in May 2001 and remembers the feelings of abandonment within the camp after Ian's death: 'When Ian died virtually everyone who had anything to do with getting them work jumped ship. There was no Ian character around, so the whole dynamic of the band had changed and they needed a sort of "personal manager". On *Where's The Party?* I've got a credit as "Damage Control". I can deal with each one individually and then as a group and manage things, I hope, effectively.'

The band are all fulsome in their praise of Lee. 'He's been marvellous for us, full of enthusiasm, and a lovely fella to boot,' said Mickey.

Writing their first album without Ian was a difficult process, and Mickey recalls the stark reality of the situation hitting home in late 2001. The band had recorded 21 songs in the studio but decided that just three were up to The Blockheads' high standards. 'It was a great leveller, and we knew we'd have to think harder.'

Having returned to the drawing board, the band spent 2002 writing new material and came up with 13 tracks that make up their new album, *Where's The Party?*, to be released at the time of this book going to press. Johnny, Chaz, Mickey and Derek were forced to brush up their lyric-writing skills, in some cases after a lull of many years.

Johnny explained, 'I used to write a lot of the lyrics in Loving Awareness but after I met Ian I didn't write a lyric for about 17 years, because he was the best lyric writer around. Towards the end of his life I started writing lyrics again and now I write frequently.'

One of the songs written by Johnny for *Where's The Party?* is 'Mona', arguably the rockiest track on the album, and one that owes much to his love of The Beatles. Along with 'Mona', 'Feel The Funk' has been a popular feature of The Blockheads' live set for more than a year and was one of the first songs written by The Blockheads after Ian's death. 'Spread It' sees Derek on vocals, having penned the lyric himself as a piece of political commentary on 21st-century Britain.

One song on the album was inspired by Ian, entitled 'I Wish It Was The Days'. Mickey explained, 'On the list that Ian left us, one of the song titles was "I Wish It Was The Days", which was a phrase he used often. Ian died before he ever managed to write a lyric, so we wrote the song ourselves to say thank you to him.'

'Where's The Party?', the album's title track, went through a number of alterations before the band declared themselves happy. The words and music were both written by Mickey who, having studied Ian at close hand for many years, was able to construct a lyric eerily similar in its Cockney vernacular.

After Chaz had made some alterations to the arrangement, the lyric was handed over to Derek to sing. In July 2003 the band declared the album complete but, on reflection, Chaz suggested they return to the studio and remix it again. Over the next two months the album was given a more distinctive, contemporary sound, while retaining its Blockheads' character.

Judging that 'Where's The Party?' was 'too rocky', Chaz gave the song to a DJ who made the song more accessible. Having produced a shorter edit for radio play, the band are hopeful of releasing it as a single in 2004. The song was immediately jumped on by The Blockheads' loyal following when it was played live during 2002. According to Lee, 'I know people who have come to gigs and two months later have sung the chorus to me. It's very catchy and won't sound at all out of place in the charts.'

In its entirety the album took a year to record, from September 2002 until September 2003, although the actual time involved was four weeks' recording and three weeks' post-production work. The Blockheads are still a formidable live act, although the various commitments of band members means they can only accept live dates sporadically. Norman still plays with Wilko Johnson, Mickey tours with The Animals, Johnny plays and records with Bob Geldof, while Chaz continues to make solo records, his latest album a jazz composition called *Zoom*.

The four original Blockheads, plus Derek, Dylan, Gilad and second saxophonists Dave Lewis are hopeful that *Where's The Party?* will be successful enough for them to devote the majority of their time to the band.

According to Derek, 'It's all very well other musicians saying how fantastic The Blockheads are, but it doesn't actually pay the rent. Most of the band are all forced to earn peripheral livings with other jobs, but their hearts lie in the band and when they come together they make a special kind of music. If they could afford to, they'd be doing it all the time but at the moment they can't.

'It's weird really that they can spend 30 years honing their skills to be the top of their tree and then some little whippersnapper with about as much talent as a dog turd can make millions. But musicians just accept it.'

Lee is full of optimism for the future and wants The Blockheads to try and break into the States, a marketplace stubbornly scorned by Ian. He believes that The Blockheads' funk-based music would go down a storm across the Atlantic and points to the fact that the band is attracting a younger fan base. He added, 'What we have now is a much more universal audience. It's not just the geezers we attracted with Ian any more. You see women coming to gigs in pairs, which was unheard of in the past, and lots of young guys follow us. We've got a reputation for being a happening, funky band, and we hope that continues.'

The band have a natural chemistry and clearly relish every moment spent onstage together. There are no cliques within the camp and each Blockhead holds a genuine affection for his colleagues, undimmed by more than 25 years spent riding the rollercoaster of rock 'n' roll.

Mickey believes the group has blossomed both musically and on a personal level since Ian's death. He said, 'It wasn't until Ian died that we started socialising together. John and Chaz have lived within two miles for years and had never been to each other's house until Ian died. Ian's death brought us all closer together in a way and we're joined at the hip now.'

The world of music will certainly be a poorer place the day The Blockheads finally hang up their instruments. In the meantime, they will continue to entertain and enjoy themselves, while attempting to play their way back in to the nation's consciousness with their extraordinary 'debut' album.

Having lost Ian Dury, one of the best songwriters of his, and indeed any, generation the band deserves enormous credit for forging a separate identity and continuing to write challenging new material. An easy option would have been to hire another singer and gone on the 'cabaret circuit', singing tried and tested songs from three decades ago. That The Blockheads have taken on Ian's mantle by writing heartfelt and witty lyrics, while retaining the gift of making accessible dance music, is something that should be cherished in an age dominated by meaningless, plastic pop.

As a certain singer might have said, 'There ain't half been some clever bastards.'

References

1. *On My Life,* BBC2 documentary, screened 25 September 1999.

2. Peter Erskine, *NME,* 2 August 1975.

3. Will Stout, *Cirkus* magazine, September 1973.

4. Interview with MT Laverty, *Trouser Press* magazine, July 1978.

5. *Ian Dury And The Blockheads,* Channel 5 Special, documentary, screened in autumn 1999.

6. Interview with Kozmo Vinyl, *New Boots And Panties* reissue, 1986.

7. *Penthouse,* Vol. 9, No. 1, January 1974.

8. BBC Radio 2 documentary, aired May 1999.

9. Monty Smith, *NME,* 18 August 1979.

10. *Reasons To Be Cheerful* CD compilation sleeve notes, released 1996.

11. Nick Kent, *NME,* 25 October 1980.

12. *Penthouse,* Vol. 19, No. 3, March 1984.

13. Will Birch, *Mojo,* December 1998.

14. Will Birch, *No Sleep Till Canvey Island: The Great Pub Rock Revolution,* Virgin, 2000.

15. *Smash Hits,* issue date unknown, 1979.

16. Interview with Brian Case, *NME,* 15 April 1978.

17. Interview with Danny Baker, *NME,* 8 August 1981.

18. Channel 4 documentary, screened 1984.

19. Interview with Brian Case, *Time Out,* October 1998.

20. Interview with Simon Hattenstone, *Guardian,* 19 June 1998.

21. Interview with BP Fallon, at *Bpfallon.com,* 1999.

22. Robin Denselow, *Guardian* obituary, 28 March 2000.

Discography

IAN DURY

<u>Singles</u>
'Sex & Drugs & Rock & Roll'/'Razzle In My Pocket'
(Stiff 7", August 1977)

'Sweet Gene Vincent'/'You're More Than Fair'
(Stiff 7", November 1977)

'Sex & Drugs & Rock & Roll'/'Two Stiff Steep Hills'/'England's Glory'
(Stiff 7", December 1977 – 1,000 copies pressed for NME Christmas
Party and 500 for Blockheads/NME competition)

'Spasticus Autisticus'/'Spasticus Autisticus (Instrumental)'
(Polydor 7" & 12", August 1981)

'Profoundly In Love With Pandora'/'Eugenius (You're A Genius)'
(EMI 7", October 1985)

'Apples'/'Byline Browne'
(WEA 7", October 1989)

<u>Albums</u>
New Boots And Panties (Stiff, September 1977)

Lord Upminster (Polydor, September 1981)

Apples (WEA, October 1989)

The Bus Driver's Prayer & Other Stories (Demon, October 1992)

IAN DURY AND THE BLOCKHEADS

<u>Singles</u>
'What A Waste'/'Wake Up And Make Love With Me'
(Stiff 7" & 12", April 1978)

'Hit Me With Your Rhythm Stick'/'There Ain't Half Been Some Clever Bastards'
(Stiff 7" & 12", November 1978)

'Reasons To Be Cheerful (Part 3)'/'Common As Muck'
(Stiff 7" & 12", July 1979)

'I Want To Be Straight'/'That's Not All'
(Stiff 7" & 12", April 1980)

'Sueperman's Big Sister'/'You'll See Glimpses'
(Stiff 7", October 1980)

'Sueperman's Big Sister'/'Fucking Ada'
(Stiff 12", October 1980)

'Hit Me With Your Rhythm Stick'/'Sex & Drugs & Rock & Roll'/'Reasons To Be Cheerful (Part 3)'/'Wake Up And Make Love With Me' (Remixed by Paul Hardcastle)
(Stiff 12", May 1985)

<u>Albums</u>
Do It Yourself (Stiff, May 1979)

Laughter (Stiff, November 1980)

Warts 'n' Audience (Demon, April 1991)
Included free single, 'If I Was With A Woman'/'Inbetweenies'

Mr Love Pants (East Central One, June 1998)

Ten More Turnips From The Tip (East Central One, March 2002)

IAN DURY AND THE MUSIC STUDENTS

Singles
'Really Glad You Came'/'You're My Inspiration'
(Polydor 7" & 12", November 1983)

'Very Personal'/'Ban The Bomb'
(Polydor 7", February 1984)

'Very Personal'/'Ban The Bomb'/'The Sky's The Limit'
(Polydor 12", February 1984)

Albums
4,000 Weeks Holiday (Polydor, January 1984)

THE BLOCKHEADS

Singles
'Where's The Party?'/'Where's The Party? (ed. version)'/'Feel The Funk'
(Blockheads Ltd [Radio CD], February 2004)

Albums
Where's The Party? (Blockheads Ltd, February 2004)

Lyrics

RAZZLE IN MY POCKET

In my yellow jersey, I went out on the nick
South Street Romford, shopping arcade
Got a Razzle magazine, I never paid
Inside my jacket and away double quick

Good sense told me, once was enough
But I had a cocky eye on more of this stuff
With the Razzle in my pocket, back to have another peek

Instead of being sneaky I strolled inside,
I put my thieving hand on something rude
I walked right out with a silhouette of nudes
'Hold on sonny' said a voice at my side
'I think you've taken one of my books'
Passers by gave me dirty looks 'Not me mister' I bravely lied

We stopped by the window of a jeweller's shop
'If it's money for your lunch, I'd have given you a loan
Have you got any form, were you on your own?
Round to the station and we'll tell the cops'
'I'm ever so ashamed, it was wicked and rash
Here's the book back, and here's the cash
I never stole before, I promise I'll stop'

'Crime doesn't pay, you've got honest eyes
If we go to the law another thief is born
And I'll get the book back, creased and torn
So return what you've taken and apologise'

I gave him back his nudie book
I said I was sorry, I slung my hook
With the Razzle in my pocket as the second prize

SEX AND DRUGS AND ROCK AND ROLL

Sex and drugs and rock and roll
Is all my brain and body needs
Sex and drugs and rock and roll
Is very good indeed

Keep your silly ways
Or throw them out the window
The wisdom of your ways
I've been there and I know
Lots of other ways
What a jolly bad show
If all you ever do is business you don't like

Sex and drugs and rock and roll
Sex and drugs and rock and roll
Sex and drugs and rock and roll
Is very good indeed

Every bit of clothing ought to make you pretty
You should cut the clothing grey is such a pity
I could wear the clothing of Mr Walter Mitty
See my tailor he's called Simon
I know it's going to fit

Here's a little bit of advice
You're quite welcome it is free
Don't do nothing that is cut price
You know what that'll make you be
They will try their tricky device
Trap you with the ordinary
Get your teeth into a small slice
The cake of liberty

YOU'RE MORE THAN FAIR

You're more than fair, you got a gorgeous bum
Why don't you come to my house and meet my mum

I like your titties, they're nice and small
Let me have a squeeze in my front hall

Satin drawers I want to run a hand in
I want to snap them off you as we reach the landing

A tender moment, don't let nothing spoil it
I shall caress your clitoris as we reach the toilet

You're more than fair, you're warm and soft
Remove the trousers as we reach the loft

To taste the pudding, you've got to try the proof
You can try the pudding on the roof
The roof's the only place I know

SPASTICUS (AUTISTICUS)

I'm spasticus, I'm spasticus
I'm spasticus autisticus
I'm spasticus, I'm spasticus
I'm spasticus autisticus
I'm spasticus, I'm spasticus
I'm spasticus autisticus

I widdle when I piddle
Cos my middle is a riddle

I'm spasticus, I'm spasticus
I'm spasticus autisticus
I'm spasticus, I'm spasticus
I'm spasticus autisticus

I'm spasticus, I'm spasticus
I'm spasticus autisticus

I dribble when I nibble
And I quibble when I scribble

Hello to you out there in Normal Land
You may not comprehend my tale or understand
As I crawl past your window give me lucky looks
You can read my body but you'll never read my books

I'm spasticus, I'm spasticus
I'm spasticus autisticus
I'm spasticus, I'm spasticus
I'm spasticus autisticus
I'm spasticus, I'm spasticus
I'm spasticus autisticus

I'm knobbled on the cobbles
Cos I hobble when I wobble

Swim!

Get up get up get up get down fall over... Woo

So place your hard-earned peanuts in my tin
And thank the Creator you're not in the state I'm in
So long have I been languished on the shelf
I must give all proceedings to myself

I'm spasticus, I'm spasticus
I'm spasticus autisticus
I'm spasticus, I'm spasticus
I'm spasticus autisticus
I'm spasticus, I'm spasticus
I'm spasticus autisticus

54 appliances in leather and elastic
100,000 thank yous from 27 spastics

Spasticus, spasticus
Spasticus autisticus
Spasticus, spasticus
Spasticus autisticus
Spasticus, spasticus
Spasticus autisticus

Widdling, griddling, skittling, diddling, fiddling, diddling, widdling,
diddling spasticus

I'm spasticus, spasticus
Spasticus autisticus
Spasticus, spasticus
Spasticus autisticus
Spasticus, spasticus
Spasticus autisticus

Spasticus, spasticus
Spasticus autisticus

I'm spasticus!
I'm spasticus!
I'm spasticus!
I'm spasticus!
I'm spasticus!
I'm spasticus!
I'm spasticus!
Spasticus!

WHAT A WASTE

I could be the driver of an articulated lorry
I could be a poet I wouldn't need to worry
I could be a teacher in a classroom full of scholars
I could be the sergeant in a squadron full of wallah's
What a waste

Because I chose to play the fool in a six piece band
First night nerves every one night stand
I should be glad to be so inclined
What a waste what a waste
Rock 'n roll don't mind
(Schtum)

I could be a lawyer with stratagems and ruses
I could be a doctor with poultices and bruises
I could be a writer with a growing reputation
I could be the ticket man at Fulham Broadway station
What a waste

I could be the catalyst that sparks the revolution
I could be an inmate in a long-term institution
I could lead to wild extremes I could do or die
I could yawn and be withdrawn and watch them gallop by
What a waste

HIT ME WITH YOUR RHYTHM STICK

In the deserts of Sudan
And the gardens of Japan
From Milan to Yucatan
Every womans' every man
Hit me with your rhythm stick
Hit me! Hit me!
Je t'adore, ich liebe dich
Hit me! Hit me! Hit me!
Hit me with your rhythm stick
Hit me slowly, hit me quick
Hit me! Hit me! Hit me!

In the wilds of Borneo
And the vineyards of Bordeaux
Eskimo, Arapaho
Move their body to and fro

Hit me with your rhythm stick
Hit me! Hit me!
Das ist gut, c'est fantastique
Hit me! Hit me! Hit me!
Hit me with your rhythm stick
It's nice to be a lunatic
Hit me! Hit me! Hit me!
Hit me! Hit me! Hit ...... me! .... (*Instrumental*)

In the dock of Tiger Bay
On the road to Mandalay
From Bombay to Santa Fe
O'er the hills and far away
Hit me with your rhythm stick
Hit me! Hit me!
C'est si bon, ist es nicht
Hit me! Hit me! Hit me!
Hit me with your rhythm stick
Two fat persons click, click, click
Hit me! Hit me! Hit me!
Hit me! Hit me! Hit me!
Hit me!
Hit me!
Hit me!
Hit me!
Hit me!
Hit me! Hit me!
Hit me!

THERE AIN'T HALF BEEN SOME CLEVER BASTARDS

Noel Coward was a charmer
As a writer he was Brahma
Velvet jackets and pyjamas
The Gay Divorce and other dramas

There ain't half been some clever bastards

Lucky bleeders, lucky bleeders
There ain't half been some clever bastards

Van Gogh did some eye-ball pleasers
He must have been a pencil squeezer
He didn't do the Mona Lisa
That was an Italian geezer

There ain't half been some clever bastards
Lucky bleeders, lucky bleeders
There ain't half been some clever bastards

Einstein can't be classed as witless
He claimed atoms were the littlest
When you did a bit of splitness
Frightened everybody shitless

There ain't half been some clever bastards
Probably got help from their mum who had help from her mum
There ain't half been some clever bastards
Now that we've had some let's hope that there's lots more to come!

There ain't half been some clever bastards
Lucky bleeders, lucky bleeders
There ain't half been some clever bastards

Okey dokey
Oh
Segovia
La da da da da da da dee
Tick tum di dum tick tum di diddle di dee

There ain't half been some clever bastards
Lucky bleeders, lucky bleeders
There ain't half been some clever bastards
Lucky bleeders, lucky bleeders
There ain't half been some clever bastards
Lucky bleeders, lucky bleeders
There ain't half been some clever bastards

REASONS TO BE CHEERFUL (PART III)

(*4 Bar Intro*)
(*4 Bars*) Why don't you get back into bed (*x 4 B/V's*)
Reasons to be cheerful Part three
Some of Buddy Holly, the working folly,
Good Golly Miss Molly and boats
Hammersmith Palais, the Bolshoi Ballet
Jump back in the alley, add nanny goats
Eighteen wheeler Scammels, Domineker camels
All other mammals plus equal votes
Seeing Piccadilly, Fanny Smith and Willy
Being rather silly and porridge oats
A bit of grin and bear it, a bit of come and share it
You're welcome we can spare it
Yellow socks
Too shorty to be haughty, too nutty to be naughty
Going on forty no electric shocks
The juice of the carrot, the smile of the parrot
A little drop of claret, anything that rocks
Elvis and Scotty, the days when I ain't spotty
Sitting on the potty, curing smallpox
Reasons to be cheerful part three (*x 4*)... 1... 2... 3...
Health Service glasses, gigolos and brasses
Round or skinny bottoms
Taking Mum to Paris, lighting up the chalice
Wee Willie Harris
Bantu Steven Biko, listening to Rico
Harpo, Groucho, Chico
Cheddar cheese and pickle, the Vincent motor *sickle*
Slap and tickle
Woody Allen, Dali, Dimitri and Pasquale
Balabalabala and Volare
Something nice to study, phoning up a buddy
Being in my nuddy
Saying okey dokey, sing-a-long-a-Smokey
Coming out of chokey
John Coltrane's soprano, Ade Celantano
Bonar Colleano

Reasons to be cheerful part three (x 4)... 1... 2... 3...
Yes yes, dear dear, perhaps next year or maybe even never
In which case.. *(Instrumental)*
Woody Allen, Dali etc.
Reasons to be cheerful part three (x 4)... 1... 2... 3...

COMMON AS MUCK

You're not Brigitte Bardot
I'm not Jack Palance
I'm not Shirley Temple
On any circumstance
Or Fred Astaire

You're not Sydney Taphler
I'm not Dirk Bogarde
I'm not very stylish
And you're not avant garde
Or Lionel Blair

We're as common as muck
Bon chance, viel glück, good luck
Where bold is beautiful we don't give a damn
Love a duck we're as common as muck

You're not Victor Hugo
I'm not Patience Strong
I'm not Rodney Rygate
Or Yvonne Goolagong
Shirley Abacair

I'm not Nelly Melba
You're not Nelly Dean
We do our best endeavours
To keep our doobries clean
Cause we care!

We're as common as muck
Buona fortuna, vayas con dios, good luck
Where bold is beautiful we don't give a damn
Love a duck we're as common as muck

We're as common as muck
Bon chance, viel glück, good luck
Where bold is beautiful we don't give a damn
Love a duck we're as common as muck

I WANT TO BE STRAIGHT

I want to be straight, I want to be straight
I'm sick and tired of taking drugs and staying up late
I want to confirm I want to conform
I want to be safe and I want to be snug and I want to be warm

I want to be straight, I want to be straight
I want to create a place of my own in the Welfare State
Brrr gonna be good, brrr gonna be kind
It might be a wrench but think of the stench I'm leaving behind

I want to be straight, I want to be straight
Come out of the cold and do what I'm told and don't deviate
I wanna give, I wanna give, I wanna give my consent
I'm learning to hate all the things that were great when I used to be
bent

Could be that straightness
Might lead to greatness
Owing to lateness
My chance has only just arrived ah haha!

I want to be straight, I want to be straight
I'm sick and tired of taking drugs and staying up late
I know that you're right, I know I was wrong
So thanks very much and please keep in touch I'll be running along

THAT'S NOT ALL

While these minutes of no good
Bloody slowly drip away
It's you that comes to help him now
That's not all he wants to say

Tomorrow
And Tomorrow
And Tomorrow
And Tomorrow
Tomorrow
And Tomorrow
Tomorrow

Tries to keep himself in shape
Washed and cleaned and acting cool
Lonely as a homeless fish
Swimming in an empty pool

Never wants to let you down
Trying hard for fighting fit
Patient as the day allows
Calls you his survival Kitt

And Tomorrow
Tomorrow
And Tomorrow
Tomorrow!

Of course you know it's actually me
Embarrassed by this wet bouquet
I love you till the cows come home
That's not all I want to say

New Boots and Panties (1977)

WAKE UP AND MAKE LOVE WITH ME

I come awake with a gift for womankind
You're still asleep but the gift don't seem to mind
Rise on this occasion halfway up your back
Sliding down your body touching your behind

You look so self-possessed
I won't disturb your rest
It's lovely when you're sleeping
But wide awake is best

Wake up and make love with me
Wake up and make love
Wake up and make love with me
I don't want to make you... I'll let the fancy take you
And you'll wake up and make love

You come awake in a horny morning mood
And have a proper wriggle in the naughty naked nude
Roll against my body get me where you want me
What happens next is private it's also very rude

I'll go and get the post and make some tea and toast
You have another sleep love it's me that needs it most

Wake up and make love with me
Wake up and make love
Wake up and make love with me
I don't want to make you I'll let the fancy take you
And you'll wake up and make love

Wake up and make love with me
Wake up and make love
Wake up and make love with me
Wake up and make love
Wake up
Wake up
Wake up
Wake up

SWEET GENE VINCENT

Blue Gene Baby
Skinny white sailor the chances were slender the beauties were brief
Shall I mourn your decline with some Thunderbird wine and a black
handkerchief
I miss your sad Virginia whisper
I miss the voice that called my heart
Sweet Gene Vincent
Young and old and gone
Sweet Gene Vincent
Who, Who, Who Slapped John!

White face black shirt
White socks black shoes
Black hair white strat
Bled white, dyed black
Sweet Gene Vincent
Let the Blue Caps roll tonight
At the Sock Hop Ball in the Union Hall
The bop is their delight
Here come duck-tail Danny dragging uncanny Annie
She's the one with the flying feet
You can break the peace daddy sickle grease
The beat is reet complete
And the jump-back honey in the dungarees tight sweater and a pony
tail

Will you guess her age when she comes back-stage
The hoodlums bite their nails

Black gloves, white frost
Black crepe, white lead
White sheet, black knight
Jet black, dead white
Sweet Gene Vincent
There's one in every town
And the devil drives 'til the hearse arrives
And you lay the pistol down
Sweet Gene Vincent
With nowhere left to hide
With lazy skin and ashtray eyes
And perforated pride

So farewell mademoiselle knicker-bocker hotel
Goodbye to money owed
But your leg still hurts and you need more shirts
You got to get back on the road

I'M PARTIAL TO YOUR ABRACADABRA

Partial to your abracadabra
Enraptured by the joy of it all
So stop me where you start
The cockles of his heart
The panties sends it right up the wall

Please please stop it - it likes it
Tickles it to death either way
These lovely boots exist
To drive it round the twist
The call of nature must be obeyed

Glad it's over, but this is worse
Could hardly say it had been coerced

Stop it cos it likes it, it's worse

I'm partial to your abracadabra
The unforeseen erogenous zones
Stop, it insists
Slap it with your wrists
It likes it when you leave it alone

There's been a manifestation
Nature made it answer the call
It simply can't resist
Boots and pants like this
Abracadabra for all

Glad that's over but this is worse
Roll it over - too perverse
Stop it cos it likes it, it's worse

I'm partial to your abracadabra

MY OLD MAN

My old man wore three piece whistles
He was never home for long
Drove a bus for London Transport
He knew where he belonged
Number 18 down to Euston
Double decker move along
Double decker move along
My old man

Later on he drove a Roller
Chauffeuring for foreign men
Dropped his aitches on occasion
Said cor blimey now and then
Did the crossword in the Standard
At the airport in the rain
At the airport in the rain

My old man
Wouldn't ever let his governers
Call him Billy - he was proud
Personal reasons make a difference
His last boss was allowed
Perhaps he had to keep his distance
Made a racket when he rowed
Made a racket when he rowed
My old man
My old man

My old man was fairly handsome
He smoked too many cigs
Lived in one room in Victoria
He was tidy in his digs
Had to have an operation
When his ulcer got too big
When his ulcer got too big
My old man
My old man

Seven years went out the window
We met as one to one
Died before we'd done much talking
Relations had begun
All the while we thought about each other
All the best mate from your son
All the best mate from your son
My old man
My old man

BILLERICAY DICKIE

Good evening, I'm from Essex in case you couldn't tell
My given name is Dickie I come from Billericay
And I'm doing very well
Had a love affair with Nina in the back of my Cortina

A seasoned-up hyena could not have been more obscener
She took me to the cleaners and other misdemeanours
But I got right up between her rum and her Ribena
Well, you ask Joyce and Vicky if candy-floss is sticky
I'm not a blinking thicky I'm Billericay Dickie
And I'm doing very well
I bought a lot of Brandy when I was courting Sandy
Took eight to make her randy and all I had was shandy
Another thing with Sandy what often came in handy
Was passing her a mandy - she didn't half go bandy
So, you ask Joyce and Vicky if I ever took the mickey
I'm not a flipping thicky I'm Billericay Dickie
And I'm doing very well
I'd rendez-vous with Janet quite near the Isle of Thanet
She looked more like a gannet she wasn't half a prannet
Her mother tried to ban it - her father helped me plan it
And when I captured Janet she bruised her pomegranate
Oh, you ask Joyce and Vicky if I ever shaped up tricky
I'm not a blooming thicky I'm Billericay Dickie
And I'm doing very well
You should never hold a candle if you don't know where it's been
The jackpot is in the handle on a normal fruit machine
So, you ask Joyce and Vicky who's their favourite brickie
I'm not a common thicky I'm Billericay Dickie
And I'm doing very well
I know a lovely old toe-rag obliging and noblesse
Kindly charming shag from Shoeburyness
My given name is Dickie I come from Billericay
I thought you'd never guess
So, you ask Joyce and Vicky a pair of squeaky chickies
I'm not a flaming thicky I'm Billericay Dickie
And I'm doing very well
Oh golly oh gosh come and lie on the couch
With a nice bit of posh from Burnham-on-Crouch
My given name is Dickie I come from Billericay
And I ain't a slouch
So, you ask Joyce and Vicky about Billericay Dickie
I ain't an effing thicky - you ask Joyce and Vicky
And I'm doing very well

CLEVOR TREVER

Just cos I ain't never had no nothing worth having never ever never ever
You ain't got no call not to think I wouldn't fall into thinking that I
ain't too clevor
And it ain't not having one thing nor not another neither either is it
anything whatever
And it's not not knowing that there ain't nothing showing and I answer
to the name of Trever
However

Just cos I ain't never said no nothing worth saying never ever never
never ever
Things have got read into what I never said till me mouth becomes me
head which ain't not all that clevor
And it's not not saying one thing nor not another neither either is it
anything I haven't said whatever
And it ain't not proving that my mind ain't moving and I answer to the
name of Trever
However

Knock me down with a feather Clevor Trever
Widebrows wonder whether Clevor Trever's clever
Either have they got nor neither haven't not
Got no right to make a clot out of Trever

Why should I feel bad about something I ain't had
Such stupidness is mad
Cos nothing underfoot comes to nothing left to add
To a load of old toot
And I ain't half not half glad cos there's nowhere to put it
Even if I had
I'm a bit of a Jack the Lad

Knock me down with a feather Clevor Trever
Widebrows wonder whether Clevor Trever's clever
Either have they got nor neither haven't not
Got no right to make a clot out of Trever
Also - it takes much longer to get up North the slow way

IF I WAS WITH A WOMAN

If I was with a woman she'd wonder what was happening
Little things would slowly go askew
If I was with a woman I'd make her quite unhappy
Specially when she did not want me to

If I was with a woman I'd make believe I loved her
All the time I would not like her much
If I was with a woman she'd soon become unsettled
I'd show her but I would not let her touch

Look at them laughing
Look at them laughing
Look at them laughing
Laughing laughing

If I was with a woman I'd never ask her questions
But if she did not want me to I would
If I was with a woman I'd offer my indifference
And make quite sure she never understood

If I was with a woman I'd threaten to unload her
Every time she asked me to explain
If I was with a woman she'd have to learn to cherish
The purity and depth of my disdain

Look at them laughing (x3)
Laughing, laughing

I've been with a woman she took away my spirit
No woman's coming close to me again
I've been with a woman she took away my spirit
No woman's coming close to me again

Look at them laughing (x3)
Laughing, laughing, laughing, laughing, laughing
Laughing, laughing, laughing, laughing, laughing...

BLOCKHEADS

You must have seen parties of Blockheads
With blotched and lagered skin
Blockheads with food particles in their teeth
What a horrible state they're in
They've got womanly breasts under pale mauve vests
Shoes like dead pigs' noses
Cornflake packet jackets catalogue trousers
A mouth what never closes
You must have seen Blockheads in raucous teams
Dressed up after work
Who screw their poor old Eileens
Get sloshed and go berserk
Rotary accessory watches
Hire-purchase signet rings
Beauty to the bully boys
No lonely vestige clings
Why bother at all about Blockheads?
Why shouldn't they do as they please?
You know if it came to a brainy game
You could baffle a Blockhead with ease

How would you like one puffing and blowing in your ear-hole?
Or pissing in your swimming pool?

Bigger brained Blockheads often acquire
Black and orange cars
Premature ejaculation drivers
Their soft-top's got roll-bars
'Fill her up' they say the Blockhead
'Go on - stick it where it hurts'
Their shapeless haircuts can't enhance
Their ghastly patterned shirts
Why bother at all about Blockheads?
Superior as you are
You're thoughtful and kind with a well-stocked mind
A Blockhead can't think very far

Imagine finding one in your laundry basket
Or banging nails in your big black dog

Why bother at all about Blockheads?
Why should you care what they do?
Cos after all is said and done
You're all Blockheads too
Blockheads
Blockheads
Blockheads...

PLAISTOW PATRICIA

Arseholes bastards fucking cunts and pricks
Aerosol
The bricks
A lawless brat from a council flat
Oh oh
A little bit of this and a little bit of that
Oh oh
Dirty tricks

From the Mile End Road
To the Matchstick Beacontree
Pulling strokes and taking liberties
She liked it best when she went up west
Oh oh
You can go to hell with your 'well well well'
Oh oh

Who said good things always come in threes?
Reds and yellows purples blues and greens
She turned the corner before she turned 15
She got into a mess on the NHS
Oh oh
It runs down your arms and settles in your palms
Oh oh

Keep your eyeballs white and keep your needle clean
Plaistow Patricia Plaistow Patricia
Plaistow Patricia Plaistow Patricia

Her tits had dropped
Her arse was getting spread
She lost some teeth
She nearly lost the thread
And then she did some smack with a Chinese chap
Oh oh
An affair began with Charlie Chan
Oh oh

Well that was just before she really lost her head
Now she owns a showroom down the Mile End Road
And her outer garments are the latest mode
And there's a Siamese cat in the council flat
Oh oh
The finest grains for my lady's veins
Oh oh

And when it gets out of order she goes away for a bit
Plaistow Patricia Plaistow Patricia
Plaistow Patricia Plaistow Patricia
Plaistow Patricia Plaistow Patricia
Go on girl

BLACKMAIL MAN

I'm an Irish cripple a Scottish Jew
I'm the blackmail man
A raspberry ripple a buckle my shoe
I'm the blackmail man
I'm a dead fish coon a pikey Greek
I'm the blackmail man
A silvery spoon a bubble and squeak
I'm the blackmail man

Well, I'm the blackmail man and I know what you do
Every one of you
I'm the blackmail man
You make me sick make me Tom and Dick
I'll put the black on you
I'm the blackmail man
Blackmail man
I'm a Paki Chink a half-cocked ponce
I'm the blackmail man
A tiddly-wink a Charlie Ronce
I'm the blackmail man
I'm a no socks tramp a cavalier drunk
I'm the blackmail man
A paraffin lamp an elephant's trunk
I'm the blackmail man
I'm the blackmail man and I think you stink
You pen and ink
Blackmail man
I hate your guts your Newington Butts
I'll put the black on you
I'm the blackmail man
Hampton Wick Berkshire Hunt
Fraser and Nash pony and trap
Blackmail man
Up your 'arris
In your mince
Hamptons don't leave fingerprints
I'm the blackmail man
I'm the blackmail man and I think you stink
You pen and ink
I'm the blackmail man
I hate your guts your Newington Butts
I put the black on you
I'm the blackmail man

Do It Yourself (1979)

INBETWEENIES

In the mirror, when I'm debonair
My reactions are my own affair
A body likes to be near the bone
Oh Nancy, Leslie, Jack and Joan
I die when I'm alone, alone

Shake your booty when your back is bent
Put your feelings where my mouth just went
As serious as things do seem
At least you've put me on the team
And friends do rule supreme, ok

Oh, pardon you, me
With a capital 'C'
And who would have thought
With a capital nought?
In between the lines

Ohhhhhhhhhh

Spread your chickens when you think of next
What the Dickens if they're highly-sexed?
Through channels that were once canals
Do lift the heart of my morale
To know that we are pals, yes

Oh, vanity fair
With a capital 'V'
You give me a share
You take it from me

Oh, jolly good show
With a capital 'O'
It's terrific to go
Hellooo

Hello, hello, hello
Hello, hello, hello

QUIET

Excuse me... Excuse me
Get right out of the way
Quiet!

I'm sorry... Beg pardon
The fault's entirely yours
Quiet!

Your Highness... Your Worship
You silly pompous ass
Quiet!

Quiet! You're making such a racket
Quiet! Why must you be so loud?
Quiet! It's costing me a packet
Quiet! Persistent louts and clowns

Hello there... How are you?
Pee off!
Quiet!

Look, honest... Really
Lies
Quiet!

How lovely!... How charming!
Horrible

Quiet!

Quiet! Or else there will be measures
Quiet! Stop this unholy row
Quiet! Shut up, you little treasures
Quiet! When you've been told, and how

Alright little chap get back on mummy's lap
There may well be chastisements if you do not shut your trap
Just sit quite still
Fold arms face front

Quiet! You're making such a din din
Quiet! Why don't you please keep quiet?
Quiet! No one else is listening
Quiet! Utterly sick and tired
Quiet!

Sh, sh, sh, sh...

DON'T ASK ME

Here I stand with a doughnut for a brain
On my life, I must see you again
I should think that's made it very plain
Is it is
Is it is or is it ain't?
Don't ask me to leave it out
Or turn it up or pack it in
Don't ask me
Don't ask me
Don't ask

Don't ask me I'm an ignorant, I'm afraid
On my life, I believe we're tailor made
I should worry if the weather spoils the trade
I'm a crumb

And I'm in your lemonade

Don't ask me to knock it off
Or cut it short or jack it in
Don't ask me
Don't ask me
Don't ask

Let me offer you my life and all my love
Let me offer you a bargain
What a lovely range don't forget the change
Don't ask
Don't ask
Don't ask

Don't ask me to make a sacrifice
On my life, I'm cheap at half the price.
Won't you try a portion or a slice?
Slightly warm but very, very nice

Don't ask me to leave it out
Or turn it up or pack it in
Don't ask me
Don't ask me
Don't ask

Don't ask...

SINK MY BOATS

I've got the feeling but I ain't got the skill
And I don't like your suggestion
Will you still love me when I'm over the hill
Is another stupid question

Don't deny that I show disrespect
Ask me why I don't change the subject

Justify, but it has no effect
My reply is that I've been ship-wrecked

You try to be sly but you're so overt
And you know the main objection
It's the passionate pressure that you exert
In the opposite direction

I'm afraid that it seems evident
Though you stay now it's time that you went
Don't persuade me with your blandishment
The old maid's had her bad accident

Sink my boats
Once again
Sink my boats
Crash my plane

Justify, but it has no effect
My reply is that I've been shipwrecked

Sink my boats
Once again
Sink my boats

Sink my boats
Once again
Sink my boats
Crash...

WAITING FOR YOUR TAXI

Waiting for your taxi
Which taxi never comes
Waiting for your taxi

THIS IS WHAT WE FIND

Morning Reg, meat and two veg?
He done him with a ten pound sledge he done himself a favour *crash*
Forty-year-old housewife, Mrs Elizabeth Walk of Lambeth Walk
Had a husband who was jubblified with only half a stalk
So she had a milk of magnesia and curry powder sandwich, half a
pound of uncut pork
Took an overdose of Omo, this made the neighbours talk
Could have been watching Frankie Vaughan on the telly and giving
herself a scratch
This is what we find... this is what we find
This is what we find
A sense of humour is required... amongst the bacon rind
Hello, Brian, wash and iron?
Try it on, it's only nylon
Single bachelor with little dog, Tony Green of Turnham Green
Said, 'Who's a clever boy then, girl, yes you know whom I mean'
Cos the mongrel laid a cable in the sandpit of the playground of the
park where they had been
And with a bit of tissue, he wiped its bum-hole clean
A bit of claggy on the waggy
This is what we find... this is what we find
This is what we find
They must have had a funny time
On the Golden Hind

O vanitas vanitatum
Which of us is happy in this life?
Which of us has our desire, or having it, is gratified?

Hello, Mrs Wood this boy looks familiar, they used to call him Robin
Hood
Now he's robbin' fuckin' shit cunt

Home improvement expert Harold Hill of Harold Hill
Of do-it-yourself dexterity and double-glazing skill
Came home to find another gentleman's kippers in the grill
So he sanded off his winkle with his Black and Decker drill

This is what we find... this is what we find
This is what we find... the hope that springs eternal
Springs right up your behind
This is what we find... this is what we find
This is what we find
This is what we find
This is what we find

UNEASY SUNNY DAY HOTSY TOTSY

Bankrupt the banks withhold the rent
Shitters are a wank and the landlord's bent
It's time that the babies kept quiet
No it ain't
Open up the nicks close down the schools
The law is a prick not fit to write the rules
It's time that the babies kept quiet
No, they're cool
Time that the babies kept quiet
No it isn't, don't be silly
Uneasy sunny day hotsy totsy
Uneasy hotsy totsy sonny Jim
Question your besotment with a manky job
Squat on your allotment for thirty bob
It's time that the babies kept quiet
Shut your gob!
Melt the guns dismantle the bombs
Love your neighbour wherever they're from
It's time that the babies kept quiet
Up your bum!
Time that the babies kept quiet
No it isn't, don't be silly
Uneasy sunny day hotsy totsy
Uneasy hotsy totsy sonny Jim
London going junkie young and full of spunky
Don't care what you tell us old and fat and jealous
Uneasy hotsy totsy sunny day

Pills for fun damn the news
Different choice different things to choose
It's time that the babies kept quiet
Drink your booze!

Time that the babies kept quiet
No it isn't, don't be daft

Uneasy sunny day hotsy totsy
Uneasy hotsy totsy sunny
Uneasy sunny day hotsy totsy
Uneasy hotsy totsy porkie pies!

MISCHIEF

Popeye Pearce is pimple, Laurence Smith is hard
Ricky loves a kicking and he wants to join the guards
Barry breaks the windows of his broken home
Have a guess. His tiny mind's been scarred
Lionel touches women when they're walking through the park
He goes in people's gardens nicking laundry in the dark
Roger left a sleeper across the District Line
His dad's a shipping clerk
Boys let's have a laugh
Let's have some mischief
Fill a Durex full of water
And throw it on a bus
That would be mischief
Take a pigeon to the pictures
Let's cause a bit of fuss
A bit of mischief
Let's go bloody raving mad
Let's do something really bad
They won't forget the day you had
Some mischief
Jack and Stan are tossing pals like monkeys in the zoo
When they got caught by gonad Gibbs they had to wank him too

Incentive didn't want two of Dave (Get it?)
He failed his interview (Oh yeah?)

She's got crinkly hair
Underneath her underwear
I know because I've been there

Wow!
Wow!

Don't let's hang about
Let's have some mischief

Here, pour a locking fluid on a Bentley, then let down his tyres
Hahahahaha
Let's go and kill some kiosks, start a few more fires
Could this be mischief?

Let's go completely over the top
Let's do the bop that just won't stop
Let's go and have another drop
Of mischief
I'm sorry I done it... I'm sorry I done it... I'm sorry I done it
I'm sorry I done it... I'm sorry I done it... I'm sorry I done it

DANCE OF THE SCREAMERS

So I'm screaming this to you. Wah!
From the last place in the queue. Wah wah wah!
I really think you'd like me given half the chance
And since you ain't got that I'll do the screamers dance

Some of us are ugly angel some of us are only small
Some of us are useless, say they haven't got the wherewithal
We went and missed the end bit, but we never quite caught the bus
We never speak our minds, my love, we ain't got nothing to discuss

Some of us are witty love, it comes from facing up to facts
It's hard to be a hero, handsome, when you've had your helmet cracked
Cheerfulness is catching, sweetie, when the fevers you have got
We've got a proper chill, my dear, we simply haven't got the hots

So I'm screaming next to you. Wah!
Silly season, skies are blue. Wah wah wah wah wah wah wah!
I hardly ever think I've made a small advance
I keep my elbows in and do the screamers dance

Don't!

Some of us are stupid, sister, some of us are very shy
Some of us get nervous, chicken, when you look us in the eye
We're ever so pathetic, d'you know, we know quite well we try too
hard
Some of us were born like this, boss, others got it by the yard

So I'm screaming this to you. Wah!
Cos I haven't got a clue. Wah!
I really know I'd like you given half a chance
And since we ain't got that I'll do the screamers dance

Wah!
Wah wah wah wah!
Wah!
Wah wah wah wah wah wah....!

LULLABY FOR FRANC(I/E)S

Go to sleep now, Frances
You've done all you can with the day
Safe and sound, that's a promise
You'll be welcome in the Milky Way

Tumble down, tired and true
Spirit to restore, a balance is due

Go to sleep now, Frances
Close your eyes

Hang your thoughts up, shut the index
It's time to impose a curfew
And you'll get up, fresh and ready
With a hundred and one things to do

Drowsy now, here comes a space
Call a halt to the steeple chase
Go to sleep Frances
Close your eyes

If your life or some old lover cause concern
Or puzzle or perturb
The more you discover, the more you learn
Go to sleep now - please do not disturb

Tumble down, tired and true
Spirit to restore, a balance is due
Go to sleep now, Frances
Close your eyes

Go to sleep now, Frances
Close your eyes
Go to sleep now, Frances
Go to sleep
Frances
Frances

Laughter (1980)

SUEPERMAN'S BIG SISTER

Till I met her, I thought I knew the answers
I thought a bit of treatment was all a body needs
I'll take you where the haps are
All the handsome chaps are
Squeeze you till I make your feelings bleed

She put me right in under fifteen minutes
She could have had my things off, so sadly was I raised
I had a lot to learn, dear
If I'd gone on the turn, dear
It wouldn't be surprising nowadays

You know she's Sueperman's big sister
Her x-ray eyes see through my silly ways
Sueperman's big sister, superior skin and blister
It doesn't seem surprising nowadays... yeah!

Sueperman's big sister
Sueperman's big sister
Sueperman's big sister
Sueperman's big sister
I said she's Sueperman's big sister
It doesn't seem surprising nowadays

And now I've had the sense to keep her friendship
And though I nearly miffed it in many little ways
The story's got no sequel
Cos me and her are equal
Is that so surprising nowadays?

Because she's Sueperman's big sister
Her x-ray eyes see through my silly ways
I said she's Sueperman's big sister, his grown up skin and blister
Is that so surprising nowadays?

PARDON

New digs and prospects of a job
New digs and prospects

(*whispered*) Have I been of interest 'til now

Breath and armpits feet for Christ's sake please stay sweet
An ever present threat of hands that want to sweat
My head aches and I'm bursting for a piss
Why should I subject myself to this

Pardon... sort of... Oh
Pardon... you know... Oh
Pardon... Um... Oh
Pardon... er... Oh

(*whispered*) My dreams could come true if I make the right impression

Hope it looks okay I had it done today
Was that me who laughed oh god I feel so daft
Think I've got a new one on my nose
Don't I look a lemon in these clothes

Pardon... sort of... Oh
Pardon... you know... Oh
Pardon... ugh... Oh
Pardon... er... Oh

(*whispered*) Do these smells belong to me

Must not laugh or crawl dear dandruff do not fall

My stomach heaving chap make me a proper prat
My head aches and I need to be excused
Tell the truth you don't seem too amused

Pardon... sort of... Oh
Pardon... you know... Oh
Pardon... um... Oh
Pardon... er... Oh

DELUSIONS OF GRANDEUR

Bee aye bickybye bo bo bo
I've got a girl that I love so

Delusions of grandeur delusions of grandeur
I'm a dedicated follower of my own success
I can handle the glamour and cope with the stress
Deal with the doughnuts and please all the rest
I'm polite to the punters and I'm street to the press

I just won a trophy from a radio station
I'm leaving my bat and my balls to the nation

I've got megalomania I've got megalomania
To be a twinkle in the showbiz dream
To which effect I do connive and scheme
I dive into the dairy and I lap up all the cream
I'm up to the armpits in self-esteem

Stick me hype me up the charts
Then I can go public with my private parts

And here is me oh look at me
Just another pathetic pop star
I love you Greta what else is there
Won't you please accept my hand?

Delusions of grandeur delusions of grandeur
Megalomania megalomania

YES AND NO (PAULA)

Hey Paula come here
When I see you not to look at
And all that and so on
And that's a fact and so forth
And all that and thereabouts
And that's the truth
And not to look at either
No fear

You think I'm wrong I think
I think you're right
I think I think you're wrong
You think I think again
And then again again
And then and then
And then and then
Again again and then
And then again again
And then and then again
Again again
And if not why not
If
And if not why why
Why not
And if not why not
Of course it might be old
Course it might be busy
Being as it might be
As it could be new

Hey Paula
I'm hoping desperately that

You will take me to see a good
And also you and me might want to share a flat together
If I get one fitted

And if not why not not
Not if or why
Or if not not
And then again again again
First thing first thing first thing to go
And why not if not if not why not why
To go first
Yes and no
Yes and no
Yes and no

I'm not going to

Have you got a party hat
Can't you show more restraint
Have you got a clarinet
Have you got a box of paint
Yes and no
Yes and no
Yes and no
What what what what what what what what what what
what what what what what what what what what
what what what...

DANCE OF THE CRACKPOTS

Oh, let's get up and let's get excited
It's a public party and you're all invited
Let's cut the custard, see the mustard
Please hold steady till we're maladjusted
Sing boop-ba-de-boop, sing twiddle-de-de
Invite the Germans home for tea
Let them mock and let them sneer

The wise young crackpot knows no fear

The emancipation that's sweeping the nation
When it seemed the world was sunk
You can bet your boots on your own pursuits
History is bunk
From Rosemary Clooney to Jerry Lee Lewis
From Debussy to Thelonius Monk
It's the modern art of the human heart
The shape of things to funk, funk, funk

Let's see you do it, you always knew it
It's totally impossible to misconstrue it
In sight of the fact and in spite of the fashion
Living is a lap-top animated fashion
Pay no attention to the bones of contention
To the new-age boogie for the old-age pension
Let them stop and let them score
We'll get madder - we were born

Motivation is the new sensation
The fantasy keeps you fit
On the human assumption, you don't have the gumption
Get up and do your bit
Being daft is a therapy class
Which sharpens up your wits
Totally enthusic about the music
And it shows in the face you sit, sit, sit

Oh, let's get up and let's get excited
It's a public party and you're all invited
Let's cut the custard, see the mustard
Please hold steady till we're maladjusted
Sing boop-ba-de-boop, sing twiddle-de-de
Invite the Germans home for tea
Let them mock and let them sneer
Wise young crackpots know no fear

Emancipation that's sweeping the nation

Worldwide tonic funk
You can bet your boots on your own pursuits
History is bunk
From Rosemary Clooney to Jerry Lee Looney
From Debussy to Thelonius Monk
It's the modern art in the human heart
The shape of things to funk, funk, funk, funk, funk

OVER THE POINTS

Thank you
I am an actual train
Believe it or not believe it or not
I carry you backwards and forth south and north
On down the line and up
Before they shunt me into the final siding
I wish to make a few points
Whenever I have a breakdown
All my passengers start talking each other
They can sit walk sleep or have a tidy as I hurtle along
Sometimes we track this line with decapitated schoolboys' heads
Still wearing their caps
Upon me at any given moment ten or twelve people might be taking
craps
Over the points
I've transported enormous frivolity and fearful violence in my carriages
I've got compartments for sex, birth, death and occasional train
spotters marriages
Believe you me there are some right eccentrics walking up and down
my corridors
Picture the consternation in my bogies when my drivers' had a drink
All over the shop hundreds of people invariably male write our
numbers down
We as trains are agreed that this is because we are extremely phallic
Nobody seems frightened aboard us 'cos we hardly ever crash
We've been squashing pennies for well over a century
People love it when they're robbed and they wave at us and are happy

watching us going passed
Can you imagine how pleasant it is in general being an iron horse
I'm quite chuffed

Last train to Wanking Panda
Last train to Wanking Panda
If you miss this one you'll never get another one
Iddybiddy arseholes to Wanking Panda

(TAKE YOUR ELBOW OUT OF THE SOUP) YOU'RE SITTING ON THE CHICKEN

To be simple and wise never tell lies
Always pick on someone my own size
Could be quite a thing
If I make it swing
I'll write you a letter or I'll give you a ring
Take your elbow out of the soup
You're sitting on the chicken
Take your elbow out of the soup
You're sitting on the chicken
Take your elbow out of the soup
You're sitting on the chicken
Holding you tight is extremely all right
If it ain't called love then it ain't worth a light
Sailor

To be sweet and true to the likes of you
I promise that time will not undo
It would be truly smart and when I make a start
I'll come and pick you up in my horse and cart
When the mouse runs up your leg
It's one o'clock in China
When the mouse runs up your leg Ooh
It's one o'clock in China
When the mouse runs up your leg Ooh
It's one o'clock in China

Oh for the wings of a dove
Goodness me I'm in love

Arms of love are open always
All around you closing theirs
You're a darling and I love you
Signed politely
One who cares

Take your elbow out of the soup
You're sitting on the kittens
Take your elbow out of the soup
You're sitting on the kittens
Take your elbow out of the soup
You're sitting on the kittens
To be simple and wise

UNCOOLOHOL

The war cry of the raging drunken sot
That sends unwelcome pangs right up your bot
It bellows forth from open windows all night long
Puts up on the thought of right and wrong

Uncoolohol
Uncoolohol

The war cry of the drinker of the drink
Can send your senses reeling to the brink
What's your poison breath and outlook puke and bile
Lose all sense of reason, humour, style

Uncoolohol
Uncoolohol

Uncool

The war cry of the boozer of the booze
In normal state of little left to lose
Pissed and witless blood and bandage not a care
Splashing noxious liquids everywhere

Uncoolohol
Uncoolohol
Uncoolohol
Uncoolohol
Uncoolohol
Uncoolohol
Uncoolohol
Uncoolohol
Uncoolohol
Uncoolohol
Uncoolohol
Uncoolohol
Uncool

HEY, HEY, TAKE ME AWAY

What's all this spunk on the duckboards?
Come on Lawrence... come on Lawrence...
Let's go out and have a prayer meeting
Take a chance with our new shotgun
Hey! Come on Lawrence!
It's time we escaped again, my son
Oi!
Come on!

Hey, hey, take me away
I hate waking up in this place
There's nutters in here who whistle and cheer
When they're watching a one-legged race
And a one-legged prefect gets me in bed
Makes me play with his dick
One legged horn and he's shouting the odds

Driving me bloody well sick

When I get better, when I get strong
Will I be alright in the head?
They're making me well, if they're caring for me
Why do they boot me and punch me?
Why do they bash me and crunch me?
Some of the counterpanes are pink and other ones are blue

Hey, hey, take me away
From the ones that go mad every night
They're crazy and dangerous one-legged sods
Who have to sit down when they bite
One-legged Peter who knows bloody well
He's got worse ever since he came in
This other poor cunt, he was born back-to-front
And he's always got stuff on his chin

When I get better, when I get strong
Will I be alright in the head?
Give me a sweet and accost me
I'll do hope that God hasn't lost me
The lino is brown and the walls have been scraped with blood where
someone has hanged themselves

I hope so!

Get it?

Hey, hey, take me away
I'm the first to put last in the past
Take the handcuffs away and please do what I say
'Cos I hate the untouchable cast
I want to be normal in body and soul
And normal in thought word and in deed
And everyone here will whistle and cheer
And be happy to see me succeed

Cheerful Charlie Ashforth

Now that I'm better, now that I'm strong
Will I be alright in the head?
Grey worry lines in all my designs
And life isn't rosy, it's red
As to why I wrote this song
I ain't done nothing wrong, but I'm unhappy
Question: Do you blame your life on life
And say it all began before the nappy?

Hey, hey, take me away...

MANIC DEPRESSION (JIMI)

The mind is a very precious flower
That finds itself a strand amongst the weeds
The cause and effect is what you might expect
And going round the bend is where it leads

The elephant provides the ivory tower
It's better left to wander to and fro
Jumbo's got no chance when the poacher doth advance
With a ghastly poison arrow in his bow

Sometimes it all falls into place
Other times it sploshes in your face
On occasion grafting wins the day
Usually you wear yourself away

Is this fair we ask ourselves as we get our headaches bad backs and
complaints
Is this fair my little ones is this fair?
Oh no it fucking ain't

It's the way the cripple crumbles
It's the flaw of the jungle
Be reliable and humble
You'll be beggared if you bumble

A merry making catchall phrase
Twentieth century malaise
It's on everybody's lips
I'm afraid you've had your chips

Manic depression manic depression
It's not a pleasant fucker pheasant plucker
Manic depression manic depression
It's a hole full of soap soul full of hope
Manic depression manic depression
Life is all a bloody rush a ruddy blush
Manic depression manic depression
Memories are shoot and hip hoot and shit

OH MR PEANUT

Oi! Rotten hat
Where'd you get that haircut
Brent Cross Shopping Centre?
I bet your mother fed you with a catapult

Oh Mr Shagnasty a bit of give and take
You call me a divvy and I think you're a snake
Oh Mr Knittingcrutch come on for heaven's sake
Stick your finger up your nose 'cos you give me the ache

Oh Mr Peanut I don't like you at all
Not only are they poisonous but your eyes are much too small
Oh Mr Pastrydraws you haven't got a clue
So stick your finger up your nose and paint your money blue

I'm sure monsieur of course you must be joking
Oh yeah mein hier you must be up the creek
What's more signor the finger that you're poking
That finger stands for reason so to speak

Oh Mr Horribleness that's enough of that

You call me a ninny and you're a stupid twat
Oh Mr Horsebreath why don't you piss right off
Stick your finger up your nose you toff

I'm sure monsieur I know that you're a jubbly
Oh yeah mien hier for suddenly you're cracked
What's more signor you look a little bit wobbly
And we suggest you put your finger back

For all your life's offences you ain't nothing but a creep
Your mouth is full of sugar you're guts are fast asleep
So stick your finger up your nose so leave it there for keeps
I hate you Mr Peanut you really make me weep ha ha ha ha

FUCKING ADA

Moments of sadness moments of guilt
Stains on the memory stains on the quilt
Chapter of incidence chapter and verse
Subheading chronic paragraph worse

Lost in the limelight baked in the blaze
Did it for nine pence those were the days
Give me my acre and give me my plough
Tell me tomorrow don't bother me now

Fucking Ada, fucking Ada
Fucking Ada, fucking Ada

Times at a distance times without touch
Greed forms the habit of asking too much
Follow at bedtime by builders and bells
Wait 'til the doldrums which nothing dispels

Bodily mentally doubtful and dread
Who runs with the beans shall go stale with the bread
Let me lie fallow in dormant dismay

Tell me tomorrow don't bother today

Fucking Ada, fucking Ada
Fucking Ada, fucking Ada

Tried like a good 'un did it all wrong
Thought that the hard way was taking too long
Too late for regret or chemical change
Yesterday's targets have gone out of range

Failure enfolds me with clammy green arms
Damn the excursions and blast the alarms
For the rest of what's natural I'll lay on the ground
Tell me tomorrow if I'm still around

Fucking Ada, fucking Ada

Mr Love Pants (1998)

JACK SHIT GEORGE

What did you learn at school today?
Jack shit
The minute the teacher turns away
That's it
How many times were you truly intrigued?
Not any
Is boredom a symptom of mental fatigue?
Not many
When have you ever been top of the class?
Not once
What will you be when you're out on your arse?
A dunce
What are your prospects of doing quite well?
Too small

And what will you have at the very last Bell?
Fuck all

You can't bear another's beauty, you can't emulate a grace
You can't filch another's mystery, occupy another's space
You can't do another's duty, or take a special place
In another person's history when they've sunk without a trace

What's the reward for being a berk?
A blank
Thick as a plank and looking for work
What a wank
What do you think of the Welfare State?
It's a fake
What have they handed you on a plate?
The ache
Have you considered how lucky you are?
Well shucks
What do you think of the system so far?
It sucks
Aren't you endowed with the patience of Job?
I wish
Don't you feel ready to conquer the globe?
Oh fish

You can't steal another's thunder, you can't fill a great divide
You can't steer another's fancy, you can't change another's side
Not undo another's blunder nor pretend another's pride
You can't offer necromancy till the final hope has died

I'm a second-class person citizen-wise,
This is something I must recognise
It's not my place to make complaint,
But am I happy? No, I ain't
I missed my chance when I was young,
Now I live below the bottom rung
I was put on earth to discover my niche;
Oh Lord, won't you make me Nouveau Riche?

THE PASSING SHOW

When we were simple and naïve
We wore our feelings on our sleeve
As we've grown jaded and corrupt
Our manner's guarded and abrupt

Oh, how we'd smile most readily
Whilst ploughing on unsteadily
Now frowns are etched upon our face
We can no longer stand the pace

Although we've got to go with the passing show
It doesn't ever mean we haven't made the scene
And what we think we know to what is really so
Is but a smithereen of what it might have been

We'd sing in gay abandon then
We'd get it wrong and try again
As here we brood with doubts assailed
Nothing ventured, nothing failed

When life itself can chart the course
Then life's the product we endorse
When circumstances tell of death
We keep our counsel, save our breath

Our laughter rang around the world
When we were happy boys and girls
As now we balk and hesitate
Encumbrance comes to those who wait

But when we're torn from mortal coil
We leave behind a counterfoil
It's what we did and who we knew
And that's what makes this story true

YOU'RE MY BABY

Every day I look at you
And every day there's something new about you
When I look into your eyes
There's many things I recognise about you
Every time I hold your hand
I'm learning how to understand about you
Got more than love enough to spare
And I'm not going anywhere without you
You're my baby

Come excursions or alarms
I'll be there to put my arms around you
The joy I get to see you smile
There'll be gladness all the while around you
Proudly at your beck and call
I'll make sure that love is all around you
Loving you is purity
Blankets of security surround you
You're my baby
You're my baby

Every day I look at you
And every day there's something new about you
Got more than love enough to spare
And I'm not going anywhere without you
You're my baby

HONEYSUCKLE HIGHWAY

Exploring every avenue of love on the honeysuckle highway
Eschewing every vestige of regret we gaily slip along
Displaying all the evidence of mirth on the daffodyllic byway
And needing no excuse to have a laugh 'cos we're doing nothing wrong

You want magic? I'll provide it
You want daydream? You're inside it
You want mystery? It will find you
You've got moonbeam right behind you

Cruising down carnality canal in my canoe can I canoodle?
Rounding every bending that we're wending in a loopy disarray
Evincing all the properties of rapture with a sybaritic splendour
And shedding every nagging little footle that is getting in the way

You want magic? I can do it
You want lovelight? Nothing to it
You want everything to be groovy?
You got me now, let's get moving

Come with me where the air is free
And spirits can in harmony unite
Swim with me in the rainbow sea
We're strangers to catastrophe tonight

Where all the clocks tell different times
And no-one finds the time to be uptight
Where sweet suggestions grow on trees
And love explodes as well indeed it might

Exploring every avenue of love on the honeysuckle highway
And needing no excuse to have a laugh 'cos we're doing nothing wrong

You want magic? Well, you've got it
You want licence? I forgot it
You want romance? Let's get busy
I've got magic to make you dizzy

Come with me to the special place
The first thing you get on your face, a smile
As secrets flourish in their space
So love will cherish every grace and style

When pressure's on another case
We get along without a trace of bile
Though memories we'll ne'er erase
Our happiness can run apace meanwhile

You wore a bandana, I wore navy blue
We met in Havana at quarter past two
Across the Savannah and down to the beach
You munched a banana, I nibbled a peach

You played a small solo, I muffled my drum
You offered a polo, I stuck with my gum
I danced a light polka, you threw a few hoops
I was Oscar Homolka, you were Marjorie Proops

ITINERANT CHILD

I took out all the seats and away I went
It's a right old banger and the chassis' bent
It's got a great big peace sign across the back
And most of the windows have been painted black

The windshield's cracked, it's a bugger to drive
It starts making smoke over 35
It's a psychedelic nightmare with a million leaks
It's home sweet home to some sweet arse freaks

Slow down itinerant child, the road is full of danger
Slow down itinerant child, there's no more welcome, stranger

Soon I was rumbling through the morning fog
With my long-haired children and my one-eyed dog
With the trucks and the buses and the trailer-vans
And my long throw horns playing Steely Dan

We straggled out for miles along the Beggar's Hill
And the word came down that we'd lost Old Bill

You can bet your boots I'm coming when the times are hard
That's why they keep my dossier at Scotland Yard

Slow down itinerant child, you're still accelerating
Slow down itinerant child, the boys in blue were waiting
Itinerant child, don't do what you're doing
Itinerant child, you'd better slow down

We drove into Happy Valley seeking peace and love
With a lone helicopter hanging up above
We didn't realise until we hit the field
There were four hundred cozzers holding riot shields

They terrorised our babies and they broke our heads
It's a stone fucking miracle there's no-one dead
They turned my ramshackle home into a burning wreck
My one-eyed dog got a broken neck

Slow down itinerant child, the road is full of danger
Slow down itinerant child, there's no more welcome, stranger
Slow down itinerant child, you're still accelerating
Slow down itinerant child, the boys in blue were waiting

GERALDINE

I'm in love with the person in the sandwich centre
If she didn't exist I'd have to invent her
There isn't any secret to my frequent visits
It's the way she makes them and they're all exquisite

I'm in love with the person in the sandwich centre
I'm enamoured of the magic of her fresh polenta
My temperature rises and my pulses quicken
When she gets cracking with the coronation chicken
Geraldine, Geraldine

I know there's much more to life than the physical side

And I should put these thoughts on hold
But when she's buttering my baguette
My blood runs hot and cold
Geraldine, G-G-G-G-G-G-G-G-Geraldine
Geraldine, G-G-G-G-G-G-G-G

I'm in love with the person in the sandwich centre
I'm living for the moment that I next frequent her
In beauty's eyes beholding my inamorata
As she works her wonders on a dried tomata
Geraldine, Geraldine

I know there's much more to life than the sensual side
And the spiritual should come first
But when she's buttering my baguette
I think I'm going to burst
Geraldine, that's the nicest badge I've ever seen
Geraldine, you make the world seem fresh and clean
Geraldine, G-G-G-G-G-G-G-G-Geraldine
Geraldine, G-G-G-G-G-G-G-G

CACKA BOOM

If you're cold, well here's a plan:
Pull the plug out of your fan
If you're hot, now here's a scheme:
Park your botty in the stream
If you're tired, check this plot:
Seek a source that hits the spot
If you're snooty, here's a ploy:
Stroll along the hoi polloi
You'll not have owt to show for it
If you don't go for it
You'll have to come to terms with it
Get on the firm with it
If you don't get to grips with it
You've had your chips with it

You'll only come to rue it if you don't do it

If you're lost, well try this notion:
Find yourself a magic potion
If you're angry, check this wheeze:
Count to ten and then say, 'cheese'
If you're uptight here's the answer:
Learn to be a belly-dancer
If you're concerned, suss a wangle:
Try it from a different angle
Now you can put a name to it
You must lay claim to it
You'll have time to regret it
If you don't go and get it
You won't have much to talk about
If you don't go on walkabout
Don't think you won't mind it
If you don't try and find it

No-one said you must be good as gold
It's what you haven't done
That matters when you're old
No-one said these things are pre-ordained
Nothing ventured...

If you're guilty, cop a stroke:
You only did it for a joke
If you're dozy, here's a tactic:
Tell 'em all they're too didactic
If you're fed up, here's a wrinkle:
Let your pianoforte tinkle
If you're wobbling here's a trick:
Happy go toilet, click, click, click

BED O' ROSES NO 9

I've done a lot of things I wished I hadn't
There's other things I never hope to do
But sliding off the map in both directions
Is the sorry mess I made of knowing you

I've seen a lot of things I wished I hadn't
There's other things I never hope to see
But no-one left alive could paint the picture
Of the mess that knowing you has made of me

I knew it wouldn't be a bed of roses
I've seen the bloody grind that love entails
But one door shuts and then another closes
And now I'm on a bloody bed of nails

Been told a lot of things I wished I hadn't
There's other things I never want to know
But sliding off the scale of least remembrance
Is the way you chose to tell me where to go

I've been a lot of things I wished I hadn't
There's other things I never hope to be
But no-one left alive could tell the story
Of what I was once you'd got done with me

I knew it might turn out to be a schtumer
Nothing would surprise me anymore
You robbed me of my natural sense of humour
And then you nailed my bollocks to the door

I knew it might turn out to be a schtumer
Nothing would surprise me anymore
You robbed me of my natural sense of humour
And nailed my poor cojones to the door

HEAVY LIVING

Heavy living is the life that I've led
See the daylight through a curtain of red
Stands to reason why I'm staying in bed
Heavy living off the top of my head

Heavy living, uh, I know it too well
Every creak on the stairway to hell
Double vision and a terrible smell
Heavy living at the Hard Luck Hotel

Heavy sausage is the price you pay when you're on a corroder
Heavy bangers is another way to let yourself go

Heavy living's the condition I'm in
I'd wish I hadn't if I knew where I'd been
The air is cold, the membrane is thin
Heavy living's getting under my skin

Heavy sausage is the price you pay at the cafe doolally
Heavy bangers has a special way of saying hello
Heavy cricket on a cloudy day
Heavy chukkas 'til the close of play
Heavy living is the way I'll stay
As if I don't know

Heavy living is the life that I've led
Passion spent, nobility fled
Stands to reason why I'm staying in bed
Heavy living off the top of my head

Heavy shitters is the price you pay when you're on a corroder
Heavy bangers is another way to let yourself go
Heavy make-up for the matinee
Heavy curtains at the cabaret
Heavy living is the way I'll stay
As if I don't know

Heavy sausage is the dish of the day
Heavy bangers on the roundelay
Heavy living is the way I'll stay
As if I don't know
As if I don't know
As if I don't know
As if I don't know

MASH IT UP HARRY

He's got his little Y-fronts and he's got his little vest
He's got his little parting in his hair
He's got his little trousers and he's got his little shoes
And he wants a bit of Wembley up his 'you-know-where'

He's got his little jacket and he's got his little shirt
He's got his little motif on his tie
He's got his little raincoat and he's got his little hat
And he wants a bit of Wembley up his 'I yi yi'

Don't call Harry a human potato, don't call Harry a spud
Don't call Harry a walking King Edward, Harry's made of flesh and
blood

He's got his little office and he's got his little chair
He's got his little cactus in its pot
He's got his little memos and he's got his little job
And he wants a bit of Wembley up his 'you-know-what'

He's got his little pension and he's got his little plan
He's got his little policy in hand
He's got his little laptop and he's got his little pen
And he wants a bit of Wembley up his Rio Grande

Don't call Harry a human potato, don't fry Harry tonight
Don't give Harry a chip on his shoulder, Harry's doing alright

Mash it up, mash it up, mash it up Harry
Mash it up, mash it up, mash it up Harry
Mash it up, mash it up, mash it up Harry
Mash it up, mash it up, mash it up Harry

He's got his little mortgage and he's got his little lounge
He's got his little bit of England to defend
He's got his little telly and he's got his little phone
And he wants a bit of Wembley up his Ponder's End

He's got his little garden and he's got his little shed
He's got his little mower on the grass
He's got his little garage and he's got his little car
And he wants a bit of Wembley up his Khyber Pass

Don't call Harry a human potato, don't roast him on a spike
I think Harry's a real Golden Wonder, let Harry be the spud you like
Don't call Harry a human potato, don't call Harry a spud
Don't call Harry a walking King Edward, Harry's made of flesh and
blood

Mash it up, mash it up, mash it up Harry
Mash it up, mash it up, mash it up Harry
Mash it up, mash it up, mash it up Harry
Mash it up, mash it up, mash it up Harry

We're on our way to Wembley, we're on the Wembley Way
We're on our way to Wembley, we're on the Wembley Way
We're on our way to Wembley, we're on the Wembley Way
We're on our way to Wembley, we're on the Wembley Way
We're on our way to Wembley, we're on the Wembley Way
We're on our way to Wembley, we're on the Wembley Way
We're on our way to Wembley, we're on the Wembley Way
We're on our way to Wembley, we're on the Wembley Way...

Ten More Turnips From the Tip (2002)

DANCE LITTLE RUDE BOY

Hey...
With your natty threads and your nifty dreads
And the Dagenham royal swagger
With your tricky spiels and your Cuban heels
And the face of a carpetbagger

With your sweet cologne and your mobile phone
And the moves of a desperado
You will cut a swathe on your gangster's lathe
With an overdose of bravado

We see you're double hip to the trippy tip
And you're searching every quarter
You can throw more shapes than a jack-a-napes
For someone's lovely daughter

So dance little rude boy dance
Dance little rude boy dance
Dance little rude boy dance
You've got to know something

Drive me to distraction drive me raving mad
Drive me to the action take me one more tad
Drive me to the west wing drive me to the right
Drive me to the best thing that has happened to me all night

Hey...
You turned up trumps in your purple pumps
And a little bit of made to measure
With your shiny frock and your yellow socks

You're addressing it to your pleasure

With a urchin crop and a skimpy top
You've got to have a good thing going
With your lazy grace and your crazy face
Who cares if your slip is showing

Now we can see you're hip to the Mother Ship
When you pop it to the north horizon
You're the one who's having all the fun
With everybody's eyes on

So dance little rude girl dance
Dance little rude girl dance
Dance little rude girl dance
You've got to know something

Make me go bananas make me feel so right
Take me to Nirvana and leave me there all night
Make me hit the ceiling send me round the bend
Take me back to Ealing when the evening ends

Hey...
With your natty threads and your nifty dreads
And the Dagenham royal swagger
With your tricky spiels and your Cuban heels
And the face of a carpetbagger

With your sweet cologne and your mobile phone
And the moves of a desperado
You will cut a swathe on your gangsters lathe
In an overdose of bravado

So dance little rude boy dance
Dance little rude boy dance
Dance little rude boy dance
You've got to know something

Drive me to distraction drive me raving mad

Drive me to the action take me one more tad
Drive me to the west wing drive me to the right
Drive me to the best thing that has happened to me all night

Make me go bananas make me feel so right
Take me to Nirvana and leave me there all night
Make me hit the ceiling send me round the bend
Take me back to Ealing when the evening ends

I BELIEVE

I believe in bottle banks and beauty from within
I believe in saying thanks and fresh air on the skin
I believe in healthy walks as tonic for the feet
I believe in serious talks and just enough to eat

That's what I believe although it seems naïve
I believe in Santa Claus to give is to receive
That's what I believe
I believe in Bob-a-job and life in Outer Space
I believe an open gob does nothing for your face
I believe in being nice in spite of what you think
I believe in good advice and not too much to drink

That's what I believe surprising as it seems
I believe that happiness is well within our dreams
That's what I believe although it seems naïve
I believe that peace and love are there to be achieved

I believe in being fair St Pancras station from the air
I believe in taking care moonshine sparkles in your hair
I believe in being true in everything you try to do
I believe in me and you and I hope you share my point of view

I believe in being kind especially when it's hard
I believe an open mind can show a fine regard
I believe that manners make a person good to know

I believe in birthday cake and going with the flow

That's what I believe as strange as it may be
I believe this attitude is good enough for me
That's what I believe although it seems naïve
I believe it simplifies the tangled web we weave

That's what I believe
That's what I believe
That's what I believe
That's what I believe
That's what I believe
That's what I believe

IT AIN'T COOL

You think it's cool to make me wait with bated breath
for what you'll say
You think it's cool to be the overlord of all that you survey
You think it's clever being clever that you wear your fortune well
You think it's cool to be the foxy one time alone will tell
That it ain't cool
It ain't cool

You think it's cool to be the comic making cracks at my expense
You think it's cool to sit in judgement when I ain't got no defence
You think it's witty being witty when you know my tongue is tied
You think it's cool to be a prankster but your jokes are passing wide
It ain't cool
It ain't cool

It ain't cool to count your blessings one by one
It ain't cool to say you've done what you ain't done
It ain't cool to claim your winnings
When you poop on your beginnings
And another person's innings has begun

You think it's cool to be a sharpy as you cut me down to size but it
ain't cool
You think it's cool to brush aside the little people you despise but it
ain't cool
You think it's nifty being nifty and you think you're no-ones fool you
ain't cool
You think it's cool to hold your victim up to cruel ridicule but it ain't
cool

It ain't cool to be a cucker it ain't cool to be a crut
It ain't cool to make your mucker wait upon their if, you, but
It ain't cool to think you're pucker when you're tearing off a sheet
It ain't cool to make a sucker out of everyone you meet
It ain't cool

It ain't cool to count your blessings one by one
It ain't cool to say you've done what you ain't done
It ain't cool to do subtraction when you're checking every fraction
Now your little piece of action has begun

It ain't cool
It ain't cool
It ain't cool
It ain't cool
It ain't cool
It ain't cool
It ain't cool
It ain't cool
It ain't cool

COWBOYS

They say it's tough out there and that's for sure
You pay your way twice over if not more
They say that that's the price of fame and now you've made your name
Your friends don't even treat you like they used to do before

They quote the many stars who died so young
From the firmament you seek to walk among
They tell you who went mad who went from good to bad
And they warn you of the dangers that await the highly-strung

Who the hell are they and who cares what they say?
Who only seek to worry and alarm
Don't give those dogs their day don't let them get their way
'Cos I can see that fame's done you no harm

They say what you sacrifice to be the best
Means you lose all other purpose in your quest
They say if fame's your only goal, then it messes up your soul
Then they mention Elvis Presley and you're s'posed to know the rest

They tell you cherish every minute that you're hot
So at least you'll have some memories when you're not
They say when fame becomes the spur you abandon what you were
Which makes it that much harder to give up what you've got

Who the hell are they and who cares what they say?
Who only deal in envy and despair
Don't give those dogs their day don't let them get their way
I'm glad to see your picture everywhere

They say celebrity extracts a heavy toll
That the devil soon appears to take control
They say it leads you by the nose and they recite the names of those
Who've bled upon the altar of the demon Rock and Roll

Who the hell are they and who cares what they say?
Who only seek to worry and alarm
Don't give those dogs their day don't let them get their way
'Cos I can see that fame's done you no harm

BALLAD OF THE SULPHATE STRANGLER

A boy was born to Jack and Marge in 1951
And what is love is love is love and what is done is done
The baby grew in size and rage beyond his normal years
And when there's blood on every page the diary ends in tears

One! Two! Three! Four!

And I won't forget the strangler he's a lesson to us all
A knight in shining armour and nearly ten feet tall
I won't forget the Strangler he's the Bournemouth Buck-a-roo
His friends will always weep for him and this I tell you true

I met him up in Finchley the man from T.F.A.
He drove a black three tonner containing our P.A.
He wore a thousand earrings and a diamond on his tooth
His multi hued proboscis betrayed a stormy youth
The Strangler on his roller skates was over six foot ten
He had a double set of documents in the names of other men
Been on the road or off the road a thousand times since then
I only wish there'd come a chance to do it all again

And I won't forget the Strangler and nor will many more
Salute the mighty Strangler hear the mighty Strangler roar
I won't forget the Strangler he's as volatile as wind
If no one's getting loopy then no one's getting chinned

Later in our saga we come to chapter two
Of big Pete Rush the Strangler the Bournemouth Buck-a-roo
We hit the road together The Blockheads and their crew
A gram of whiz, a drop of vod, a can of Special Brew
From Spain to San Francisco we blazed a funky trail
With occasional disbursements to keep the Strangler out of jail
When we got to New York City we had to let him go
'Cos the dramas going on backstage were better than the show

And I won't forget the Strangler at this point we drift apart
He said you placed a dagger now right in my strawberry tart

Full bound for death or glory and worth his weight in gold
When the Devil made the Strangler he threw away the mould
These are the scars of the life that I lead
The veins are from drink and the nose is from speed
A Stanley knife here which had me well geed
Do I get cut and do I not bleed?
Each purple patch upon my face shall rudely chart my fall from grace
I will not pass the Loving Cup until the patches all join up

Then Jenny came and told the news that big Pete Rush had died
And me and Baxter were so sad it was a pity how we cried
The mighty Sulphate Strangler was the last one of his breed
Now he's got a white three tonner and he's knocking out Godspeed

And I won't forget the Strangler and nor will many more
Salute the mighty Strangler hear the mighty Strangler roar
I won't forget the Strangler he's as volatile as wind
He takes the world's encumbrance when it wasn't him who sinned
I won't forget the Strangler I wish he hadn't died
Now he's hanging out with Lynott across the Great Divide
I won't forget the Strangler he's worth his weight in gold
When the Devil made the Strangler he threw away the mould

I won't forget the Strangler (*x* 4)

I COULD LIE

I could lie before I could talk
Run away before I could walk
I could cheat before I could play
I was gone before I could stay
I could curse before I could cry
I could sneer before I could sigh
I could want before I could need
I was awful in thought word and deed

I could hate before I could feel
I could sell before I could steal
I could creep before I could crawl
I was big before I was small
I could curse before I could cry
I could sneer before I could sigh
I could want before I could need
I was awful in thought word and deed

Lah la la lah la lah
Lah la la lah la la lah
Lah la la lah la lah
Lah la la lah la la lah

I could lie before I could talk
Run away before I could walk
I could cheat before I could play
I was gone before I could stay
I could hate before I could feel
I could sell before I could steal
I could creep before I could crawl
I was big before I was small
I could curse before I could cry
I could sneer before I could sigh
I could want before I could need
I was awful in thought word and deed

Lah la la lah la lah
Lah la la lah la la lah
Lah la la lah la lah
Lah la la lah la la lah

Lah la la lah la lah
Lah la la lah la la lah
Lah la la lah la lah
Lah la la lah la la lah

ONE LOVE

One looks for happiness one longs to find a partner
One knows that nowadays one love will be the answer
One sees a crazy world one needs a fresh perspective
One comes to realise one love's a true objective

One seeks a perfect love one learns to tell the difference
One finds in consequence, one love is all that makes sense
One hopes there'll be a way one peers into the distance
One thinks that come what may one love will be the best chance

One love and only one
One love to last forever
One love only one love
One love it's now or never

One tries to draw a line one draws a swift conclusion
One tells oneself in life, one love is the solution
One falls in love at last one celebrates the meeting
One always will because one love cannot be beaten

One love and only one
One love with no misgivings
One love only one love
One love while we're still living

One tries to draw the line one draws a swift conclusion
One tells oneself in life, one love is the solution
One falls in love at last one celebrates the meeting
One always will because one love cannot be beaten

One love and only one
One love to last forever
One love only one love
One love it's now or never

One love and only one
One love with no misgivings

One love only one love
One love while we're still living

HAPPY HIPPY

I'm hanging up my hang ups ere I turn into a blank automaton
You won't find me on the treadmill you can tell em Willie Boy has been
and gone
Yes Mogadon time's over there'll be an empty bed in Babylon
'Cos I'm a happy hippy it's beads and Roman sandals from now on

Yes I'm a happy hippy they call me Mr Whippy
When everything is crappy being hippy makes you happy
Yes I'm a happy hippy and you can bet your bippy
That everybody's happy 'cos everything is trippy

I've found a new position I don't use chairs and tables anymore
I focus my attention from a lovely purple cushion on the floor
When I look back on the rat race I don't regret a thing I've disavowed
With the freedom of an eagle I can always keep my head above the
clouds

Yes I'm a happy hippy they call me MrWhippy
When everything is crappy being hippy makes you happy
Yes I'm a happy hippy and you can bet your bippy
That everybody's happy 'cos everything is trippy

Now I'm a jolly beatnik I haven't got a worry in the way
My hair grows long and shaggy as I savour every minute of the day
Immune from all achievement since I threw away my telly and my
phone
In my pastel pyjamas spending every waking moment getting stoned

'Cos I'm a happy hippy they call me MrWhippy
When everything is crappy being hippy makes you happy
Yes I'm a happy hippy and you can bet your bippy

That everybody's happy 'cos everything is trippy
I'm a happy hippy and everything is trippy
I'm a happy hippy and everything is trippy
I'm a happy hippy and everything is trippy
I'm a happy hippy and everything is trippy —— yipee

BOOKS AND WATER

On your nineteenth bump you got the rising hump
As the fruity squalls about to soil your smalls
So take a flying jump at the stirrup pump
Or the Priory walls will have your cobblers alls
You'll never light the lamp when your match is damp
And it's the sea green snot that really hits the spot
You put the rubber stamp on your stomach cramp
And what has time forgot is better not or what?

Books and water
Bricks and mortar
Books and water
You can do what you like on a Saturday night
But you ain't coming home if you feel alright

You take a sherbert dab 'til the next rehab
Tie the nuptial knot of never will ain't got
And under every slab there's even more kebab
Whereby you lose the plot about the truth, so what?
And when they stop the clock upon the disused stock
The only common ground is at the lost and found
And with your arse in hock say thanks a lot old cock
For only fourteen pound I'm Alabamy bound

Books and water
Pigs and slaughter
Books and water
Take a pipe on this and run like hell
If you ain't seen nothin' like a ne'er do well

On your nineteenth bump you got the rising hump
You play the bing-bang stakes whatever else it takes
So do a flying jump at the stirrup pump
As Zaroathustra spake thus are the breaks
You'll never light the lamp when your match is damp
And it's the sea green snot that really hits the spot
You put the rubber stamp on your stomach cramp
And what has time forgot is better not, or what?

Books and water
Bricks and mortar
Books and water
You can do what you like on a Saturday night
But you ain't coming home if you feel alright

Books and water
Pigs and slaughter
Books and water
Take a pipe on this and run like hell
If you ain't seen nothing like a ne'er do well… well well well well

Books and water
Books and water

YOU'RE THE WHY

I shuffled through the modes of bad behaviour
And hankered for the desolated dawn
I couldn't cope with yet another saviour
To steer me from the way that I was born

Then like a ton of bricks the dawn descended
Recalcitrance was hurtled to the floor
The citadel lay breached and undefended
You brought a love I'd never known before

I want you till the seasons lose their mystery
I need you till the birds forget to fly
I love you more than anyone in history
Wherever there's a wherefore you're the why

Index